# Betty Crocker's
# NEW
# GOOD
## AND
# EASY
## COOK BOOK

*Illustrated by Rudi Trautmann*

FIRST EDITION
SEVENTH PRINTING

© COPYRIGHT 1962 BY GENERAL MILLS, INC., MINNEAPOLIS, MINNESOTA. ALL RIGHTS RESERVED. NO PORTION OF THIS BOOK MAY BE REPRINTED OR REPRODUCED IN ANY FORM OR ANY MANNER WITHOUT THE WRITTEN PERMISSION OF THE PUBLISHERS, EXCEPT BY A REVIEWER WHO WISHES TO QUOTE BRIEF PASSAGES IN CONNECTION WITH A REVIEW. BETTY CROCKER IS A TRADE NAME OF GENERAL MILLS. PRINTED IN THE U.S.A. BY WESTERN PRINTING AND LITHOGRAPHING COMPANY.

LIBRARY OF CONGRESS CATALOG CARD NUMBER: 62-15434

GOLDEN PRESS  NEW YORK

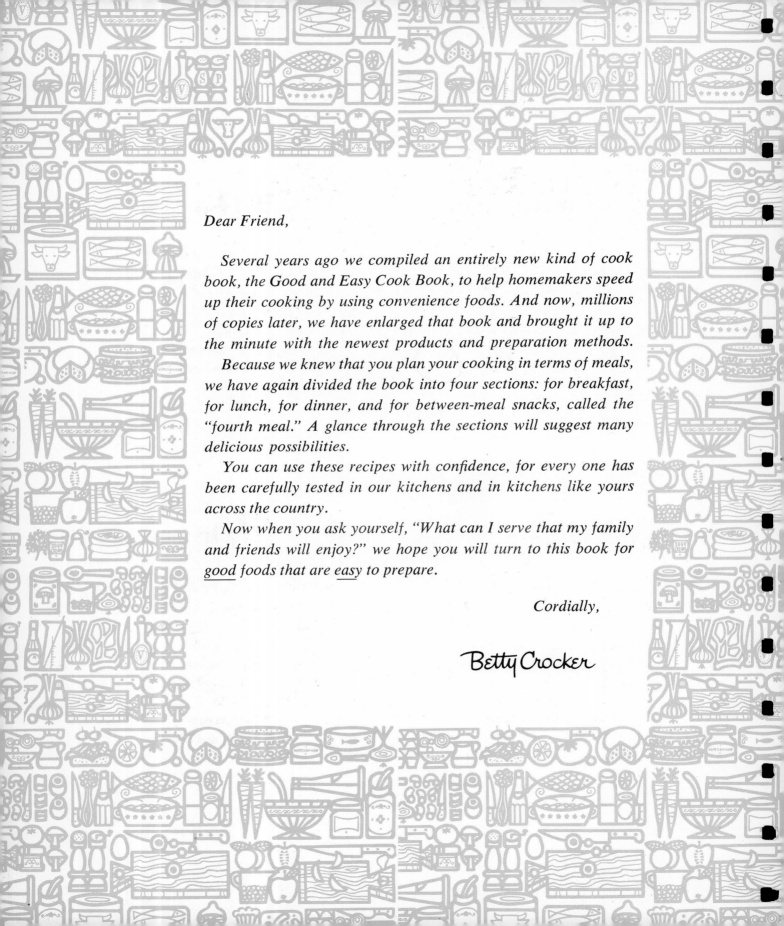

Dear Friend,

Several years ago we compiled an entirely new kind of cook book, the Good and Easy Cook Book, to help homemakers speed up their cooking by using convenience foods. And now, millions of copies later, we have enlarged that book and brought it up to the minute with the newest products and preparation methods.

Because we knew that you plan your cooking in terms of meals, we have again divided the book into four sections: for breakfast, for lunch, for dinner, and for between-meal snacks, called the "fourth meal." A glance through the sections will suggest many delicious possibilities.

You can use these recipes with confidence, for every one has been carefully tested in our kitchens and in kitchens like yours across the country.

Now when you ask yourself, "What can I serve that my family and friends will enjoy?" we hope you will turn to this book for _good_ foods that are _easy_ to prepare.

Cordially,

Betty Crocker

# CONTENTS

# Breakfast

Start the day with a song and a good breakfast and nothing will go wrong—or, should we say, more things will go right.

At breakfast we "break" our "fast," for during the night's rest our bodies are without food for the longest time in the 24-hour span. So it is important that the family be served an appetizing breakfast, including one-fourth to one-third of the day's food requirements.

Serving a well-balanced breakfast is easier than ever today, thanks to canned and frozen fruits and juices, ready-to-eat cereals, and prepared mixes for quick breads. And automatic cooking appliances are wonderful breakfast-time helpers.

This breakfast section features colorful fruit go-togethers, special cereal suggestions, six ways to prepare breakfast eggs, a luscious array of hot breads, hearty breakfast meats, even coffee brewing directions. Scattered throughout the pages are suggestions for gay garnishes and savory accompaniments to tempt breakfast-skippers or -skimpers.

In addition to new ideas for weekday breakfasts that must be truly meals-in-minutes, we have included menus and recipes for weekend and holiday breakfasts, when the family spends a leisurely hour together, and for brunches, the increasingly popular combination meal that is so often used for entertaining friends.

## FAVORITE FRUIT JUICES

Breakfast fruits are a wonderful way to get your daily quota of vitamin C. Many fruit juices are naturally rich in this "sunshine" vitamin, others have been enriched with it.

| **Grapefruit** | **Lemon** | **Tomato** |
|---|---|---|
| **Orange** | **Pineapple** | **Prune** |

For variety, try:

| **Apple** | **Apricot** | **Carrot** |
|---|---|---|
| **Cranberry** | **Grape** | **Tangerine** |

## FRUIT AND JUICE TOGETHER

*Serve in pretty frosty dishes or compotes (dip rims in lemon juice, then in sugar for interest).*

Bananas in cranberry or other fruit juice
Orange juice over orange sections
Cantaloupe balls in grapefruit juice
Prunes soaked in pineapple juice
Apricots or prunes soaked in apple cider
Orange juice over blueberries

## WARM FRUITS FOR BREAKFAST

For a warm and hearty beginning for cool weather breakfasts, try serving Baked Apples or Baked Peaches and Pears (p. 47). Apples could be baked the evening before along with a meat, then reheated in the morning. Grapefruit is also wonderful served warm; broil it as directed on p. 46. Another warm breakfast fruit that's sure to appeal to the youngsters is applesauce heated with a little butter and sprinkled with cinnamon or topped with red cinnamon candies.

### FRUIT GO-TOGETHERS

Sliced bananas in fruit juice
Applesauce with raisins
Strawberries or raspberries and
  pineapple cubes
Sliced peaches and blueberries
Grapes with orange slices

**Grapefruit New Orleans:** Grapefruit half on glass plate with vine-like garnish of mint or water cress around it.
**Golden Glow:** Mix mandarin oranges and another golden or yellow fruit (pineapple, peaches, pears, banana slices) in pretty compote. Garnish with cherries.
**Ruby Delight:** Strawberry-rhubarb sauce spooned into frosty sherbet dishes. Garnish with pineapple chunk, slit so that it sits over rim.
**Brown-eyed Susan:** Orange slices or sections around cooked prunes.
**Melon Divine:** Fill melon half or wedge with sweetened raspberries or strawberries.
**Grapefruit Surprise:** Section grapefruit half; remove several sections and replace with mandarin oranges.

## GARNISHES FOR BREAKFAST FRUITS

Lemon or orange slices . . . Pineapple cubes . . . Mint or lemon leaves . . . Big whole strawberries . . . Pomegranate seeds . . . Sugar-coated grapes, strawberries, or Bing cherries . . . Shredded or grated coconut (toasted or tinted) . . . Chopped dates, nuts, or raisins . . . Kumquats, lingonberries, blueberries, or raspberries . . . Maraschino cherries.

### HAPPY CEREAL-FRUIT COMBINATIONS

*Serve with cream or milk.*

. . . strawberries on Wheaties
. . . blueberries and Twinkles
. . . applesauce on corn flakes
. . . apricot halves on Jets
. . . peach slices and Trix
. . . crushed pineapple on hot oatmeal
. . . chopped prunes or raisins in hot Wheat Hearts
. . . banana slices with Cocoa Puffs and Kix
. . . chopped dried apricots stirred into cooked cereal
(add before cooking)
. . . raspberries and Cheerios

For the Gourmet

**Green Grapes folded into Lemon Ice**
**Strawberry Garnish**
**Hot Wheat Cereal**
**Cinnamon Sour Cream (below, left)**
**Thin Slices of Rye Toast**
**Butter          Raspberry Preserves**
**Café au Lait (p. 168)**

### INSTEAD OF MILK

*Try pouring these over cereal (when using sweetened liquids you will not need additional sugar).*

Eggnog
Flavored milks (p. 178)
Softened ice cream
Whipped cream
Softened fruit-flavored sherbets
Cinnamon Sour Cream: blend ½ cup commercial sour cream, 2 tbsp. sugar, ¼ tsp. cinnamon and ¼ cup apricot nectar thoroughly. Serve on hot cereal.

## TEMPTING, SWEET CEREAL TOPPINGS

*To substitute for sugar.*

Flaked or grated coconut

Brown sugar with or without nuts

Honey (warm or cold)

Sweetened cocoa mix or mixture of half sugar and half cocoa

Cinnamon and sugar mixture

Tiny cubes of sparkling jelly (or, jelly may be melted and drizzled on cereal)

Maple syrup

Semi-sweet chocolate pieces or miniature marshmallows (especially good swirled into hot cereal)

## CHILD-PLEASER CEREAL BOWLS

Teddy Bear in a Bowl—Half pear on Wheaties with raisin face and banana slice ears.

Jack Horner Bowl—Hide a cooked prune in a bowl of Cheerios.

His Very Own—Form child's initials with raspberries or strawberries on Trix.

Raisin Face—Raisin eyes, nose, and mouth on hot cooked cereal.

Jack O'Lantern—Peach half on Kix with maraschino cherry nose and mouth, raisin eyes.

## SERVING SUGGESTIONS FOR FUN

Put dry cereal in attractive pitcher at the table. Let family or guests "pour out" the amount they'd like.

Serve cereals in lovely compote or other dessert-type dishes for breakfast elegance.

Make a cereal buffet! Have several kinds of dry cereal handy . . . along with sugar, cream or milk (or other interesting substitutes above and left), and fruit. Spread on a bright cloth at a side table or counter. Let family "make their own," then take to table (uncluttered by packages and pitchers).

## HOW TO SOFT-COOK EGGS

**Cold Water Start:** Have eggs at room temperature (prevents cracking). Cover completely with cold water . . . do not pile up. Heat until water boils. Remove from heat. Cover pan. Let stand off heat 2 to 4 min.

**Boiling Water Start:** Have eggs at room temperature (prevents cracking). Bring enough water to cover eggs to boil in large saucepan. To prevent cracking shells, carefully lower eggs into water with spoon. Reduce heat. Keep water simmering 3 to 5 min.

## HOW TO HARD-COOK EGGS

**Cold Water Start:** Follow directions for soft-cooked eggs—except let stand off heat 23 to 25 min.

**Boiling Water Start:** Follow directions for soft-cooked eggs—except keep water simmering 18 to 20 min.

### Breakfast Children Can Prepare

**Orange Juice**

**Wheaties      Sugar      Cream or Milk**

**Scrambled Eggs (p. 9) or Eggs in a Frame**

**Toast**

**Honey or Strawberry Preserves**

**Milk          Coffee**

## HOW TO FRY EGGS

Heat a thin layer of butter or bacon fat in heavy skillet until moderately hot. Break eggs, one at a time, into saucer; slip into skillet. Immediately reduce heat to low. Cook slowly, spooning fat over eggs until whites are set and a film forms over yolks, 3 to 4 min. Or, turn eggs over quickly when whites are set and cook until done as desired. Sprinkle with salt and pepper. Serve at once on a warm plate.

**Poached-Fried Eggs:** Fry eggs (above)—except use just enough fat to coat skillet. Immediately add ½ tsp. water or cream for each egg. Cover tightly. Cook to desired firmness, 5 to 6 min.

**Eggs in a Frame:** Cut a circle from a slice of bread. Butter the rest of the slice (not circle) generously on both sides. Place in hot buttered skillet over low heat. Drop an egg into the center. Cook slowly until egg is set and underside of bread is brown. Turn. Brown other side. Season with salt and pepper.

## HOW TO POACH EGGS

Fill greased skillet with hot water about 1½″ deep. Bring to boil; then reduce to simmering. Break each egg into a saucer and slip, one at a time, into the water. Slide egg toward side of pan to keep yolk in center. Cook below simmering 3 to 5 min. Lift from water, one at a time, with slotted turner. Drain; season with salt and pepper. Serve at once on hot buttered toast, ham-covered toast rounds, toasted split corn bread, or corned beef hash slices.

**Eggs Poached in Milk:** Poach eggs (above)—except use milk or cream in place of water. Pour the hot milk over eggs on the hot toast.

## HOW TO SCRAMBLE EGGS

Break eggs into a bowl with 1 tbsp. milk or cream for each egg; add salt and pepper. Beat with fork. Heat butter or other fat (½ tbsp. for each egg) in moderately hot skillet. Pour in egg mixture and reduce heat to low. (Eggs should be scrambled slowly and gently.) When mixture starts to set at bottom and sides, lift cooked portions with spatula and turn gently to cook all portions evenly. As soon as eggs are almost cooked through but are still moist and glossy, 5 to 8 min., quickly remove to hot platter and serve at once.

**Herb Scrambled Eggs:** Add minced fresh herbs (chives, parsley, tarragon, or chervil) to eggs.

**Scrambled Eggs with Cheese:** For each egg, add 1 tbsp. grated Cheddar cheese and ¼ tsp. minced onion. Serve with tomato sauce, if desired.

**With Mushrooms:** First sauté sliced fresh or canned mushrooms (1 to 2 tbsp. for each egg) in the hot fat. Add eggs and scramble.

**With Dried Beef or Ham:** Frizzle flaked pieces of dried beef or boiled ham in hot fat before adding eggs. Serve with mushroom sauce, if desired.

## HOW TO BAKE OR SHIRR EGGS

Break and slip 1 or 2 eggs into a greased individual shallow baking dish. Dot with butter. Sprinkle with salt and pepper. Add 1 tbsp. cream or milk, if desired. Bake at 350° (mod.) 15 to 20 min., or until set. Serve hot in the dish as an individual serving, garnished with parsley or water cress.

**Eggs Baked on Beef Hash:** Spread warm, moist corned beef or roast beef hash (homemade or canned) in greased shallow baking dish. With bottom of custard cup, make deep hollows in hash. Dot with butter. Break an egg into each hollow. Season with salt and pepper; cover with 1 tbsp. cream. Bake as above. *(See picture, p. 10.)*

**Eggs Baked in Bacon Rings:** Bake or shirr eggs (above) —except circle inside of each baking dish with a partially cooked bacon strip (not crisp) before adding egg.

## FRENCH OMELET

*Easier to make than it sounds! See picture opposite.*

| | |
|---|---|
| **3 eggs** | **dash of salt and pepper** |
| **3 tbsp. milk or cream** | **1 tbsp. fat** |

Beat eggs until fluffy. Beat in milk or cream and seasonings. Pour into hot fat in skillet over low heat. Cook slowly . . . keeping heat low. As undersurface becomes set, start lifting it slightly with spatula to let uncooked portion flow underneath and cook. To add herbs, cheese, or meat, sprinkle ½ tbsp. per egg over top of eggs while cooking. As soon as all of mixture seems set, fold or roll it; serve immediately. *2 servings.*

### FAVORITE OMELET TOPPINGS

| | |
|---|---|
| **Cheese Sauce** | **Chicken à la King** |
| **Mushroom Sauce** | **Creamed Asparagus** |
| **Tomato Sauce** | |

## BUFFET EGGS

*Try this for supper, too.*

| | |
|---|---|
| **3 tbsp. butter** | **4 oz. (about 1⅓ cups) dried beef, cut in small strips** |
| **¼ cup finely chopped green onion tops** | |
| **9 eggs** | **1 cup cottage cheese (cream-style or dry)** |

Melt butter in large skillet. Add onion tops and cook until tender. Beat eggs thoroughly; blend in dried beef and cottage cheese. Add egg mixture to onion and cook like scrambled eggs. *6 servings.*

## QUICK WAYS TO COOK BACON

**Pan-Fried:** Place slices in cold skillet. Heat slowly. As bacon heats, separate slices. Do not overcrowd. Turn to cook evenly. Drain on absorbent paper.

**Broiled:** Place separated slices on broiling rack 3″ away from heat. Turn once to brown evenly.

**Baked:** Place separated slices on rack in pan. Bake in oven at 400° (mod. hot) about 10 min. Do not turn.

## QUICK WAYS TO COOK CANADIAN BACON

Canadian bacon (smoked boneless pork loin) comes sliced, 22 to 26 slices per lb., or in a piece (for baking). Allow 2 to 4 oz. for each serving.

**Pan-Fried:** Follow directions for bacon (above).

**Broiled:** Follow directions for bacon (above).

**Baked:** Canadian bacon in the piece may be roasted in 325° oven like ham. Remove casing. For 2-lb. piece, roast 1½ hr.; for a 4-lb. piece, 2⅓ hr. or 170° on meat thermometer. Glaze with 1 cup cranberry or currant jelly or with a mixture of 1 cup brown sugar and ¾ cup crushed pineapple during last 15 min. of baking, if desired.

*Come over for Brunch*

**Golden Glow Fruit Cocktail (p. 5)**
**Eggs Baked on Beef Hash (p. 9)**
**Biscuits**

## QUICK WAYS TO COOK HAM

**Pan-Fried:** Slice ham ¼ to ½″ thick. Trim off some fat to rub hot skillet. Cook ham slowly until brown on one side, 4 to 8 min. Turn and brown on second side.

**Broiled:** Slash edges of fat on ½ to 1″ thick slice of ham. Place on broiling rack 3″ below heat. Broil until tender, 5 to 10 min. on each side. Serve on hot platter garnished with peach or apricot halves, broiled a few minutes.

**Frizzled:** Lay boiled ham in lightly greased hot skillet. Pan-fry quickly until edges curl and look crisp. Remove to hot platter. Eat with fingers like bacon.

*Fisherman's Luck*

**Sliced Peaches and Blueberries with Milk or Cream**
**Pan-fried Fish (p. 84)**
**Corn Bread (p. 119)**

*Morning Meal at the Ranch*

**Stewed Prunes**
**Hot Oatmeal with Brown Sugar**
**Fried Eggs (p. 8)     Thick-sliced Bacon**
**Buttermilk Pancakes with Syrup**

## QUICK WAYS TO COOK PORK SAUSAGE

**Pork Sausage Links:** Place in skillet; add small amount of water. Cover and simmer 5 min. Never prick. Drain. Pan-fry until brown on all sides or bake in oven at 400° (mod. hot) 20 to 30 min.

**Pork Sausage Patties:** Form bulk pork sausage into patties or cut from roll. Place in cold skillet; cook over low heat 12 to 15 min., or until brown, turning once. Pour off fat as it gathers. Or bake as for Pork Sausage Links (above).

*Meant for Men*

**Cranberry-Orange Cocktail**
**Sunday Morning Sausage Ring**
**with Eggs à la King**
**Wild Blueberry Muffins**

## SUNDAY MORNING SAUSAGE RING

| | |
|---|---|
| **2 lb. bulk pork sausage** | **1½ cups fine dry toast or bread crumbs** |
| **2 eggs, beaten** | |
| **2 tbsp. grated onion** | **¼ cup chopped parsley, if desired** |

Heat oven to 350° (mod.). Lightly butter a 9″ ring mold. Mix ingredients well and pack into mold. Bake 20 min., take from oven and pour off excess fat. Bake 20 min. more. Turn onto heated platter and fill with scrambled eggs (8 to 12 eggs) or Eggs à la King (p. 37). *8 servings.*

**Supper Sausage Ring:** Make Sausage Ring (above)—except do not fill with scrambled eggs. Instead, fill with buttered mashed squash or cooked apples sprinkled with cinnamon.

## MUFFINS

| | |
|---|---|
| 2 tbsp. sugar | 1 egg |
| 2 cups Bisquick | ¾ cup milk |

Heat oven to 400° (mod. hot). Blend ingredients, then beat vigorously 30 seconds. Fill well-greased muffin pans ⅔ full. Bake 15 min. *Makes 12 muffins.*

**Fruit Muffins:** Make Muffins (above)—except fold 1 cup fresh berries or 1 cup cut-up dates or figs carefully into batter.

**Orange Muffins:** Make Muffins (above)—except use ½ cup orange juice for ½ cup of milk. After filling muffin cups, sprinkle batter with sugar.

**Butterscotch Pecan Muffins:** Place 1½ tsp. butter, 1½ tsp. brown sugar, and 2 or 3 pecan halves in each of 12 greased muffin cups. Spoon in Muffin batter (above) and bake as directed.

**Surprise Muffins:** Make Muffins (above)—except fill muffin cups ½ full of batter, drop scant teaspoonful of jelly in center, add more batter to fill cup ⅔ full. Open the baked muffin—and surprise!—there's jelly in the center!

## DROP BISCUITS

Heat oven to 450° (hot). Add ⅔ cup milk all at once to 2 cups Bisquick. Stir with fork into soft dough. Beat vigorously 20 strokes. Drop dough with spoon onto ungreased baking sheet. Bake 10 to 15 min. Serve with butter, jelly, jam, marmalade, or Honey Butter (p. 19). *Makes 12 biscuits.*

**Bacon Biscuits:** Add ⅓ cup crisply cooked diced bacon to Drop Biscuit batter (above).

**Cinnamon Biscuit Balls:** Make small balls of Drop Biscuit dough (above) and roll them in mixture of 2 tbsp. sugar and 1 tsp. cinnamon. Bake 8 to 10 min. *Makes 2 doz. balls.*

*EXTRA-QUICK MUFFINS—Wonderful, tender muffins can be made from muffin mixes. Take your choice of a variety of delicious flavors. So good...and so easy! To vary these flavorful muffins, sprinkle the top with cinnamon and sugar mixture (nuts, too!) before baking; or dip in butter and roll in cinnamon and sugar mixture after baking. Or, nuts can be added to the batter, if desired.*

## FRENCH TOAST

| | |
|---|---|
| 6 slices stale bread | ¼ tsp. salt |
| 2 beaten eggs | ½ cup milk |

Mix eggs, milk, and salt. Dip each slice of bread into mixture. Brown both sides in butter or other fat on hot griddle. Serve hot with maple syrup, jelly, or honey.

**Continental French Toast:** Use French bread. Serve more this way, since more of the little slices will fit on your griddle!

**Oahu Toast:** Drain 1 can (8½ oz.) pineapple slices, saving juice. In small pan, boil juice 10 min. at medium heat to thicken for use as syrup. Meanwhile make French Toast (above). Sauté pineapple slices in hot fat as toast browns. Serve toast hot with half slices of pineapple and pineapple syrup.

**Waffled French Toast:** Make French Toast (above)—except butter bread on both sides before dipping into egg-milk mixture. Toast in waffle baker until crisp.

## LIGHTNING-QUICK WAFFLES

Save time and work by using Bisquick or our butter-milk pancake mix. For variety, have chopped nuts, blueberries, and/or coconut ready to sprinkle over batter in waffle baker just before baking. To bake waffles correctly, close the iron quickly after pouring on the batter, and bake until steaming stops.

**Bacon Waffles:** Lay short strips of bacon over the grids of a heated waffle baker. Close about 1 min. Then pour waffle batter—minus melted shortening or oil—over cooked bacon and bake.

**Cheese-and-Bacon Waffles:** Fold ½ cup grated Cheddar cheese into batter. Pour onto iron. Lay short strips of crisp bacon across batter. Bake.

> *LEFTOVER WAFFLES? — Wrap and freeze. When needed, simply unwrap them and toast.*

## SPECIAL SYRUPS FOR PANCAKES AND WAFFLES

**Butter-kissed:** Melt butter over very low heat and mix with warm syrup—a perfect topping.

**Orange Honey:** Dilute honey with orange juice concentrate to taste. Spice with cloves and cinnamon. Heat before serving this delectable treat.

**Maple Whip:** Cream ½ cup soft butter. Add 1 cup maple-blended syrup gradually. Beat until smooth and of spreading consistency.

**Maple Apricot Syrup:** Blend ¾ cup maple-blended syrup, 1 tbsp. butter, and ¼ cup apricot nectar; heat.

*A Day in the Country*
**Pineapple-Grapefruit Juice**
**Your-choice Waffles**
**(sprinkle chopped nuts, blueberries, or grated cheese on batter in iron)**
**Butter            Syrup**

## FAVORITE PANCAKES

Warm, old-fashioned goodness in minutes...from Bisquick or our buttermilk pancake mix. Follow package directions for 2-cup recipe pancakes, then try these luscious variations:

**Corn Meal Pancakes:** Use ½ cup corn meal in place of ½ cup of mix. Bake. Serve with syrup or jelly and Frizzled Ham (p. 11) or bacon, or with grilled sausage and apple rings.

**Banana Pancakes:** Add 1 cup mashed ripe bananas (2 medium), 1 tbsp. lemon juice, and 2 tbsp. sugar. Serve with butter and honey or currant jelly.

**Spicy Pancakes:** Add 1 tsp. cinnamon, ½ tsp. allspice, ½ tsp. cloves, and ½ tsp. nutmeg. Serve with syrup or sweetened applesauce.

## SOUR CREAM PANCAKES

*A cross between an omelet and a pancake.*

Mix 3 eggs, 1 cup commercial sour cream, and 1 cup of our buttermilk pancake mix until smooth. Batter will be thick. Bake on medium-hot griddle or electric skillet (380°). These pancakes take longer to bake through. Serve with warm syrup. *Makes 10 to 12 pancakes.*

## PUFF PANCAKES

| | |
|---|---|
| **2 eggs** | **2 tbsp. sugar** |
| **1 cup milk** | **¼ cup melted** |
| **2⅓ cups Bisquick** | **shortening** |

Beat eggs with rotary beater or mixer until soft peaks form. Blend in milk; add Bisquick and sugar. Mix just until well dampened, then fold in shortening. Spoon onto ungreased medium-hot griddle. Turn when puffed up and bubbles begin to break. Cook other side. *Makes 15 to 20 pancakes.*

> *PANCAKE POINTERS—To save dishes, mix batter in wide-mouthed pitcher ready to pour onto griddle. Leftover batter can be stored, covered, in refrigerator and thinned with milk when used again.*

## EASY COFFEE CAKE

| | |
|---|---|
| 2 tbsp. sugar | 1 egg |
| 2 cups Bisquick | ¾ cup milk |

Heat oven to 400° (mod. hot). Blend ingredients. Beat vigorously 30 seconds. Spread batter into greased 9" round layer pan or 8 or 9" sq. pan. Sprinkle with mixture of ⅓ cup brown sugar, ⅓ cup Bisquick, ¼ cup cold butter, and ½ tsp. cinnamon; blended with fork until crumbly. Bake 20 to 25 min. *8 servings.*

**Berry or Fruit Coffee Cake:** Fold 1 cup fresh berries or ¾ cup well-drained canned berries or 1 cup cut-up dates or figs into Coffee Cake batter (above).

**Prune, Apricot, or Pineapple Coffee Cake:** When Coffee Cake batter (above) is in the pan, spread over it 2 tbsp. melted butter and sprinkle with ¼ cup granulated or brown sugar (add ¾ tsp. cinnamon for prune variation). Arrange over top 1 cup chopped drained cooked prunes or apricots or 1 cup drained crushed pineapple. Bake.

**Apple Chip Coffee Cake:** Fold 1 cup finely chopped pared apples into Coffee Cake batter (above). Sprinkle with topping and bake as above.

**Almond Crunch Coffee Cake:** Combine 2 tbsp. grated lemon rind, ¼ cup roasted chopped almonds, and 3 tbsp. sugar. Sprinkle over Coffee Cake batter (above) in pan. Bake.

**Brazil Nut Coffee Cake:** Make Coffee Cake batter (above). Sprinkle with mixture of ½ cup brown sugar (packed), 2 tbsp. Bisquick, 2 tbsp. vegetable oil or melted shortening, and ½ cup chopped Brazil nuts. *(See picture opposite.)*

*Some Sunny Morning*

**Chilled Tomato Juice**
**Trix with Milk**
**Scrambled Eggs (p. 9)**
**Brazil Nut Coffee Cake**

## DOUBLE-QUICK COFFEE BREAD

*Cake-like . . . delicious served warm. And, best of all, only one bowl for everything!*

| | |
|---|---|
| ¾ cup warm water (not hot—110 to 115°) | 2¼ cups Gold Medal Flour |
| 1 pkg. active dry yeast | 1 egg |
| ¼ cup sugar | ¼ cup soft shortening or butter |
| 1 tsp. salt | |

Choose a topping (below); grease pan and have topping ready. In mixing bowl, dissolve yeast in warm water. Measure flour by dip-level-pour method. Add sugar, salt, and about half the flour. Beat thoroughly 2 min. Add egg and shortening. Gradually beat in remaining flour until smooth. Drop small spoonfuls over topping in bottom of pan. Cover. Let rise in warm place (85°) until double in bulk, 50 to 60 min. (If kitchen is cool, place dough on a rack over a bowl of hot water and cover completely with a towel.) Heat oven to 375° (quick mod.). Bake 30 to 35 min., or until brown. Immediately turn out to avoid sticking. Serve warm. *9 to 12 servings.*

**Cherry Butterscotch Ring:** Melt in 9" ring mold ⅓ cup butter and ½ cup brown sugar (packed) with 1 tbsp. corn syrup. Decorate with walnut or pecan halves and candied or maraschino cherries. Cool slightly before spooning in dough. *(See picture, p. 156.)*

**Browned Butter Almond Buns:** Melt ⅓ cup butter in 8 or 9" sq. pan. Add ½ cup slivered blanched almonds. Heat until butter foams up in pan and browns and almonds are a light golden brown. (Almonds brown a little more while cooling.) Cool slightly. Mix in 2 tbsp. light corn syrup, ½ cup sugar, and ½ tsp. almond extract. Spoon in dough.

**Cinnamon Streusel Coffee Bread:** Mix thoroughly 2 tbsp. butter, ⅓ cup granulated or brown sugar, 2 tbsp. flour, 2 tsp. cinnamon, and ½ cup chopped nuts. Spoon dough into an 8 or 9" sq. pan. Sprinkle with streusel mixture.

**Marmalade Coffee Bread:** Sprinkle ¼ cup brown sugar (packed) in 8 or 9" sq. pan. Add ½ cup pineapple or orange marmalade. Spoon in dough.

## HAWAIIAN YEAST ROLLS

*Made with Bisquick and yeast . . . sticky-rich and good. Only 1 hour rising time.*

| | |
|---|---|
| ¾ cup drained crushed pineapple | 1 egg |
| ½ cup brown sugar (packed) | 1 tbsp. granulated sugar |
| ¼ cup soft butter | 2½ cups Bisquick |
| 1 pkg. active dry yeast | 2 tbsp. butter |
| ½ cup warm water (not hot—105 to 115°) | ¼ cup brown sugar (packed) |

Mix pineapple, ½ cup brown sugar, and ¼ cup butter. Divide among 12 large greased muffin cups. Dissolve yeast in water. Mix in egg, granulated sugar, and Bisquick; beat vigorously. Turn dough onto surface well dusted with Bisquick. Knead until smooth, 20 times. Roll into a rectangle, 16x9″. Spread with rest of ingredients. Roll up tightly beginning at wide side. Seal well by pinching edge of dough into roll. Slice into 12. Place in prepared muffin cups. Place pan of rolls on wire rack over bowl of hot water and cover with towel; let rise 1 hr. Heat oven to 400° (mod. hot). Bake 15 min. Invert pan; serve. *Makes 12 rolls.*

## JAM DANDIES

| | |
|---|---|
| 2 cups Bisquick | 2 tbsp. sugar |
| ⅔ cup milk | ½ cup thick strawberry jam |

Heat oven to 400° (mod. hot). Mix Bisquick, milk, and sugar to stiff dough. Beat vigorously 20 strokes. Roll around on board lightly dusted with Bisquick. Knead to smooth up. Divide in half. Pat each to fit 8″ layer pan. Fit one piece into greased pan, pressing about ¼″ up sides. Spread with jam. Cover with other circle. Sprinkle top with ¼ cup each sugar and chopped nuts. Cut with sharp knife into 8 wedges. Bake 20 to 25 min. Serve warm. *8 servings.*

## CARAMEL BUNS

| | |
|---|---|
| ¼ cup soft butter | ¾ cup warm water (not hot—105 to 115°) |
| ⅓ cup brown sugar (packed) | 2½ cups Bisquick |
| 1 tsp. light corn syrup | 2 tbsp. soft butter |
| ⅓ cup pecans or walnuts | ¼ cup brown sugar (packed) |
| 1 pkg. active dry yeast | 1 tsp. cinnamon |

Melt ¼ cup butter; add ⅓ cup brown sugar and corn syrup. Bring syrup mixture to a rolling boil. Spread in 8″ round layer pan. Add pecans. Dissolve yeast in water. Mix in Bisquick and beat vigorously. Turn dough onto surface well dusted with Bisquick. Knead until smooth, 20 times. Roll out into rectangle, 16x9″. Spread with remaining ingredients. Roll up tightly, beginning at wide side. Seal well by pinching edge of dough into roll. Slice into 10 slices. Place in pan. Place pan of buns on wire rack over bowl of hot water and cover with towel; let rise 1 hr. Heat oven to 400° (mod. hot); bake 20 to 25 min. Invert pan and serve buns warm. *Makes 10 buns.*

## SPICY MARMALADE BREAD

Spread 1″ thick slices of French bread with soft butter, then with orange marmalade (don't skimp!). Sprinkle generously with cinnamon. Place on baking sheet. Heat in 400° oven about 8 min., until hot.

### GINGERBREAD FOR BREAKFAST

Ever try it? With golden butter melting over the top and a sprinkle of sugar . . . warm and tender. Midwestern farmers eat it often for breakfast. And, when you try it, you'll see why. Make it from your favorite recipe or with gingerbread mix.

## HONEY BUTTER BRUNCH RING

*Rich and tender, it is best eaten with a fork.*

| | |
|---|---|
| 2 tbsp. sugar | Date-Nut Mixture (below) |
| 2 tbsp. butter | 2 tbsp. butter, melted |
| 2 cups Bisquick | ⅓ cup honey |
| ⅔ cup milk | |

Heat oven to 350° (mod.). Stir sugar and butter into Bisquick. Add milk all at once and beat to a soft dough. Drop about half of dough into 10 mounds on floured board; roll into balls. Place around bottom of 9″ ring mold and cover with Date-Nut Mixture. Make rest of dough into 10 more balls; place in mold. Mix butter and honey; pour over top. Bake 25 min., until golden brown. Remove from mold immediately after baking. *8 servings.*

**Date-Nut Mixture:** Mix ½ cup light brown sugar (packed), ¼ cup chopped dates, ¼ cup chopped nuts, 1 tsp. cinnamon, and ¼ cup butter, melted.

## DOUGHNUTS

| | |
|---|---|
| 2 cups Bisquick | 1 tsp. vanilla |
| ¼ cup sugar | 1 egg |
| ⅓ cup milk | ¼ tsp. each cinnamon and nutmeg, if desired |

Fill heavy kettle or deep fat fryer with fat or oil to depth of 3″. Heat fat to 375° (temp. at which a small bread cube browns in 50 sec.). Mix ingredients until well blended. Turn dough onto lightly floured surface and knead about 10 times. Roll out ⅜″ thick. Cut with floured doughnut cutter. Drop into hot fat. Fry until golden brown on both sides, about 1 min. to a side. Remove from fat and drain on absorbent paper. Shake one at a time in a small paper bag containing sugar—and, if desired, a dash of cinnamon. *Makes about 12 doughnuts.*

## BAKED CORN FRITTER

*New-fashioned fritters. The same hearty eating without the fuss of deep fat frying.*

Heat oven to 400° (mod. hot). Grease an oblong pan, 13x9½x2″. Drain 1 can (1 lb.) whole-kernel corn, reserving juice. Prepare 1 pkg. (14 oz.) of our corn muffin mix, using ⅔ cup corn juice for liquid in batter. Add corn. Pour into prepared pan. Bake 20 to 25 min. Serve hot with butter, syrup, and crisp bacon or sausage. *9 to 12 servings.*

## WONDERFUL BUTTER SPREADS FOR MUFFINS, ROLLS, OR BISCUITS

**Honey Butter:** Beat ½ cup honey into ½ cup butter. Add 1 tsp. grated orange rind and beat until fluffy.

**Marmalade Butter:** Mix equal portions of sweet orange marmalade and butter together until blended. Makes orange muffins doubly good.

## TEMPTING TOUCHES FOR BROWN 'N SERVE ROLLS

**Cinnamon-topped Rolls:** Butter rolls; then sprinkle with sugar-and-cinnamon mixture (¼ cup granulated or brown sugar to 1 tsp. cinnamon). Bake in 400° oven 8 to 10 min.

**Streusel-topped Rolls:** Spread rolls with a mixture of 2 tbsp. butter or margarine, 5 tbsp. sugar, 2 tbsp. flour, and ½ tsp. cinnamon. Bake in 400° oven 8 to 10 min.

**Orange-glazed Rolls:** Bring to a boil ½ cup sugar, 2 tbsp. water, and ¼ cup orange juice; simmer for 5 min. Stir in grated rind of 1 orange and cool. Spread on fresh rolls while still warm.

**Frosted Rolls:** Mix sifted confectioners' sugar with cream or milk to spreading consistency. Add flavoring, if desired. Spread over freshly baked rolls while still warm.

## BASIC RULES FOR A GOOD CUP OF COFFEE

**1.** Use fresh coffee. Keep tightly covered—it loses its flavor when exposed to air.

**2.** Use the correct grind for your coffee maker. "Drip" for glass vacuum makers or dripolators; "regular" or "steel cut" for percolators or steeped (boiled) coffee.

**3.** Be sure coffee maker is sparkling clean. Wash well after each use.

**4.** Start with fresh cold water from the tap.

**5.** Make at least ¾ capacity of the pot. Smaller quantity minimizes the "real coffee" flavor.

**6.** Measure coffee and water carefully—2 tbsp. coffee to ¾ cup water for medium strength.

**7.** Serve it fresh! If necessary that it stand, remove grounds. Keep hot on asbestos pad over very low heat, or in pan of hot water.

## UNUSUAL AND DELICIOUS BREAKFAST BEVERAGES

Cranberry juice adds zip and pretty pink color to pineapple, orange, or apple juice . . . or to apricot nectar.

Tangy grapefruit or pineapple juice does wonders to the everyday orange juice.

Spark sweet apricot or peach nectar with a drop or two of lemon juice.

On a cold, cold morning, serve extra-nourishing cups of bouillon or consommé with salty crackers for a breakfast starter.

For extra-special breakfast or brunch, serve chilled eggnog—fluffy and foamy—with nutmeg on top.

Vegetable cocktail, tomato juice, or carrot juice are enhanced with lemon or lime slices or a dash of lemon or lime juice, sugar, salt, or Tabasco.

## HOT CHOCOLATE

| | |
|---|---|
| 2 sq. unsweetened chocolate (2 oz.) | pinch of salt |
| | 3 tbsp. sugar |
| 1 cup water | 3 cups milk |

Heat chocolate and water over low heat, stirring until chocolate melts and mixture is smooth. Add salt and sugar. Boil 4 min., stirring. Then slowly stir in milk. Cover and heat until scalded. Do not boil. Just before serving, beat with rotary beater until smooth. Serve hot, topped with whipped cream. *6 servings.*

## SOUTH AMERICAN CHOCOLATE

*Coffee and chocolate, smoothly blended for an unusual mid-morning drink.*

Melt over hot water ½ lb. sweet cooking chocolate or 1 pkg. (6 oz.) semi-sweet chocolate pieces. Add 1 cup strong hot coffee. Stir well and heat on low for 1 min. Scald 6 cups milk (1½ qt.); add to chocolate. Simmer until very hot. Beat with rotary beater until frothy. Set over hot water 10 min. to blend flavors. Just before serving, beat again with rotary beater. *8 servings.*

## HOT COCOA

| | |
|---|---|
| ¼ cup sugar | 1½ cups water |
| ¼ cup cocoa | 6 cups milk |

Mix sugar and cocoa. Add water; place over low heat until mixture boils, about 4 min. Add milk; cover and heat until scalded. Do not boil. Add a pinch of salt and a drop of vanilla, if desired. Just before serving, stir until smooth or beat with rotary beater. Serve hot with marshmallows or whipped cream. *6 to 8 servings.*

**Spicy Cocoa:** Just before serving cocoa, add a dash of either cinnamon or nutmeg.

*READY-TO-SERVE COCOA — Some powdered forms have sweetening, powdered milk, and flavoring already mixed. You need add only hot water or milk, mix well, and serve. It can also be used for nutritious cold chocolate-flavored drinks.*

# Hearty Weekend Breakfasts for the Family

### *Pancake Party*

**Grapefruit Halves**
**Puff Pancakes (p. 15)**
**with Maple Whip (p. 15)**

### *Southern Special*

**Wedges of Honeydew Melon**
**Fried Ham**      **Hot Grits**
**Biscuits**      **Honey Butter (p. 19)**

### *Hawaiian Style*

**Sliced Bananas in Orange Juice**
**with Shredded Coconut**
**Oahu Toast (p. 13)**
**Sausage Patties (p. 12)**

### *Breakfast Buffet*

**Cantaloupe Halves**
**Choice of Ready-to-Eat Cereals**
**Bacon and Fried Egg Platter**
**Browned Butter Almond Buns (p. 17)**

# Festive Brunches for Family and Friends

### *Strawberry Festival*

**Orange Nog**
**(beat orange juice and**
**raw egg together)**
**Strawberry Shortcake (p. 48)**
**Crisp Bacon**

### *Favorite for Fall*

**Autumn Fruit Cup**
**(diced apple and melon balls)**
**Soft-cooked Eggs (p. 8)**
**Pork Sausage Links (p. 12)**
**Caramel Buns (p. 18)**

### *Holiday Breakfast*

**Brown-eyed Susans (p. 5)**
**Cheerios with Eggnog**
**Shirred Eggs (p. 9)**      **Bacon**
**Cherry Butterscotch Ring (p. 17)**
**or Jam Dandies (p. 18)**

### *It's Spring*

**Strawberry-Rhubarb Sauce**
**French Omelet (p. 9)**
**with Creamed Asparagus**
**Toasted English Muffins**
**Marmalade Butter (p. 19)**

# Lunch

Lunch is the noon meal in many American homes while dinner is served in the evening; in other homes, dinner is at noon and supper is the light meal of the day. Although the easy recipes and menus in this chapter have been titled "Lunch," they will be just as good for supper—if that is what you and your family have.

Variety is the spice of lunch—and lending variety is fun when you use lunch patterns. Soup-sandwich-salad, sandwich-dessert, soup-cookies-fruit, casserole-relishes-ice cream, and salad-rolls-dessert are just a few of today's popular lunch patterns. One day serve a new soup with a favorite sandwich, another time prepare a new dessert to follow a tried-and-true salad.

We've filled the pages that follow with lunch-time foods that take very little time to prepare, special touches to add to canned, packaged, and frozen foods, and suggestions for using up food from other meals as "put-togethers" or "made-overs." Menu plans for colorful and nutritious lunches will help you decide what to serve with what. There are ideas, too, for meals-in-a-box, lunches to be carried to school or job.

And for the days when company comes for lunch or supper, you will find quick-to-fix foods to add a festive touch to the meal yet leave you free to enjoy the occasion.

## SOUTH-OF-THE-BORDER SUPPER SOUP

| | |
|---|---|
| 1 can (10½ oz.) bean with bacon soup | 1 soup can water |
| 1 can (10½ oz.) tomato soup | ⅛ to ¼ tsp. garlic powder, if desired |
| 1 can (10½ oz.) chili without beans | corn chips |

Combine soups and chili. Stir in water; blend in garlic powder. Heat to boil. Ladle into bowls. Top with corn chips. *4 to 6 servings.*

## SPLIT PEA SOUP

| | |
|---|---|
| 2 cups dried split peas (1 lb.) | 1 large onion, minced |
| 3 qt. water | 3 stalks celery (with tops), chopped fine |
| 1 ham bone or small shank end of ham | 1 sprig parsley |
| | salt and pepper |

Soak peas in water in large kettle. Bring to boil and boil gently 2 min. Remove from heat; cover and let stand 1 hr. Add ham, onion, celery, and parsley. Heat to boil; cover and simmer 2 to 2½ hr., until peas are tender and liquid is partially cooked down. Season to taste with salt and pepper. For a smooth soup, put through a sieve. Dilute as desired with additional milk or water. *8 servings.*

## QUICK VEGETABLE SOUP WITH FRANK SLICES

| | |
|---|---|
| 2 cans (10½ oz. each) condensed beef bouillon | 4 zucchini squash, sliced |
| 1 soup can water | 2 onions, cut in chunks |
| 2 cloves garlic, minced | 3 ripe tomatoes, quartered |
| 1 tsp. monosodium glutamate | 2 tbsp. butter |
| 4 carrots, pared and cut in small pieces | 1 tsp. salt |
| | 3 frankfurters, cut in slices |

Combine bouillon, water, garlic, monosodium glutamate, and carrots in large saucepan. Cook over medium heat 15 min. Add remaining ingredients and simmer another 30 min. *6 to 8 servings.*

## OLD-FASHIONED VEGETABLE SOUP

| | |
|---|---|
| 1 lb. shin beef with bone | 3 sprigs parsley, cut fine |
| 4 cups water | 1 tbsp. salt |
| 1 medium onion, chopped | ½ bay leaf, crumbled* |
| 1 cup sliced carrots | 3 peppercorns* |
| 1 cup cut-up celery and leaves | ¼ tsp. marjoram |
| 1 can (1 lb.) tomatoes (2 cups) | ¼ tsp. thyme |

Cut meat off soup bone; cut in small chunks. Brown in 1 or 2 tbsp. hot fat in large kettle. Add water and bone; simmer, covered, 1½ to 2 hr. Remove bone and skim fat from top of soup. Add vegetables and seasonings and cook an additional 20 to 30 min., or until vegetables are tender. *6 to 8 servings.*

*Place whole herbs and spices in 6x4″ piece of clean new cheesecloth or muslin and tie with white string; cook with meat and vegetables; remove when desired flavor is obtained.

## CORN-TOMATO CHOWDER

| | |
|---|---|
| ¼ lb. bacon or salt pork | 1 tbsp. sugar |
| 1 small onion, diced | 2 tsp. salt |
| 1 can (1 lb.) whole-kernel corn (2 cups) | ½ tsp. paprika |
| 1 can (1 lb.) tomatoes (2 cups) | ⅛ tsp. pepper |
| 2 cups diced potatoes | 3 cups boiling water |
| | 1 cup evaporated milk |

Cut bacon into small pieces and fry slowly to a golden brown in a 3- to 4-qt. saucepan. Add onion and cook slowly, without browning, 5 min. Add corn (including liquid), tomatoes, and potatoes. Sprinkle with seasonings. Add boiling water and cook slowly until potatoes are tender, 20 to 25 min. Remove from heat and slowly stir in milk. *6 to 8 servings.*

**Note:** *When salt pork is used, reduce salt to 1 tsp.*

# Start with a Can of Soup

**Cream of Corn Soup:** Combine 1 can (10½ oz.) cream of chicken soup, ½ cup mayonnaise, 1½ to 2½ cups milk, and 1 can (1 lb.) whole-kernel corn (2 cups). Heat to steaming. Garnish with pimiento. *4 to 6 servings.*

**Savory Cream of Chicken Soup:** Mix 1 can (10½ oz.) each cream of chicken soup and chicken with rice soup. Add ½ cup milk and 1 tsp. tarragon. Heat over low heat, stirring occasionally. Garnish with whipped cream sprinkled with paprika. *4 servings.*

**Quick Cream of Vegetable Soup:** Use 1 can (10½ oz.) diluted cream of chicken soup or make 2 cups Thin Cream Sauce (p. 103), using chicken broth or consommé as part of liquid. Add ½ pkg. frozen mixed vegetables, cooked, or half of 1-lb. can mixed vegetables. (Use the other half pkg. or can for salad on another day.) Heat to boiling. *4 servings.*

**Madrilene:** Heat together equal amounts beef consommé or bouillon (diluted as directed on can), chicken broth, and tomato juice. Garnish with lemon slice; serve.

**Lobster Bisque:** Heat 1 can (10½ oz.) cream of chicken soup and 1 soup can milk. Add 1 can (5 oz.) lobster, cut in pieces, ¼ to ½ tsp. paprika, ⅛ tsp. nutmeg, and a few grains cayenne pepper. *4 servings.*

**Rich Chicken and Clam Soup:** Combine 1 can (13¾ oz.) chicken broth with 1 can (7½ oz.) minced clams (including juice). Simmer 5 min. Add ½ cup cream (20% butterfat). Heat but do not boil. Garnish with chopped parsley. *4 servings.*

**Clam-Tomato Bisque:** Combine 1 can (10½ oz.) tomato soup and 1 can (7½ oz.) minced clams, using the juice of clams as part of liquid. Add salt, pepper, and lemon juice to taste. Simmer 5 min. Just before serving, add 1 soup can milk. Heat but do not boil. *4 servings.*

**Quick Russian Borsch:** Add 2 finely shredded small raw beets, 1 cup finely shredded cabbage, and 2 to 4 tbsp. chopped onion to 1 can (10½ oz.) bouillon (diluted according to directions on can). Bring to boiling and simmer 10 min. Serve topped with a spoonful of sour cream. *4 servings.*

## CHEESE CHOWDER

1 pkg. (10 oz.) frozen
   mixed vegetables

1 can (10½ oz.) cream of
   chicken soup, undiluted

1 soup can milk

1 cup grated processed
   Cheddar cheese

Cook vegetables as directed on pkg. Add soup and milk; heat slowly, stirring occasionally. Serve with grated cheese on top. *4 servings.*

**Note:** *Just heat to simmering, do not boil.*

## EASY CORN-CLAM CHOWDER

Follow directions on 1 can (10 oz.) frozen clam chowder adding 1 can (7 oz.) whole-kernel corn, drained, 1 tsp. onion flakes, ¼ tsp. salt, and ⅛ tsp. pepper, if desired. Garnish with paprika or chopped parsley. *3 servings.*

*REMEMBER DEHYDRATED SOUPS—in their easy-to-store envelopes. They can be prepared in minutes, yet have that delicious cooked-for-hours flavor.*

BORSCH

## CREAM OF POTATO SOUP

| | |
|---|---|
| 2 tbsp. butter | 4 cups milk (1 qt.) |
| 2 tbsp. chopped onion | Enough of our mashed |
| 1½ tsp. salt | Potato Buds (dry) |
| ¼ tsp. celery salt | for 4 servings |
| ⅛ tsp. pepper | |

Combine ingredients in medium saucepan. Heat to boiling, stirring occasionally. Remove from heat. Strain into serving dishes. (Soup should be consistency of heavy cream. If thicker, add more milk.) Garnish with paprika and parsley. *4 to 5 servings.*

## CREAM OF CARROT SOUP

| | |
|---|---|
| ½ cup chopped onion | ⅛ tsp. pepper |
| 2 tbsp. butter | ⅛ tsp. celery salt |
| 2 tbsp. flour | 2½ cups milk |
| 1 tsp. salt | 1 cup carrot juice (12-oz. can) |

Sauté onion in butter until golden. Blend in flour and seasonings. Cook over low heat, stirring until mixture is smooth and bubbly. Remove from heat. Stir in milk and carrot juice. Bring to boil; boil 1 min., stirring constantly. Serve topped with crisp croutons or minced parsley. *4 servings.*

## SPINACH SOUP

| | |
|---|---|
| 1 tsp. finely chopped onion | 1 pkg. (10 oz.) frozen chopped spinach, thawed |
| 2 tbsp. butter | |
| 2 tbsp. flour | 2 cups milk |
| 1 tsp. salt | 2 cups chicken broth |
| ⅛ tsp. pepper | |

Sauté onion in butter. Blend in flour and seasonings. Stir over medium heat until smooth and bubbly. Stir in spinach. Bring to boil; boil 1 min., stirring constantly. Remove from heat. Gradually stir in milk and chicken broth. Heat to serving temperature. *6 servings.*

**Blender Spinach Soup:** Follow directions above—except put 1 lb. fresh spinach, cooked, through food blender with 1 medium onion in place of frozen chopped spinach. Omit finely chopped onion.

## OYSTER STEW

| | |
|---|---|
| 1 pt. milk (2 cups) | 1 pt. oysters (with liquor) |
| ½ cup cream (20% butterfat) | 1 tsp. salt |
| ¼ cup butter | dash of pepper |

Heat milk and cream to scalding. Just before serving, melt butter in saucepan; add oysters and oyster liquor. Cook gently just until oyster edges curl. Add to scalded milk and cream. Season with salt and pepper; serve immediately with oyster crackers. *4 servings.*

## CALIFORNIA CREAM SOUP

| | |
|---|---|
| 1 can (10½ oz.) cream of celery soup | ¾ tsp. salt |
| 1 can (10½ oz.) cream of chicken soup | ⅛ tsp. pepper |
| ⅔ cup cream (20% butterfat) | ¾ cup chopped avocado |
| 2 cups milk | ¼ cup ripe olives, sliced |
| | ¼ cup chopped pimiento |

In large saucepan mix soups, cream, milk, salt, and pepper. Cook over low heat to simmer. Stir in avocado, olives, and pimiento. Continue heating slowly for several minutes. *Makes 7½ cups (4 main dish servings or 6 to 8 first course servings).*

## SOUP ACCOMPANIMENTS

**Crispy Crackers:** Heat oven to 300° (slow). Brush crackers with vegetable oil or melted butter. Heat until lightly browned.

**Seeded Crackers:** Sprinkle crackers with celery, caraway, or poppy seeds before heating.

**Cheese Crackers:** Place thin slices of cheese or grated cheese on crackers. Heat until cheese melts.

**Croutons:** Cut day-old bread in ½" squares. Fry in butter until golden brown. Shake skillet or toss with fork. Serve atop cream soups.

**Cheese Nippies:** Melt ⅓ cup butter in skillet. Add 3 to 5 drops Tabasco, ½ tsp. salt, 1 tsp. paprika, and ⅓ cup grated Cheddar or Parmesan cheese. Mix in 4 cups Kix. Stir over low heat until well blended.

# Sandwich Making

**The Bread:** Use fresh or day-old bread. Leave crusts on (prevents drying). Try different breads.

**The Spread:** Have butter or margarine soft. Keep a covered bowl of odds and ends. Spread all the way to the edge on both slices to prevent filling from soaking.

**The Filling:** Have filling well seasoned before spreading (moist but not wet). Keep fillings fresh and moist in covered bowls or plastic containers in refrigerator. Wrap lettuce separately. Use several thin slices of meat rather than just one thick slice.

**The Making:** Line up matching slices; spread butter on all. Spoon on filling, then spread evenly to the edges. Wrap individually.

**The Wrapping:** Place sandwich in center of oblong of waxed paper; bring edges together, fold down several times, turn under corners, then ends. Or use handy waxed paper or plastic sandwich bags.

**For Packing a Number of Sandwiches:** Place a damp towel in shallow pan; line with waxed paper. Make double fold of paper over sandwiches, then bring towel over top (see sketch).

**If You Have a Freezer:** Make a week's supply of sandwiches at one time. Wrap in waxed paper, slipping name of sandwich under top fold. Avoid sandwiches with hard-cooked eggs, mayonnaise, or lettuce. Sandwiches will be thawed by lunch time if taken from freezer at breakfast.

# Filling Suggestions

*Sandwich fillings are seldom made from written recipes but rather from ingenuity, imagination, and whatever is on hand. Season fillings to taste.*

##  Egg

Chopped hard-cooked egg, pickle relish, pimiento, and salad dressing.

Chopped hard-cooked egg, minced ripe olives, and mayonnaise.

Chopped hard-cooked egg, chopped ham, minced onion and green pepper, and salad dressing.

##  Cheese

Cream cheese, chopped stuffed olives, and nuts.

Sliced Cheddar cheese, thinly sliced fried ham, and prepared mustard.

Swiss cheese, ham, and pickle.

Cream cheese, Roquefort cheese, and chopped nuts.

Cream cheese, drained crushed pineapple, and chopped pecans.

Swiss cheese and mustard on rye bread.

Cottage cheese, minced green pepper and onion on whole wheat bread.

##  Meat

Leftover beef roast (ground), chopped pickle and celery, mustard or horse-radish, and mayonnaise.

Leftover baked ham (ground), chopped pickle, mustard, and mayonnaise.

Ground cooked ham or canned luncheon meat, cheese, sweet pickle, and mayonnaise.

Liverwurst, slice of tomato, lettuce, and mayonnaise.

##  Fish

Flaked tuna or salmon, sweet pickle, chopped celery, and mayonnaise.

Crabmeat, chopped celery, dash of lemon juice, and mayonnaise.

## VARIETY FROM COLD CUTS

**Deviled Frankfurters:** Mix together ½ lb. frankfurters (coarsely ground), ½ tsp. dry mustard, 3 tbsp. sweet pickle relish, 2 tbsp. milk, and ⅓ cup salad dressing. *6 sandwiches.*

**Bologna-Cheese:** Grind together ¼ lb. bologna and ¼ lb. Cheddar cheese. Add ⅓ cup milk, 2 tbsp. sweet pickle relish, ¼ tsp. dry mustard, ⅛ tsp. salt, and dash of pepper. *8 sandwiches.*

## FROM THE GRILL

**French-toasted Sandwiches:** Sandwiches of cheese, meat, fish, or almost any leftover sandwiches, are delicious French-toasted. For every 3 sandwiches combine 2 beaten eggs, ¼ tsp. salt, and ½ cup milk. Dip sandwiches into egg mixture. Brown on both sides in butter on hot electric grill or in heavy skillet.

**Grilled Cheese Sandwiches:** Make cheese sandwiches. Brush lightly with melted butter or spread with soft butter on both sides and bake until golden brown on electric grill or in heavy skillet.

**Open Grilled Cheese Sandwiches:** Toast bread slices on one side. Cover lightly buttered untoasted side with Cheddar cheese. Place under broiler until cheese melts. Sprinkle with paprika; garnish with parsley, pickles, and tomato wedges. Serve at once.

## FROM THINGS ON HAND

**Carrot-Peanut:** Combine 1½ cups grated raw carrots, ½ cup finely chopped salted peanuts, ¼ cup pickle relish, and ⅓ cup salad dressing. *8 sandwiches.*

**Raisin-Peanut Butter:** Mix ¾ cup crunchy peanut butter, 6 tbsp. chopped raisins, and 6 tbsp. orange juice. *5 sandwiches.*

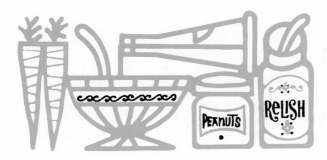

## HANDY CANNED MEATS

**Corned Beef and Egg:** Combine ¼ lb. corned beef (coarsely ground), 2 hard-cooked eggs (chopped), 1 tbsp. sweet pickle relish, ¼ cup cream, 1 tbsp. lemon juice, ¼ tsp. salt, and pepper. *8 sandwiches.*

**Salmon Salad:** Combine 1 cup flaked salmon, ¼ tsp. salt, ½ cup finely chopped celery, ¼ cup finely chopped green pepper, 2 tbsp. mayonnaise, and 2 tbsp. lemon juice. *8 sandwiches.*

**Sardine and Egg:** Combine ¼ cup mashed sardines, 2 hard-cooked eggs (chopped), 1 tbsp. pickle relish, 2 tsp. sardine or olive oil, dash of salt, and 1 tbsp. salad dressing. *3 sandwiches.*

## THE VERSATILE EGG

**Egg Salad, Garden Style:** Combine 8 slices bacon (fried crisp and crumbled), 3 hard-cooked eggs (chopped), 2 tbsp. pickle relish (drained), 2 tbsp. finely chopped radishes, 2 tbsp. finely chopped carrots, ½ tsp. salt, 1 tbsp. French dressing, and 1 to 2 tbsp. salad dressing. *6 sandwiches. (See picture, p. 55.)*

**Egg and Deviled Ham:** Combine 1 hard-cooked egg (chopped), ¼ cup deviled ham, 1 tbsp. Worcestershire sauce, and 2 tbsp. chopped pickle. *3 sandwiches.*

**Norwegian Spread:** Combine 1 pkg. (3 oz.) softened cream cheese, 2 hard-cooked eggs (chopped), 1 small onion (chopped), 1 large dill pickle (chopped), and 4 strips crisp bacon (crumbled). Chill to blend flavors. *3 sandwiches.*

# The Art of Making a Good Hamburger

### WHAT TO BUY

Ground beef made from chuck or trimmings and sold by a reliable meat dealer is juicier, less expensive, and has even more flavor than ground round because it has some fat through it.

### HOW TO STORE GROUND BEEF

For use same day or next, wrap loosely and refrigerate at once. To keep longer, shape into patties; place between waxed papers and keep in freezer. Patties can be wrapped in freezer paper and stored in freezer up to 3 months.

### BARBECUED HAMBURGERS FOR A CROWD

| | |
|---|---|
| 1 cup chopped onion | 2 tbsp. brown sugar |
| 2 tbsp. butter | 1 tbsp. Worcestershire sauce |
| 4 lb. ground beef | |
| 1 bottle (14 oz.) catsup | 1 tbsp. salt |
| 1 cup water | 2 tsp. vinegar |
| ½ cup chopped celery | 1 tsp. monosodium glutamate |
| ¼ cup lemon juice | ½ tsp. dry mustard |

Sauté onion in butter. Add ground beef; brown lightly. Drain off excess fat. Add rest of ingredients and simmer, covered, 30 min. *Use to fill 30 to 40 warm hamburger buns.*

Or, cool and freeze in five 1-pt. freezing containers. Seal and label with name and date. Freeze at 0° or lower. Before serving, heat mixture slowly in skillet. *1 pt. fills 6 to 8 hot buttered hamburger buns.*

*The Gang's All Here*

**Barbecued Hamburgers for a Crowd**
**Old-fashioned Cabbage Slaw (p. 97)**
**Lemon Macaroon Torte (p. 128)**

### JUICY HAMBURGERS

| | |
|---|---|
| 1 lb. ground beef | ¼ tsp. monosodium glutamate |
| 1 tsp. salt | |
| ¼ tsp. pepper | 1 tsp. Worcestershire sauce |
| 2 tbsp. chopped onion | |
| ½ cup water or milk | horse-radish or mustard to taste |

Toss all ingredients together lightly with a fork. Divide and form into 4 thick patties or 8 thin ones. Handle as little as possible. Pan-fry in small amount of hot fat, broil 3″ from heat, or grill on electric grill. Fry or broil 8 min. for rare, 12 min. for medium, and 16 min. for well done. Turn once but do not flatten—this presses juices out. Serve immediately on buttered toasted split buns.

**Quick Barbecued Hamburgers:** Broil, turning once. Spread with bottled barbecue sauce, catsup, or chili sauce after turning and continue broiling.

**Surprise Burgers:** Form 8 thin patties from 1 lb. ground beef. On half the patties, spread pickle relish, prepared mustard, catsup, or chopped onions. Top with remaining thin patties and seal edges. Fry or broil as desired.

**Double Decker Cheeseburgers:** Form 8 thin patties from 1 lb. ground beef. Mix 2 oz. crumbled Bleu cheese or 2 oz. shredded Cheddar cheese with 1 tsp. salt, ¼ tsp. pepper, 2 tbsp. mayonnaise, 1 tsp. Worcestershire sauce, and ½ tsp. mustard. Spread cheese filling on half the patties, top each with a second patty. Fry or broil.

**Cheeseburgers:** When second side of hamburger patty is half broiled, top with thin slice of cheese. Broil until cheese melts.

**California Hamburger:** Top cooked hamburger in bun with slice of tomato, onion, lettuce, and mayonnaise.

**Pizza Burgers:** Broil, turning once. When second side is half broiled, top with thin slice of Mozzarella cheese. Broil until cheese melts. Place in toasted bun, spoon Pizza Sauce (canned or recipe below) over patty.

> Pizza Sauce: Mix 1 can (8 oz.) tomato sauce, 1 tsp. salt, ¼ tsp. pepper, ¼ to ½ tsp. oregano, and 1 clove garlic, minced very fine or squeezed through garlic press, in pan. Heat 5 min.

## SLIM JIM BURGERS

¾ lb. ground beef
¼ lb. ground pork
1 egg, beaten
½ cup dry bread crumbs
⅓ cup milk
¾ tsp. salt
¼ tsp. pepper

⅓ cup finely chopped onion
1 tbsp. dry mustard
½ tsp. Worcestershire sauce
1 small bay leaf, crushed
8 cheese sticks, 3½ x ¼ x ¼"
8 frankfurter buns

Heat oven to 400° (mod. hot). Combine all ingredients except cheese and buns. Divide meat into 8 equal portions; mold each portion around a cheese stick. Place on lightly greased baking sheet with sides (jelly roll pan, if available). Bake about 20 min. Serve in warm split frankfurter buns. Top with Tomato Sauce (p. 103). Garnish with parsley. *8 sandwiches.*

## SPREAD-A-BURGERS

*See picture, p. 55.*

1 can (10½ oz.) tomato soup
½ cup shredded American or Cheddar cheese
¼ cup chopped onion
1½ tsp. salt
1 tsp. dry mustard

¼ tsp. pepper
1 lb. ground beef
8 hamburger buns, split and toasted
16 thin green pepper rings
stuffed green olives, sliced

Heat oven to 350° (mod.). Mix soup, cheese, onion, salt, mustard, and pepper. Blend in ground beef. Spread toasted bun halves with meat mixture, sealing to edges. Place 10 to 12 buns on a baking sheet and set on oven rack 6 to 8" from broiling unit. Bake 15 to 20 min., or until meat is done. Open oven door and turn oven to broil; broil about 3 min., or until meat is nicely browned. Repeat as above with remaining 6 to 8 Spread-A-Burgers, for second servings. Garnish each bun half with pepper ring and olives. Serve open-face. *16 open-face or 8 double servings.*

## ORIENTAL BURGERS

1 medium onion, sliced
1 lb. ground beef
2 tbsp. vegetable oil
1 can (1 lb.) bean sprouts, drained
1 can (5 oz.) water chestnuts, sliced (¾ cup)

⅓ cup soy sauce
⅓ cup water
1 tbsp. dark molasses
2 tbsp. water
2 tbsp. cornstarch
hamburger buns (about 8)

Sauté onion and beef in oil until browned. Add bean sprouts, water chestnuts, soy sauce, ⅓ cup water, and molasses. Cook about 5 min. Add 2 tbsp. water to cornstarch; mix and add to mixture. Bring to boil; boil 1 min. Salt to taste. Serve in hamburger buns. *About 8 sandwiches.*

## SOUTHERN BURGERS

1 lb. ground beef
1 medium onion, diced
3 tbsp. catsup

3 tbsp. prepared mustard
1 can (10½ oz.) chicken gumbo soup

Brown beef and onion in a little hot fat. Stir in catsup, mustard, and soup. Simmer until mixture has thickened a little, about 15 min. Spoon over toasted split buns. (May be made early, refrigerated, and reheated.) *6 servings.*

## CRUMBLED HAMBURGER

½ cup chopped onion
2 tbsp. fat
1 lb. ground beef
2 tbsp. flour
¼ cup plus 2 tbsp. catsup

1 tbsp. prepared mustard
½ tsp. salt
¼ tsp. pepper
1 cup commercial sour cream

Brown onion in hot fat. Add and brown meat, drain off excess fat. Mix in rest of ingredients except sour cream. Simmer 5 to 10 min. to thicken a little. Stir in sour cream. Heat through. Serve hot on toasted buns. *8 servings.*

# Nice for Lunch, Supper, or Quick Snacks

### REUBEN SANDWICH

1 can (1 lb.) sauer-
  kraut, drained
¼ cup plus 2 tbsp.
  mayonnaise
½ lb. sliced turkey

½ lb. Swiss cheese,
  sliced
1 pkg. (4 oz.) corned
  beef
12 slices rye bread

Marinate sauerkraut in mayonnaise 30 min. Arrange pieces of turkey, cheese, and corned beef on 6 buttered slices of bread. Arrange marinated sauerkraut atop meat and cheese (use ⅓ cup per slice). Top with second slice of bread. Sandwich will be 1½ to 2" high. *6 sandwiches.*

### HAM-PINEAPPLE SANDWICH SUPPER

favorite ham loaf
  mixture using 1 lb.
  meat
6 pineapple slices
¾ cup brown sugar
  (packed)
¼ cup vinegar

¼ cup liquid from
  pineapple
2 tbsp. prepared
  mustard
6 hamburger buns
cream cheese balls
  rolled in chopped nuts

Heat oven to 350° (mod.). Prepare ham loaf mixture; divide into 6 portions; pat out on cutting board until ½ to ¾" thick. Cut into rings with doughnut cutter. Arrange rings of meat and pineapple in baking pan (do not stack). Bake 30 min., basting occasionally with sauce made by heating brown sugar, vinegar, pineapple liquid, and mustard in pan until sugar dissolves. Butter buns and toast. Serve sandwiches open-face with meat ring on bottom half and pineapple on top half. Garnish with cream cheese balls and parsley. *6 sandwiches.*

### HAM-TOMATO-COLE SLAW SANDWICH

Split and butter buns. Fill with sliced boiled ham topped with tomato slices and spoonfuls of crispy cole slaw. Sliced roast chicken or turkey or canned luncheon meat may be used in place of ham.

### HASH PIZZA PIES

1 can (16 oz.) roast
  beef hash
⅓ cup catsup
¾ tsp. oregano
1 tsp. dried parsley
  flakes

2 tbsp. finely chopped onion
4 large English muffins,
  split and buttered
1 pkg. (8 oz.) sliced
  natural sharp Cheddar
  cheese

Mix first five ingredients. Spread to edge of each muffin half. Top with cheese slice. Broil as far from heat as possible, until cheese melts and pizzas are bubbly hot. *4 to 6 servings.*

### SAUCY SANDWICH ROLLS

1 lb. wieners, chopped
  or sliced
1 medium onion, finely
  chopped
3 tbsp. bacon fat
¼ cup Gold Medal Flour
¾ tsp. salt
dash of pepper

½ tsp. each dry mustard
  and Worcestershire
  sauce
½ cup each catsup and
  water
1 cup chopped celery
½ cup grated cheese
12 frankfurter buns

Brown wieners and onion in hot fat. Remove from heat. Blend in flour, seasonings, catsup, water, and celery. Cook about 5 min., or until celery is tender, stirring constantly. Add cheese. Heat until cheese melts. Remove from heat. Remove some of soft centers from buns. Fill pockets with mixture. Wrap in heavy waxed paper or aluminum foil, twisting ends tightly. Just before serving, heat in shallow pan at 350° (mod.) 10 to 15 min. *12 sandwich rolls.*

*Stag Supper*

**Ham-Tomato-Cole Slaw Sandwiches**
**Baked Beans or Potato Salad**
**Fresh Fruit          Coffee**

## HAM-FILLED ROLLS

½ lb. Cheddar cheese
½ lb. minced ham
2 sweet pickles
1 tsp. grated onion

2 tbsp. mayonnaise or salad dressing
8 to 10 buns, split and buttered

Heat oven to 350° (mod.). Put cheese, ham, and pickles through food chopper. Add onion and mayonnaise. Spread between bun sections. Place on baking sheet; heat in oven 15 min. *8 to 10 servings.*

*Sunday Night Supper*

**Ham-filled Rolls**
**Relishes          Beverage**
**Fruit Ambrosia (p. 46)**
**with Brownies (p. 53)**

## BACON AND TOMATO SANDWICH

Toast bread on one side and lightly on second side. Butter second side and top with thick tomato slices. Place 2 slices bacon, fried until almost crisp, on each sandwich. Top with thin slice of cheese. Broil 5″ from heat until cheese melts.

## EASY DENVER SANDWICH

¼ cup minced onion
¼ cup minced green pepper
1 tbsp. butter
4 eggs

¼ cup milk
½ cup minced cooked ham
salt and pepper

Sauté onion and green pepper slowly in hot butter in 8 or 9″ skillet until onion is yellow. Beat eggs slightly with milk. Stir in ham, salt, and pepper. Pour into skillet; scramble gently with onion-pepper mixture over low heat just until set. Spoon into hot toasted buns or serve between buttered slices of bread or toast. *4 sandwiches.*

**Deviled Denver:** Omit minced cooked ham and substitute 1 can (2¼ oz.) deviled ham and ¼ tsp. Worcestershire sauce.

## BROILED CRABMEAT BUNS

6 hamburger buns
1 can (6½ oz.) crabmeat, flaked
¼ cup mayonnaise

1 tsp. Worcestershire sauce
¼ cup diced celery
1 dill pickle, diced
6 thin slices cheese

Split and butter buns. Toast on split side. Mix remaining ingredients except cheese. Spoon onto lower half of buns; top with cheese slices. Broil 5″ from heat until cheese melts. Or heat in hot oven (400°) 15 min. Place top on each bun. *6 servings.*

**Broiled Crabmeat Appetizers:** Use this same mixture on dollar-sized toast rounds. *(See picture, p. 60.)*

## FRENCH-TOASTED HASH SANDWICHES

1 can (1 lb.) corned beef hash
12 slices bread
6 slices processed cheese

4 eggs
½ cup milk
½ tsp. salt

Spread hash on 6 bread slices (press together if it tends to be crumbly); place a slice of cheese on each and cover with remaining bread slices. Beat thoroughly eggs, milk, and salt; dip sandwiches well into this mixture. Fry in melted butter on both sides until golden brown. Serve with catsup, mustard, or horse-radish. *6 sandwiches.*

## NEW ORLEANS CLUB SANDWICH

12 slices white bread, toasted
24 shrimp, boiled (two 4½-oz. cans)
⅓ cup tartar sauce

4 slices Cheddar cheese
12 thinly sliced green peppers or ⅓ cup chopped green pepper
4 tomatoes, quartered

Butter 8 slices of toast lightly. On each of 4 buttered slices of toast, arrange 6 shrimp. Spread remaining unbuttered toast with tartar sauce and place on shrimp, sauce-side-down. On top of toast place a slice of cheese, then green peppers. Place under broiler until cheese melts and is bubbling. Top with third slice of buttered toast and fasten with toothpicks. Cut into 4 sections. Garnish with ripe tomato quarters between sections. Serve immediately. *4 sandwiches.*

## CREAMY BEEF-TOMATO SKILLET

1 lb. ground beef

½ lb. lean ground pork

1 large onion, chopped

1 medium green pepper, diced

1 clove garlic, minced

1 can (1 lb. 13 oz.) tomatoes (3½ cups)

1 can (8 oz.) tomato sauce

1 pkg. (8 oz.) uncooked elbow macaroni

1 small jar pimiento, cut up

2 tbsp. sugar

2 tsp. chili powder

2 tsp. salt

1 cup commercial sour cream

Brown meat in large heavy skillet, breaking meat up with fork as it cooks and pouring off fat occasionally (be sure meat is well drained). Stir in vegetables, macaroni, and seasonings. Bring to boil; cover. Simmer 20 min., or until macaroni is tender, stirring often to prevent sticking. Stir in sour cream. Warm. Do not boil as mixture may curdle. *6 servings.*

## DO-AHEAD DRIED BEEF CASSEROLE

1 can (11 oz.) cream of mushroom soup

1 cup milk

1 cup processed Cheddar cheese, cut fine (¼ lb.)

3 tbsp. finely chopped onion

1 cup uncooked elbow macaroni

¼ lb. dried beef, cut in bite-size pieces

2 hard-cooked eggs, sliced

Stir soup until creamy. Add milk, cheese, onion, un-cooked macaroni, and dried beef. Fold in eggs. Turn into buttered 1½-qt. baking dish. Refrigerate 3 to 4 hr. or overnight. Bake, uncovered, in 350° (mod.) oven 1 hr. *4 to 6 servings.*

**Note:** *If dried beef is very salty, pour boiling water over it and drain well before using.*

## TUNA-NOODLE BAKE

4 cups cooked noodles (8-oz. pkg.)

1 can (6½ or 7 oz.) tuna

¼ cup diced green pepper

¼ cup chopped pimiento

1 small onion, chopped

½ tsp. salt

1 can (11 oz.) cream of mushroom soup

1 can (4 oz.) mush-rooms (including liquor)

1 cup grated cheese (¼ lb.)

Heat oven to 425° (hot). Combine all ingredients, using only half the cheese. Pour into greased 1½-qt. baking dish. Sprinkle with remaining cheese. Bake 20 min. *4 to 6 servings.*

## MACARONI SAUTÉ

2 cups elbow macaroni (8 oz.), uncooked

½ cup chopped onion

½ cup chopped green pepper

1 clove garlic, minced

½ cup vegetable oil

3 cups tomato juice

1 tsp. salt

¼ tsp. pepper

2 tsp. Worcestershire sauce

Sauté macaroni, onion, green pepper, and garlic in hot oil until macaroni turns slightly yellow. Add tomato juice and seasonings; bring to boil. Cover and simmer 20 min. *6 servings.*

**Macaroni-Beef Sauté:** Sauté 1 lb. ground beef with macaroni. Increase salt to 1½ tsp.

## NOODLES WITH HERB CHEESE SAUCE

1 pkg. (8 oz.) noodles

2 cups Medium Cream Sauce (p. 103)

½ tsp. each thyme, basil, savory, minced parsley, and chives or onion

2 cups grated Cheddar cheese

Boil noodles. Meanwhile, make Cream Sauce. Stir in herbs and cheese, reserving ¼ cup cheese for topping. Stir until cheese is melted. Mix noodles and sauce. Pour into ungreased 1½-qt. baking dish. Top with reserved cheese. Broil until cheese melts. Serve immediately. *6 to 8 servings.*

**Sea Food-Cheese Sauce:** Add 1 can (7 oz.) salmon or tuna, broken in large pieces, to recipe above.

## TOMATO SPAGHETTI SAUCE

| | |
|---|---|
| 2 medium onions, diced | 1 tbsp. chili sauce |
| 1 clove garlic, minced | 1 tsp. basil |
| 2 tbsp. vegetable oil | ½ tsp. sugar |
| 1 can (1 lb. 4 oz.) tomato juice | ½ tsp. salt |
| | ¼ tsp. pepper |
| 1 can (6 oz.) tomato paste | dash cayenne pepper |

Brown onion and garlic in hot oil. Add remaining ingredients; bring to boil and simmer 30 min., stirring occasionally. Serve hot over cooked macaroni or spaghetti; sprinkle with Parmesan cheese. *4 servings.*

**Meaty Spaghetti Sauce:** Brown ½ lb. ground beef with the onions in making Tomato Spaghetti Sauce (above).

## CHICKEN-MACARONI EN CASSEROLE

| | |
|---|---|
| 3 cups cooked elbow macaroni (1½ cups uncooked) | 1 cup sliced canned mushrooms |
| | ¼ cup diced pimiento |
| 2 cups grated Cheddar cheese | 1 can (10½ oz.) cream of chicken soup plus milk to make 2 cups |
| 1½ cups cooked diced chicken | |

Heat oven to 350° (mod.). Mix all ingredients. Pour into buttered 2-qt. baking dish. Bake 60 min. *6 to 8 servings.*

**Ham-Macaroni en Casserole:** Use cooked diced ham in place of chicken in Chicken-Macaroni en Casserole (above); use 3½ to 4 cups cooked macaroni (7-oz. pkg. uncooked).

### EASY COOKING METHOD FOR MACARONI PRODUCTS

Use 7- or 8-oz. pkg. macaroni, spaghetti, or noodles (about 2 cups). Drop into 6 cups rapidly boiling water (4 tsp. salt). Bring back to rapid boil. Cook, stirring constantly, for 3 min. Cover with tight-fitting lid; remove from heat and let stand 10 min. Rinse with hot water, then drain.

**Note:** *For thicker-walled macaroni products such as lasagne or rigatoni, follow manufacturer's directions.*

## OLD-FASHIONED MACARONI AND CHEESE

| | |
|---|---|
| 1 pkg. (8 oz.) macaroni, cooked | 1 tsp. salt |
| | ¼ tsp. pepper |
| 2 cups cut-up sharp processed cheese (½″ cubes—½ lb.) | 2 cups milk |
| | paprika |

Heat oven to 350° (mod.). Place cooked macaroni, cheese, salt, and pepper in alternate layers in buttered oblong baking dish, 11½ x 7½ x 1½″, ending with layer of cheese on top. Pour milk over all. Sprinkle with paprika. Bake 35 to 45 min., or until golden brown on top. *6 to 8 servings.*

**With Sour Cream:** Use 2½ cups commercial sour cream in place of the milk; spread over macaroni, ending with remaining cheese on top of sour cream. Sprinkle with paprika.

## NOODLE-KRAUT-SAUSAGE BAKE

| | |
|---|---|
| 2 cups uncooked noodles | 1 tsp. onion salt |
| 1 cup commercial sour cream | ½ tsp. salt |
| | ¼ tsp. pepper |
| ½ cup milk | 1 tbsp. poppy seeds |
| 2 tbsp. butter | 1 lb. pork sausage links |
| 1 can (1 lb.) sauerkraut | |

Heat oven to 375° (quick mod.). Cook noodles as directed on pkg. Drain. Combine sour cream, milk, butter, sauerkraut, onion salt, salt, pepper, and poppy seeds in 2-qt. baking dish. Stir in noodles and blend well. Cook sausage in heavy covered skillet about 10 min., turning occasionally until evenly browned. Arrange sausages, pinwheel-fashion, on top of sauerkraut mixture. Bake, covered, 30 min. *6 to 8 servings.*

## BISCUIT-TOPPED VEGETABLE BEEF CASSEROLE

| | |
|---|---|
| ¼ cup chopped onion | 2 medium carrots, diced |
| 2 tbsp. fat | 3 drops Tabasco |
| 1 lb. ground beef | ½ cup catsup |
| 1 tsp. salt | ¼ cup Gold Medal Flour |
| ⅛ tsp. pepper | Easy Biscuits (p. 44) |
| 1½ cups tomato juice | |
| 3 stalks celery, chopped | |

Heat oven to 375° (quick mod.). Sauté onion in fat. Add beef and seasonings. Cook over medium heat until meat is well browned. Add 1 cup of the tomato juice, celery, carrots, and Tabasco. Simmer, covered, 15 min. Add remaining ½ cup tomato juice and catsup to flour; stir into meat mixture. Cook until thick, stirring constantly. Pour into 2-qt. baking dish. Top meat mixture with biscuits. Bake 20 to 25 min. *6 servings.*

## DOUBLE-QUICK
## FRANK-BEAN BAKE

| | |
|---|---|
| 1 can (12 oz.) red kid- ney beans, well drained | 1 small onion, minced |
| 1 can (1 lb. 1 oz.) Lima beans, drained | 1 cup grated Cheddar cheese (¼ lb.) |
| ½ cup canned spaghetti sauce with mushrooms | 4 to 6 frankfurters |

Heat oven to 375° (quick mod.). Mix beans, spaghetti sauce, onion, and cheese in 1½-qt. baking dish. Arrange whole frankfurters over the top. Bake 30 min., or until bean mixture is bubbling and the franks are lightly browned on top. *4 to 6 servings.*

## TUNA BISCUIT BRAID

| | |
|---|---|
| 2 cans (6½ or 7 oz. each) tuna, drained and flaked | ⅔ cup milk |
| ¼ cup mayonnaise | 2 cups Bisquick |
| 2 tbsp. chopped parsley | creamed peas (2 cups cooked peas in 1 cup Medium Cream Sauce, p. 103) |
| 1 tbsp. lemon juice | |
| 1 tbsp. minced onion | |
| ½ tsp. salt | |

Heat oven to 425° (hot). Mix tuna, mayonnaise, parsley, lemon juice, onion, and salt. Make rolled biscuit dough: add milk all at once to Bisquick and stir with fork into a soft dough; beat 15 strokes; turn onto floured board; knead 8 to 10 times; roll into rectangle, 12x10″. Put on baking sheet. Spread tuna mixture down center of dough. Make 7 cuts down each side from edge of dough to tuna filling. Bring first two opposite strips over filling; seal ends. Continue to crisscross remaining strips. Bake 15 to 20 min. Serve slices topped with creamed peas. *6 to 8 servings.*

## HASH SKILLET PIE

| | |
|---|---|
| 2-cup recipe Standard Pastry (p. 141) | ¼ cup milk or tomato juice |
| 1 can (1 lb.) corned beef hash, broken up | 2 tbsp. chopped onion |

Heat oven to 425° (hot). Roll pastry into a 12″ sq.; ease into heavy 10″ skillet, letting pastry hang over edge. Mix remaining ingredients; place in pastry-lined skillet. Fold pastry over filling; bake 30 to 40 min. Cut in wedges and serve with hot chili sauce or catsup. *4 to 6 servings.*

## HASH HATS

Heat oven to 350° (mod.). Break apart with a fork 1 can (1 lb.) corned beef hash; blend in ¼ cup finely chopped sweet pickle or pickle relish. Place four ¼″ slices Bermuda onion in baking dish. Season with salt and pepper; top with butter. Mold hash in rounds on onion slices. Bake 20 min. Serve with hot chili sauce. *4 servings.*

## SNOW-CAPPED FRANKS

**2 cups mashed potatoes**
**2 tbsp. grated onion**
**2 tbsp. chopped parsley**
**1 tsp. prepared mustard**

**1 pkg. frankfurters (about 10)**
**4 slices bacon, cooked and crumbled**

Use leftover potatoes or prepare our mashed Potato Buds for 4 servings as directed on pkg. Mix potatoes, onion, parsley, and mustard. Cut frankfurters lengthwise, being careful not to cut completely through. Flatten franks completely and spread with potato mixture. Garnish with crumbled bacon. Broil about 8 min., until tips of potatoes are browned. *4 servings.*

## TUNA-POTATO CASSEROLE

*New idea for Friday and Lenten suppers.*

Heat oven to 375° (quick mod.). Using our scalloped potato mix, empty potatoes into 1½-qt. baking dish. Sprinkle contents of seasonings packet over potatoes. Add 1 can (10½ oz.) cream of celery soup and 2¼ cups boiling water. Stir in 1 can (6½ or 7 oz.) tuna, drained, and 1 jar (2 oz.) pimiento, drained and chopped. Bake, covered, 35 to 40 min. *4 to 6 servings.*

## HAM-POTATO-CHEESE CASSEROLE

**2 cups diced cooked potatoes**
**1½ to 2 cups cubed cooked ham**

**¼ lb. Cheddar cheese, finely cubed or grated**
**2 tbsp. chopped pimiento**
**½ cup cream (20% butterfat)**

Heat oven to 350° (mod.). Combine ingredients and place in 1½-qt. baking dish. Cover and bake 45 min. *4 to 6 servings.*

## HAM STEAK WITH POTATOES

Follow pkg. directions on our scalloped potato mix or au gratin potato mix, using an oval 1½-qt. baking dish. Trim fat from 1" thick slice precooked ham. Place on potatoes before baking. Do not cover. Bake 30 to 35 min. If using a round dish, cut ham slice into serving-size pieces. *4 to 6 servings.*

## SAUSAGE WITH POTATOES

Prepare our scalloped potato mix or our au gratin potato mix as directed on pkg.—except omit butter. Place 1 pkg. (8 oz.) precooked brown 'n serve sausages on top of potatoes before baking. Do not cover. Bake 30 to 35 min. *4 to 6 servings.*

**Canadian Bacon with Potatoes:** Use 8 slices of Canadian bacon (¼ to ½" thick) in place of sausage.
**Franks with Potatoes:** Use 4 frankfurters, sliced, in place of sausage. Cover.
**Ham with Potatoes:** Reduce water to 2 cups and omit butter. Stir 1 cup cubed precooked ham into potatoes in place of sausage. Cover.

## PORK CHOP SCALLOP

Trim excess fat from 4 rib pork chops (¾ to 1" thick). Dip in flour. Brown chops on both sides over low heat in 10" skillet. Season with salt and pepper. Remove from skillet. Empty 1 pkg. of our scalloped potatoes and seasoned sauce mix into skillet. Stir in 2¼ cups water and ½ cup milk. Place pork chops on top. Bring to boil. Cover and simmer 30 to 35 min. Garnish with parsley. *4 servings.*

## CHINESE PORK AND RICE

| | |
|---|---|
| ⅔ cup uncooked rice | 2 tsp. soy sauce |
| 2 tbsp. vegetable oil | 1 medium onion, chopped |
| 1 tsp. salt | 2 stalks celery, chopped |
| 1½ cups boiling water | 1 green pepper, chopped |
| 1 bouillon cube | 1½ cups diced cooked pork |

Cook rice in hot oil until golden brown. Add salt, water, bouillon cube, and soy sauce. Cover; cook 20 min. Add rest of ingredients and ¼ cup more water, if necessary. Cover tightly, cook 10 min. more. *4 servings.*

## SPANISH RICE

| | |
|---|---|
| 6 slices bacon, cut up | 3 cups cooked rice (1 cup uncooked) |
| ¼ cup finely chopped onion | 2 cups cooked tomatoes |
| ¼ cup chopped green pepper | 1½ tsp. salt |
| | ⅛ tsp. pepper |

**In a Skillet:** Fry bacon until crisp; remove from skillet; drain off most of fat. Add onion and green pepper to bacon fat; cook over medium heat until onion is yellow. Add remaining ingredients and cook, uncovered, over low heat about 15 min., or until hot. *4 to 6 servings.*

**In the Oven:** Heat oven to 400° (mod. hot). Fry bacon until crisp; remove to 1½-qt. baking dish. Add onion and green pepper to bacon fat; cook until onion is yellow. Combine all ingredients in baking dish. Bake 25 to 30 min.

**Jiffy Spanish Rice:** Substitute 1⅓ cups instant rice and 1⅓ cups water for cooked rice.

**Beef Spanish Rice:** Substitute 1½ to 2 cups cut-up cooked beef or pork (from roast) for bacon, using 2 tbsp. butter or other fat to sauté onion and pepper.

**Mexican Rice:** Substitute 1 lb. ground beef for bacon, 1 small clove garlic, minced, for green pepper. Sauté onion and garlic in 1 tbsp. butter. Add meat and brown. Drain off any excess fat. Add 2 tsp. chili powder and ½ cup raisins with remaining ingredients.

## TUNA-RICE CASSEROLE

| | |
|---|---|
| ¼ cup minced onion | 2 cans (6½ or 7 oz. each) tuna, drained and flaked |
| 1 tbsp. butter | 2 tbsp. parsley |
| 1⅔ cups (13-oz. can) evaporated milk | ⅓ cup sliced stuffed olives |
| 1 tsp. salt | dash of pepper |
| 2 tsp. dry mustard | 1 egg, slightly beaten |
| 2 cups grated processed cheese | ½ cup water |
| | 1½ cups instant rice |

Heat oven to 350° (mod.). Sauté onion in butter until tender in large saucepan. Add milk, salt, mustard, and 1½ cups cheese. Heat until cheese melts. Add tuna, parsley, olives, pepper, egg, water, and rice. Blend well. Place in 2-qt. baking dish and sprinkle remaining cheese on top. Bake, covered, 20 to 25 min. Serve hot. *6 servings.*

## HAMBURGER-RICE CASSEROLE

| | |
|---|---|
| 3½ cups water | 1 cup chopped onion (2 medium) |
| 1 cup rice | 1 tbsp. butter |
| 1 tsp. salt | ¼ cup soy sauce |
| 1 lb. ground beef | 2 tbsp. brown sugar |
| 1 tsp. fat | 1 can (4 oz.) mushrooms, drained |
| 1½ cups chopped celery | 1 can (10½ oz.) chicken with rice soup |

Heat oven to 350° (mod.). Bring water to boil in saucepan. Add rice and salt. Remove from heat, cover and let stand while preparing the rest of ingredients. Brown ground beef in hot fat. Add celery and onion; cook 5 min. Add butter, soy sauce, brown sugar, mushrooms, soup, and rice (including water). Mix thoroughly. Pour into buttered 3-qt. baking dish. Cover and bake 30 min. Uncover and bake 30 min. more. *8 to 10 servings.*

## WELSH RAREBIT

| | |
|---|---|
| 2 cups grated sharp Cheddar cheese (½ lb.) | ¼ tsp. Worcestershire sauce |
| ⅔ cup milk | ⅛ tsp. salt |
| ¼ tsp. dry mustard | dash of pepper |

Melt cheese over hot water; gradually add milk and stir until smooth. Blend in seasonings. Serve on crisp crackers, toast, or potato chips. *4 servings.*

## EGGS ON DEVILED HAM TOAST

Spread toast with deviled ham. Top with a poached egg (p. 8). Add Cheese Sauce (p. 103), if desired.

## SAVORY EGGS

| | |
|---|---|
| 1 cup grated Cheddar cheese | 1 tsp. prepared mustard |
| 2 tbsp. butter | ½ tsp. salt |
| ½ cup cream (20% butterfat) | ¼ tsp. pepper |
| | 6 eggs, slightly beaten |

Heat oven to 325° (slow mod.). Sprinkle cheese in 9" sq. pan. Dot with butter. Mix cream, mustard, salt, and pepper; pour half over cheese. Pour eggs over top, then remaining cream mixture. Bake 25 min. Serve at once. *6 servings.*

## EGGS CONTINENTAL

| | |
|---|---|
| ½ cup fine soft bread crumbs | 2 tbsp. minced parsley or chives |
| 4 hard-cooked eggs, sliced | ½ tsp. salt |
| 3 slices bacon, diced | dash of pepper |
| ½ cup commercial sour cream | ¼ tsp. paprika |
| | ½ cup grated sharp Cheddar cheese |

Heat oven to 375° (quick mod.). Line 4 individual baking dishes with bread crumbs. Place sliced eggs in layer over crumbs. Fry bacon until crisp, drain off fat. Mix bacon, sour cream, parsley, and seasonings thoroughly. Spoon over eggs. Top with cheese. Sprinkle with paprika. Bake 15 to 20 min., until cheese is melted. Serve at once. *4 servings.*

## CREAMED EGGS ON TOAST

Cut 4 hard-cooked eggs in quarters; add to 1 cup well-seasoned Medium Cream Sauce (p. 103). Serve on hot buttered toast or in Toast Cups (p. 107). Sprinkle with paprika. *4 servings.*

**Eggs à la King:** Add 1 can (2 oz.) mushrooms, 2 tbsp. chopped green pepper, and 2 tbsp. chopped pimiento.

**Creamed Tuna or Salmon and Eggs:** Add 1 cup flaked tuna or salmon.

**Creamed Chipped Beef and Eggs:** Frizzle 2 oz. chipped beef in butter; add to eggs.

**Creamed Ham and Eggs:** Add 1 cup diced cooked ham and ¼ cup mushrooms (browned in butter used in making Cream Sauce) to eggs.

## POTATO-EGG SCRAMBLE

Dice 4 or 5 medium potatoes, boiled. Dice 6 slices bacon and fry until crisp; pour off half the fat. Add potatoes and onions (1 bunch green or 1 dry, finely chopped); fry until lightly browned. Add 4 eggs and seasonings. Stir gently until eggs are lightly set. *4 servings.*

## CHEESEBURGER CASSEROLE

| | |
|---|---|
| 8 slices day-old bread | 1 cup grated sharp Cheddar cheese |
| ½ lb. ground beef | 1 egg, beaten |
| ¼ cup chopped onion | ¾ cup milk |
| 2 tbsp. chopped celery | ⅛ tsp. dry mustard |
| 1 tbsp. prepared mustard | dash of pepper |
| ½ tsp. salt | ½ tsp. salt |

Heat oven to 350° (mod.). Toast bread. Butter both sides and cut diagonally. Mix ground beef, onion, celery, prepared mustard, and ½ tsp. salt in medium-sized frying pan. Cook over medium heat until meat is lightly browned. Arrange toast, cheese, and hamburger mixture in alternate layers in greased 9" sq. pan, ending with cheese as top layer. Mix egg, milk, dry mustard, pepper, and ½ tsp. salt. Pour over layers in pan. Sprinkle with paprika. Bake 30 to 35 min. *4 to 6 servings.*

# ❧ Especially for the Girls ❧

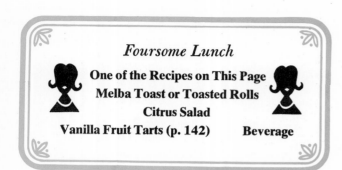

*Foursome Lunch*

**One of the Recipes on This Page**
**Melba Toast or Toasted Rolls**
**Citrus Salad**
**Vanilla Fruit Tarts (p. 142)        Beverage**

## ASPARAGUS-DRIED BEEF SAVORY

1 pkg. (10 oz.) cut-up
  frozen asparagus or
  1 lb. fresh asparagus,
  cut up
3 tbsp. butter
2 tbsp. finely chopped
  onion
1 tbsp. flour

⅔ cup milk
½ cup grated Cheddar
  cheese
4 oz. shredded dried
  beef
2 tbsp. chopped pimiento
8 Toast Cups (p. 107)

Cook asparagus in boiling salted water until barely tender, about 5 min. Drain. Melt butter in skillet and add onion. Cook until onion is tender. Blend in flour. Add milk, stirring until mixture boils and thickens. Stir in cheese, beef, asparagus, and pimiento. Heat through. Serve in Toast Cups or on toast points. *8 servings.*

## CHEESE SOUFFLÉ

1 cup grated sharp
  cheese
1 cup Thick Cream
  Sauce (p. 103)

3 egg yolks, well beaten
¼ tsp. cream of
  tartar
3 egg whites

Heat oven to 350° (mod.). Blend cheese into Cream Sauce; gradually stir into egg yolks. Add cream of tartar to egg whites; beat until stiff. Fold in cheese mixture. Pour into ungreased 1½-qt. baking dish; make groove with spoon 1″ from edge. Bake in pan of hot water (1″ deep) 50 to 60 min., or until puffed and golden brown. *4 servings.*

## SCALLOP CASSEROLE

1 pt. scallops
½ to ¾ cup cream
  (20% butterfat)
½ cup butter, melted

1 tsp. salt
¼ tsp. pepper
3 cups soft bread crumbs
1 tbsp. celery seeds

Heat oven to 375° (quick mod.). Arrange scallops in greased baking dish, 11½ x 7½ x 1½″. Over them pour thin layer of cream. Toss together remaining ingredients; sprinkle over scallops. Over this pour more cream; it should come three fourths of the way up on scallops. Sprinkle with paprika. Bake 30 to 40 min. Also attractive served in sea food shells. *4 servings.*

## HOT CHICKEN SALAD

2 cups cubed cooked
  chicken
2 cups thinly sliced
  celery
1 cup toasted bread
  cubes
1 cup mayonnaise
½ cup toasted chopped
  or slivered almonds

2 tbsp. lemon juice
2 tsp. grated onion
½ tsp. salt
½ cup grated cheese
1 cup toasted bread cubes
  or crushed potato chips

Heat oven to 450° (hot). Combine all ingredients except cheese and second cup of bread cubes. Pile lightly into individual baking dishes or ramekins. Sprinkle with cheese and bread cubes or potato chips. Bake 10 to 15 min., or until bubbly. *6 servings.*

**Hot Sea Food Salad:** Make Hot Chicken Salad (above) —except omit chicken and use tuna or crabmeat. Garnish with lemon.

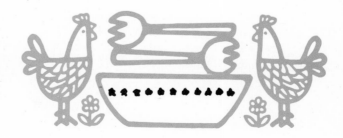

# Picture-Pretty Salad Plates

*For entertaining at lunch or supper in the summertime.*

### SUNBURST FRUIT PLATE

red apple slices

orange slices

sliced banana

green seedless grapes

melon slices

cream cheese-stuffed prunes

On individual serving plates, arrange a portion of each fruit on a leaf of garden lettuce. Center plate with orange sherbet. Pass a sweet fruit dressing or a combination of French dressing and mayonnaise. Serve with thinly sliced nut bread sandwiches and iced tea.

### THREE SALADS IN ONE

tomato salad (small tomato stuffed with cottage cheese and chives)

chicken salad sprinkled with slivered, salted almonds

grapefruit and orange salad with avocado slices

ripe olives, celery, pimiento, and water cress for garnish

On individual serving plates, arrange each salad in separate lettuce cup. Garnish with ripe olives, celery sticks, pimiento strips, and water cress. Pass double dish of mayonnaise for chicken and tomato salads, sweet fruit dressing for fruit salad. Serve with split toasted English muffins.

### GARDEN PATCH QUILT

tomato sections

notched cucumber slices

oval carrot slices (cut diagonally)

cooked or canned whole green beans

raw cauliflowerets marinated in French dressing

On individual serving plates, arrange a portion of each vegetable in a lettuce cup. Center the plate with creamy mayonnaise in a glass cup. Serve with toasted cheese-topped wiener buns and milk. Any selection of cooked or raw vegetables may be used.

### VINAIGRETTE VEGETABLE PLATE

1 lb. fresh asparagus or 1 lb. fresh green beans

1 head or 1 pkg. (10 oz.) frozen cauliflower

1 can (7 oz.) artichoke hearts, drained

Vinaigrette Dressing (below)

cherry tomatoes

parsley

1 can (7 oz.) shrimp

mayonnaise

Cook asparagus or beans and cauliflower. Pour ¼ cup Vinaigrette Dressing over each of the 3 vegetables. Chill 1 hr. Arrange artistically on individual serving plates. Garnish with cherry tomatoes and parsley. Serve with shrimp dipped in mayonnaise. *4 servings.*

**Vinaigrette Dressing:** Mix 1 cup oil-and-vinegar dressing (bottled or your favorite recipe), 2 tbsp. chopped parsley, ¼ cup finely chopped pickle, 2 tsp. chopped onion, and, if desired, 2 tsp. capers. Chill. *Makes 1½ cups.* Use remaining dressing with salad greens.

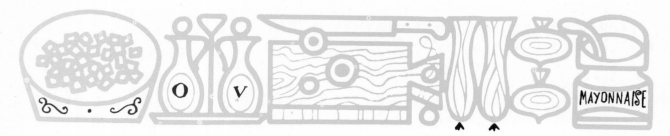

## POTATO SALAD

4 cups cubed cooked
  potatoes

¼ cup clear French dress-
  ing (or ¼ cup vegetable
  oil and 2 tbsp. vinegar)

3 hard-cooked eggs, cut up

1 cup diced celery

2 to 3 tbsp. chopped
  onion

½ cup salad dressing
  or mayonnaise

Potatoes have better flavor if cooked in skins. Cut up
potatoes while warm. Marinate potatoes in French
dressing 1 hr. Add remaining ingredients; season with
salt and pepper. Garnish with 1 hard-cooked egg, parsley, and pimiento. *6 servings.*

**Garden Potato Salad:** Add ¼ cup grated carrots,
sliced radishes, or diced cucumber.

**Ham Potato Salad:** Add 1 cup cut-up baked ham and
½ tsp. prepared mustard.

*POTATO SALAD TIPS: Potatoes have
better flavor if cooked in the skins or baked.
Cut up potatoes while warm, not cold.*

## GARDEN-STYLE COTTAGE CHEESE

1½ cups cottage
  cheese

1 cup pitted ripe olives,
  cut up (7½-oz. can)

1 cup coarsely chopped
  unpared cucumber

1 tbsp. lemon juice

½ tsp. salt

dash of freshly ground
  pepper

1/16 tsp. chili
  powder

Combine all ingredients. Serve on salad greens. If
desired, garnish with tomato wedges. *6 servings.*

## KIDNEY BEAN SALAD

2 cups drained cooked
  kidney beans (1-lb.
  4-oz. can)

¼ cup diced celery

3 dill or sweet
  pickles, chopped

1 small onion, minced

2 hard-cooked eggs,
  sliced

½ tsp. salt

⅛ tsp. pepper

about ¼ cup mayon-
  naise or commercial
  sour cream

Mix all ingredients except mayonnaise. Mix lightly
with mayonnaise. Chill thoroughly. Serve on salad
greens. Garnish with grated cheese. *6 servings.*

## GREEN AND GOLD SALAD

1½ cups cooked peas

½ cup diced Cheddar
  cheese

2 tbsp. finely chopped
  onion

¼ cup mayonnaise

1½ tsp. prepared
  mustard

Combine peas, cheese, and onion. Toss with mayonnaise and mustard. Chill. Serve on greens garnished
with radish roses. *4 servings.*

## WASHINGTON STATE BEAN SALAD

1 can (1 lb.) green beans

1 can (1 lb.) red kidney
  beans

1 green pepper, finely
  chopped

1 small onion, finely
  chopped

½ to ¾ cup sugar

1 tsp. salt

½ tsp. black pepper

½ cup vinegar

½ cup vegetable oil

Drain beans thoroughly; add green pepper and onion.
Mix well. Add remaining ingredients and toss to blend.
Refrigerate for several hours; drain and serve in lettuce
cups. *4 to 6 servings.*

## RASPBERRY-APPLESAUCE SALAD

**1 cup applesauce**
**1 pkg. (3 oz.) raspberry-flavored gelatin**
**1 pkg. (10 oz.) frozen raspberries, thawed**

Heat applesauce just to boil. Add gelatin; mix well. Stir in raspberries. Pour into 8 or 9″ ring mold or individual molds. Chill until set. Serve with sour cream or whipped cream-mayonnaise dressing. *6 servings.*

## EASY PINEAPPLE SALAD

Drain 1 can (9 oz.) sliced pineapple (4 slices), reserving juice. Blend 1 pkg. (3 oz.) cream cheese with 1 tbsp. pineapple juice. Spread pineapple slices with cheese mixture. Place on lettuce. Pile little sweet green grapes in center of each slice. *Makes 4 salads.*

## GOLDEN RING SALAD

Cut a ripe cantaloupe in rings, remove seeds and rind, and place a slice on greens on each salad plate. Top with a slice of canned pineapple. Serve with a favorite fruit salad dressing. Garnish with a sprinkling of chopped fresh mint.

## BLACK-EYED SUSAN SALAD

Arrange orange or grapefruit segments in ring on greens; center with dates. Pass a fruit dressing.

## BUTTERFLY SALAD

For each serving cut pineapple slices in half and place back to back, butterfly fashion, on a lettuce leaf. Top with half slices of jellied cranberry sauce, lapping so pineapple shows about ½″ at top. Place a spoonful of cottage cheese along center and 2 whole cloves at top in cottage cheese as antennae. Serve with French Dressing (p. 102).

## FESTIVE FRUIT SALADS

Fresh peach slices with sweet green grapes.

Pear halves topped with cottage cheese and garnished with pitted cooked prunes.

Chopped tart red apple with raisins or cut-up dates blended with salad dressing.

Peach halves filled with mayonnaise and topped with grated Cheddar cheese.

Long banana slices topped with salad dressing and chopped peanuts.

## FRUIT SALAD DRESSING

**1 cup sugar**
**3 tbsp. cornstarch**
**1 cup unsweetened pineapple juice**
**¼ cup lemon juice (2 lemons)**
**¼ cup orange juice (1 orange)**
**grated rinds of 1 lemon and 1 orange**

Combine sugar and cornstarch in saucepan. Stir in pineapple juice. Cook, stirring occasionally, over medium heat until mixture thickens and boils; boil 1 min. Add lemon and orange juice and grated rinds. Cool. *Makes 2½ cups.*

## FROZEN FRUIT SALAD

**1 pkg. (3 oz.) cream cheese**
**2 tbsp. cream**
**⅓ cup mayonnaise**
**2 tbsp. lemon juice**
**1 can (1 lb. 13 oz.) fruit cocktail, drained**
**½ cup pitted Bing cherries**
**½ cup chopped pecans**
**2 tbsp. sugar**
**1 cup whipping cream, whipped**

Mix cream cheese and cream. Blend in mayonnaise and lemon juice. Combine fruits, pecans, and sugar. Stir cream cheese-mayonnaise mixture into fruits. Fold fruit mixture into whipped cream. Pour into freezing tray. Freeze in refrigerator freezing compartment without stirring. Serve on lettuce garnished with Bing cherry halves or pecan halves. *8 to 12 servings.*

## MEXICAN GREEN BEAN SALAD

| | |
|---|---|
| 2 cups cooked French-cut or cut-up green beans | 2 tbsp. finely chopped onion |
| 2 to 3 tbsp. French dressing | 2 to 3 tbsp. grated Cheddar or Parmesan cheese |

Marinate beans in dressing with onion several hours or overnight. Add cheese. Garnish with red or white onion rings. *4 servings.*

## RANDALL HOUSE DRESSING

| | |
|---|---|
| 1 can (13 oz.) evaporated milk | ⅓ cup catsup |
| ½ cup vinegar | ½ tsp. Worcestershire sauce |
| 1 pkg. dehydrated onion soup mix | ¼ tsp. Tabasco |

Combine ingredients and shake or stir until blended. Serve over mixed greens, vegetable, or sea food salad, or toss with cabbage for slaw. *Makes 2½ cups.*

## SOUR CREAM DRESSING

Blend 1 cup commercial sour cream, 1½ tsp. salt, ⅛ tsp. pepper, 3 tbsp. minced chives or onion, and 2 tbsp. lemon juice (or 1 tbsp. vinegar). Serve over cucumbers, baked potatoes, or tomatoes. *Makes 1¼ cups.*

## WILTED GREENS

| | |
|---|---|
| 4 slices bacon, cut up | 2 green onions, chopped |
| ¼ cup vinegar | 1 tsp. salt |
| 2 tbsp. water | dash of pepper |
| 1 qt. shredded greens (lettuce or spinach) | 1 hard-cooked egg, chopped, if desired |

Fry bacon until crisp; add vinegar and water. Heat. Combine greens, onions, and seasonings. Pour hot mixture over greens; toss until wilted. Sprinkle egg over top. *6 servings.*

## COLE SLAW

| | |
|---|---|
| ½ medium head cabbage | ¼ cup salad dressing |
| 1 medium onion, chopped | ¼ tsp. salt |
| 2 tbsp. vinegar | dash of pepper |
| ¼ cup commercial sour or whipping cream | ½ tsp. dry mustard paprika |

Shred cabbage very thin; place in plastic bag in refrigerator to crisp. Combine cabbage, onion, and vinegar in bowl. Mix cream, salad dressing, and seasonings; toss with cabbage. Sprinkle with paprika. *6 servings.*

## OVERNIGHT VEGETABLE SALAD

| | |
|---|---|
| 1 can (1 lb.) French-cut green beans, drained | 1 medium onion, finely chopped |
| 1 can (1 lb.) green peas, drained | 1 stalk celery, finely chopped |
| 1 can (2 or 4 oz.) pimiento, cut up | Sweet-Sour Dressing (below) |

Toss all ingredients with Sweet-Sour Dressing and let stand overnight in refrigerator. Drain well before serving; serve in lettuce cups or salad bowl. *8 servings.*

**Sweet-Sour Dressing:** Blend 1 cup sugar, 1 cup vinegar, ½ cup vegetable oil, 1 tsp. paprika, and 1 clove garlic, minced. Shake well until sugar is dissolved.

## CHICKEN SALAD

| | |
|---|---|
| 2 cups cubed cold cooked chicken (large chunks) | salt and pepper |
| 1 cup diced celery | ½ cup mayonnaise |
| 1 tbsp. lemon juice | 2 or 3 hard-cooked eggs, cut up |

Toss together chicken, celery, lemon juice, and seasonings. Mix in mayonnaise. Carefully fold in eggs. Chill thoroughly. Arrange a mound of salad on greens. Garnish with olives, little sweet pickles, crumbled crisp bacon, or salted almonds. *6 servings.*

**Chicken-Fruit Salad:** Make Chicken Salad (above)—except omit hard-cooked eggs. Add 1 cup halved sweet green grapes.

## LIMA-SHRIMP SALAD

| | |
|---|---|
| 2 cups cooked baby green Lima beans (10-oz. pkg. frozen) | 2 tsp. tarragon vinegar |
| 1 can (4½ oz.) shrimp | 1 tsp. prepared mustard |
| 1 cup chopped celery | 1 tbsp. minced parsley |
| ⅔ cup mayonnaise | ¼ tsp. prepared horse-radish |
| 2 hard-cooked eggs, chopped | ½ tsp. salt |
| 1 tsp. lemon juice | 2 tsp. chopped capers |

Combine beans, shrimp, and celery. Mix mayonnaise with rest of ingredients and mix lightly with bean mixture. Chill. *6 servings.*

## SEA FOOD SALAD

| | |
|---|---|
| 1 cup chopped shrimp or flaked cooked crabmeat, tuna, or salmon | 1 tsp. lemon juice |
| 1 cup diced celery | 1 tsp. finely minced onion |
| 1 cup lettuce hearts, cut in small pieces | salt and paprika to taste |
| | mayonnaise |

Mix all ingredients except mayonnaise lightly. Chill. Just before serving, drain and toss with mayonnaise to moisten. Serve on crisp lettuce. Garnish with tomato sections, wedges of lemon, slices of hard-cooked egg, and ripe olives. *4 servings.*

## CHEF'S SALAD

| | |
|---|---|
| 1 head lettuce | 1 cup match-like strips of cold cooked meat (beef, ham, tongue) |
| ½ bunch romaine or endive | |
| ½ cup chopped green onion | 1 can (2 oz.) flat fillets of anchovy, if desired |
| ½ cup sliced celery | |
| 1 cup match-like strips of Swiss cheese | ½ cup mayonnaise |
| | ¼ cup French dressing |

Rub bowl with cut clove of garlic. Tear greens into bite-size pieces. Toss greens, onion, celery, cheese, and meat in bowl. Just before serving, toss with mayonnaise blended with French dressing. *4 servings.*

## MEAT-MACARONI SALAD

| | |
|---|---|
| 2 cups cooked and cooled macaroni (1 cup broken, uncooked) | 1 tbsp. grated onion |
| | 1 tbsp. minced parsley |
| 1 cup diced cucumber | ¾ cup mayonnaise |
| 1½ cups cooked chicken or veal or 1 can (7 oz.) salmon or tuna | ½ tsp. salt |
| | ¼ tsp. pepper |

Combine all ingredients; toss together until blended. Chill. Serve on lettuce. Garnish with chopped parsley and paprika. *4 to 6 servings.*

## MIROTON OF SEA FOOD

| | |
|---|---|
| 2 cups cubed cold boiled potatoes | 3 tbsp. chopped crisp pickles |
| 2 tbsp. French dressing | mayonnaise to moisten |
| 2 cups flaked tuna, salmon, crabmeat, shrimp, or lobster | fresh tomatoes and ripe olives for garnish |

Marinate potatoes by tossing with French dressing. Chill potatoes and sea food thoroughly. Mix lightly with pickles and mayonnaise. Heap in high mound on serving platter. Sprinkle with paprika and finely minced parsley. Surround with lettuce cups, each containing wedges of tomatoes and shiny ripe olives for one serving. *6 to 8 servings.*

# Breads to Serve with Soups

### ONION BISCUIT BREAD

Heat oven to 450° (hot). Add ⅔ cup milk all at once to 2 cups Bisquick. Stir with fork into a soft dough. Add 1 tbsp. instant dry onion to dough. Beat dough 20 strokes. Spread on greased baking sheet into an oblong, 10x8″. Spread top with 1 tbsp. soft butter; sprinkle top with poppy seeds. Bake 10 min. Serve hot, broken in pieces or cut into squares.

**Garlic Biscuit Bread:** Make Onion Biscuit Bread (above) omitting onion and poppy seeds. Sprinkle garlic powder or salt over butter.

### EASY BISCUITS

Heat oven to 450° (hot). Add ⅔ cup milk all at once to 2 cups Bisquick. Stir with fork into a soft dough. Beat dough vigorously 20 strokes, until stiff and slightly sticky. Roll dough around on cloth-covered board lightly dusted with Bisquick to prevent sticking. Knead gently 8 to 10 times to smooth up dough. Roll out ½″ thick. Biscuits double in size in baking. Cut close together with floured biscuit cutter. Bake on ungreased baking sheet 10 to 15 min., 1″ apart for crusty sides, close together for soft sides. Serve with butter, jam, or honey. *Makes twelve 2″ biscuits.*

**Richer Biscuits:** Mix ¼ cup soft butter or 3 tbsp. vegetable oil into Bisquick before mixing in milk.

**Buttermilk Biscuits:** Use buttermilk for liquid. It may be necessary to use a few additional tablespoons of buttermilk to make a dough of soft consistency.

**Sour Cream-Chive Biscuits:** Use ⅔ cup commercial sour cream and ⅓ cup water in place of milk. Add 1 tbsp. chopped chives.

### FAVORITE BISCUITS

| | |
|---|---|
| 2 cups Gold Medal Flour | ¼ cup shortening |
| 3 tsp. baking powder | ¾ cup milk |
| 1 tsp. salt | |

Heat oven to 450° (hot). Measure flour by dip-level-pour method. Stir dry ingredients together in bowl. Cut in shortening until mixture looks like meal. Stir in milk. Round up on lightly floured cloth-covered board. Knead lightly 20 to 25 times. Roll dough or pat out ½″ thick. Cut with floured biscuit cutter. For biscuits with soft sides, place close together on baking sheet; for crusty sides, place 1″ apart. Bake 10 to 12 min., or until golden brown. *Makes 20 biscuits.*

**Herb Biscuits:** Make Favorite Biscuits (above)—except add ¼ tsp. dry mustard, ½ tsp. crumbled dry sage, and 1¼ tsp. caraway seeds to flour.

### FLAVORTOP BISCUITS

| | |
|---|---|
| 1 tbsp. chopped pimiento | 1 pkg. (3 oz.) cream cheese |
| 1 tbsp. chopped parsley | unbaked biscuits (use Easy Biscuits, left, or Favorite Biscuits, above) |
| 2 tsp. minced onion | |
| 2 tbsp. butter | |

Heat oven to 450° (hot). Blend pimiento, parsley, onion, butter, and cheese. Spread over top of unbaked biscuits. Bake 10 to 15 min. *Makes about 12 biscuits.*

### CHEESE PUFFS

| | |
|---|---|
| 1 pkg. brown 'n serve rolls or tea biscuits (about 10) | 2 tbsp. soft butter |
| | ½ tsp. dry mustard |
| 2 cups grated cheese (½ lb.) | ½ tsp. salt |
| | ⅛ tsp. pepper |

Slice rolls in half. Mix rest of ingredients. Place a scant tablespoonful of the cheese mixture on each half. Bake as directed on pkg. *Makes about 20 puffs.*

# Breads to Serve with Salads

## NUT BREAD

| | |
|---|---|
| ½ cup sugar | 3 cups Bisquick |
| 1 egg | 1½ cups chopped nuts |
| 1¼ cups milk | |

Heat oven to 350° (mod.). Mix sugar, egg, milk, and Bisquick. Beat vigorously 30 seconds. Batter may still be slightly lumpy. Stir in nuts. Pour into well-greased loaf pan, 9x5x3″. Bake 45 to 50 min., until toothpick stuck into center comes out clean. Crack in top is typical. Cool before slicing.

**Fruit-Nut Bread** (Apricot, Raisin, Date, or Fig): Follow directions for Nut Bread (above)—except use ¾ cup sugar and use orange juice instead of milk. Use only ¾ cup chopped nuts and add 1 cup chopped dried apricots, dates, figs, or raisins. Bake 55 to 60 min.

**Banana-Nut Bread:** Follow directions for Nut Bread (above)—except use ¾ cup sugar and only ½ cup milk. Use only ¾ cup chopped nuts and add 1 cup mashed bananas (2 to 3 bananas).

**Gumdrop-Nut Bread:** Follow directions for Nut Bread (above)—except add 1 cup assorted gumdrops, cut in pieces, omitting black gumdrops. Bake 50 to 55 min.

**Cinnamon Bread:** Follow directions for Nut Bread (above)—except omit nuts. Pour ⅓ of batter into pan. Sprinkle very generously with cinnamon, covering entire surface. Add second ⅓ of batter and sprinkle on more cinnamon. Add last ⅓ of batter and add more cinnamon. Cut through whole batter with knife, swirling cinnamon through batter.

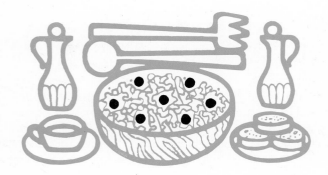

## BUTTONS AND BOWKNOTS

| | |
|---|---|
| 2 cups Bisquick | ⅔ cup cream or ½ cup milk |
| 2 tbsp. sugar | |
| 1 tsp. nutmeg | 1 egg |
| ⅛ tsp. cinnamon | ¼ cup butter, melted |
| | ½ cup sugar |

Heat oven to 400° (mod. hot). Mix Bisquick, 2 tbsp. sugar, and spices. Add cream and egg. Mix well. Dust hands and board lightly with Bisquick. Knead 2 or 3 times. Keep dough soft. Roll out ½″ thick. Cut with doughnut cutter dipped in Bisquick. Doughnut "holes" will be buttons. Holding opposite sides of ring of dough with fingers, twist to make bowknot or figure 8. Pat scraps together, reroll, and cut. Bake on ungreased baking sheet 10 to 12 min., until golden brown. Immediately after baking, dip each quickly in melted butter, then in ½ cup sugar, coating all sides. Serve warm. *Makes about 10.*

## RASPBERRY PEEK-A-BOOS

| | |
|---|---|
| 1 cup fresh raspberries | 2 tsp. lemon juice |
| 4 tbsp. sugar | 2 cups Bisquick |
| ½ tsp. nutmeg | ¼ cup soft butter |
| ½ tsp. cinnamon | ⅔ cup milk |

Heat oven to 450° (hot). Toss berries, 2 tbsp. sugar, nutmeg, cinnamon, and lemon juice. Combine Bisquick, 2 tbsp. sugar, and butter. Add milk all at once; stir with fork into soft dough. Beat 15 strokes. Place a tablespoonful of dough in bottom of each of 10 paper-lined medium muffin cups. Top with 1 tbsp. raspberry mixture. Drop a scant tablespoonful of dough onto berries. Bake 10 to 15 min. Remove from pans immediately. When slightly cool, ice with a thin confectioners' sugar icing. *Makes 10.*

**Blueberry Peek-a-boos:** Substitute blueberries for raspberries in recipe above.

### FRUIT AMBROSIA

Sprinkle cut-up fruit (oranges, bananas, apples, pineapple) with confectioners' sugar. Chill. Toss with plain or toasted shredded coconut just before serving.

### FRUIT WITH SHERBET

*Two of many delectable combinations.*

Sprinkle cubes of pineapple or other fresh fruit with a little confectioners' sugar. Chill. To serve, place scoop of lemon or lime sherbet in each individual serving dish and surround with sweetened fruit.

Place a scoop of lime or orange sherbet or ice in each sherbet glass. Garnish with orange segments (white membrane removed) or mandarin orange sections. Pour orange juice over top.

### FRUIT WITH CREAM 'N SUGAR

Cover washed berries or seedless green grapes with brown sugar. Serve cold with sweet or commercial sour cream.

### FRUIT PARFAITS

Layer fresh sweet cherry halves, fresh cantaloupe cubes, or fresh strawberries, raspberries, or blueberries with vanilla ice cream in parfait glasses, allowing about ¼ cup fruit per serving. Freeze parfaits 15 to 30 min. (If frozen longer than 1 hr., fruit will be icy and difficult to eat.)

### FROZEN LEMON CREAM

| | |
|---|---|
| 1 can (15 oz.) sweetened condensed milk | 1 cup whipping cream, whipped |
| ⅓ cup lemon juice (juice of 2 lemons) | |

Fold milk and lemon juice into whipped cream. Pour into refrigerator tray. Cover with waxed paper. Freeze until firm, several hours. *4 servings.*

### STRAWBERRIES AU NATUREL

Serve circle of washed unhulled strawberries around mound of confectioners' sugar on each dessert plate. Eat with fingers.

### PRUNE OR APRICOT WHIP

| | |
|---|---|
| 1 cup cut-up cooked prunes or apricots | ¼ tsp. salt |
| 3 egg whites | 1 tbsp. lemon juice, if desired |
| ⅓ cup sugar | |

With rotary beater or mixer, beat fruit, egg whites, sugar, and salt together until stiff enough to hold shape (5 min.). Fold in lemon juice. Fold in or garnish with sweetened whipped cream. *4 to 6 servings.*

### PINEAPPLE MARSHMALLOW CREAM

Heat 1 can (13½ oz.) crushed pineapple (about 1⅔ cups), 1 tbsp. lemon juice, and ½ lb. marshmallows (22 to 30), cut up, in saucepan over low heat. Stir until marshmallows are dissolved. Remove from heat; cool. When partially set, fold in 1 cup whipping cream, whipped. Chill 2 hr. or overnight. *8 servings.*

### BROILED GRAPEFRUIT

Remove seeds from grapefruit halves. Cut around sections, remove center. Sprinkle with a bit of sugar (brown or maple). Broil about 10 min., until top is glazed and fruit heated.

### ICE CREAM WITH CHERRY KABOBS

Scoop peppermint ice cream into sherbet glasses and freeze until very hard. Make kabobs by putting 2 or 3 dark sweet fresh cherries on wooden skewers. To serve, stick 1 or 2 kabobs into ice cream so kabob stands up at an angle. To eat, slip cherries off skewer onto ice cream. If desired, pineapple chunks, cantaloupe balls, or strawberries could be used for kabobs and served with vanilla or other favorite ice creams.

## MAGIC APPLES

Wash and core cooking apples. Remove 1″ strip of peel around middle. Place in saucepan. Fill center of each apple with 1 to 2 tbsp. brown or granulated sugar, ¼ tsp. butter, and dash of cinnamon. Pour in water ½″ deep. Cover. Cook until almost tender, about 8 min.; then remove cover and cook until tender, turning apples once in syrup to glaze.

## BAKED APPLES OR PEARS

Prepare same as Magic Apples (above)—except place apples or pears in baking dish. Heat oven to 350° (mod.). Pour in water just to cover bottom of dish. Bake, uncovered, until tender, 45 to 60 min. Cool. Serve with plain or whipped cream.

**Honey Crunch Baked Apples:** Fill center of apple with 1 tbsp. honey and 1 tbsp. slivered blanched almonds instead of butter and sugar.

## QUICK BAKED PEACHES AND PEARS

Heat oven to 425° (hot). Place drained canned fruit halves hollow-side-up in baking dish with a bit of butter in each. Sprinkle with mace and lemon rind. Bake 12 min. Serve warm, garnished with chopped nuts.

## BING CHERRY CUP

| | |
|---|---|
| **1 can (1 lb. 4 oz.) Bing cherries, drained** | **2 tbsp. cornstarch** **2 tbsp. lemon juice** |

Stir juice drained from cherries into cornstarch. Add lemon juice. Cook over low heat until thickened, stirring occasionally. Pour cherries into a 1-qt. baking dish. Pour the thickened juice over fruit. Heat 20 min. in 300° (slow) oven. Pour 2 tbsp. cooking sherry over top, if desired. Serve warm or chilled, plain or sprinkled with chopped nuts and coconut. *5 servings.*

## FRESH FRUIT SAUCE

*Apple, Peach, Pear, Plum, or Rhubarb Sauce.*

| | |
|---|---|
| **4 cups washed, peeled, cut-up fruit** | **1 tsp. lemon juice** |
| **1 cup boiling water** | **⅛ tsp. grated lemon rind** |
| **½ to 1 cup sugar** | **⅛ tsp. cinnamon or** |
| **dash of salt** | **nutmeg** |

Prepare fruit and add to boiling water in saucepan; simmer until nearly tender. Stir in sugar and salt—also, if desired, lemon juice, grated lemon rind, and spice. Cook until fruit is tender.

---

### Approximate Cooking Times

Apples—15 to 20 min.    Pears—about 15 min.
Peaches—about 10 min.   Plums—20 to 25 min.
Rhubarb—10 to 15 min.

---

## STEWED DRIED FRUIT

Packaged dried apples, apricots, figs, peaches, pears, and prunes are so tender that they do not need soaking. Cook according to pkg. directions. To sweeten dried fruits, add the following amounts of sugar or honey per cup: Apricots—¼ cup, Figs—1 tbsp., Peaches—¼ cup, Prunes—2 tbsp., Apples—¼ cup.

## STRAWBERRY SHORTCAKE

**1 qt. fresh strawberries**
**1 cup sugar**

**Bisquick Shortcake (below)**

Wash, hull, and cut up strawberries. Sprinkle with sugar and let stand 1 hr. Mix and bake Bisquick Shortcake (below). Split; fill and top with sweetened berries. Serve with cream or whipped cream. *6 servings.*

**Raspberry Shortcake:** Use 1 qt. fresh raspberries in place of strawberries in Strawberry Shortcake (above).

**Peach Shortcake:** Use 1 qt. sliced fresh peaches in place of strawberries in Strawberry Shortcake (above).

**Cranberry Festival Shortcake:** Mix 1 can (9 oz.) crushed pineapple, 1 cup finely chopped red-skinned apple, and 1 cup canned whole cranberry sauce; let stand at room temperature. Use cranberry mixture in place of strawberries in Strawberry Shortcake (above).

## BISQUICK SHORTCAKE

**¾ cup cream (or ½ cup milk plus ¼ cup butter, melted)**

**2 cups Bisquick**
**2 tbsp. sugar**

Heat oven to 450° (hot). Add cream to Bisquick and sugar. Mix thoroughly with fork. Knead 10 times on floured surface. Pat or roll dough to half the thickness desired in baked shortcakes. Cut into individual shortcakes with floured cutter. Bake 10 to 15 min. *Makes 6.*

## FRUIT OR BERRY BUTTERCAKE

**1 cup Gold Medal Flour**
**½ cup butter**

**3 tbsp. confectioners' sugar**
**sweetened sliced fruit or berries**

Heat oven to 350° (mod.). Measure flour by dip-level-pour method. Mix flour, butter, and sugar with hands until smooth. Divide into 6 equal parts. Shape into flat rounds about 3″ in diameter. Place on baking sheet. Chill 1 hr. Bake 15 to 20 min., or until very lightly browned. Serve each round topped with sweetened fruit or berries and whipped cream. *6 servings.*

## CANNED FRUIT COBBLER

*Use cherries, blueberries, or peaches.*

**2½ to 3 cups canned fruit and juice (about ¾ cup juice)**
**2 tbsp. Bisquick**

**½ to 1 cup sugar (for unsweetened fruit only)**
**½ tsp. cinnamon**
**1 tsp. to 1 tbsp. lemon juice**

Heat oven to 425° (hot). Mix ingredients in oblong baking dish, 10x6x1½″, or 8″ sq. baking dish. Top with Short Pie Dough (below). Bake 25 min. Serve warm with cream. *6 servings.*

**Short Pie Dough:** Add 3 tbsp. boiling water to 1 cup Bisquick and ¼ cup soft butter. Stir vigorously with fork until dough forms a ball and cleans the bowl. Dough will be puffy and soft. Divide into 6 parts. Press into 6 rounds (3 to 4″ across).

## APPLE CRISP

**4 cups sliced, pared, and cored baking apples (about 6 medium)**
**⅔ to ¾ cup brown sugar (packed)**

**½ cup Gold Medal Flour**
**½ cup rolled oats**
**¾ tsp. cinnamon**
**¾ tsp. nutmeg**
**⅓ cup soft butter**

Heat oven to 375° (quick mod.). Place sliced apples in greased 8″ sq. pan or baking dish, 10x6x1½″, or 1½-qt. baking dish. Blend remaining ingredients until mixture is crumbly. Spread over apples. Bake 30 to 35 min., or until apples are tender and topping is golden brown. Serve warm with cream or ice cream. *6 to 8 servings.*

**Peach Crisp:** Use 1 can (1 lb. 13 oz.) sliced peaches, drained, in place of apples. Use ⅔ cup sugar.

**Cherry Crisp:** Use 1 can cherry pie filling in place of apples. Use ⅔ cup sugar.

**Pineapple Crisp:** Use 2 cans (12 oz. each) pineapple tidbits, drained, or 2 cans (1 lb. 4 oz. each) crushed pineapple in place of apples. Use ⅔ cup sugar.

**Apricot Crisp:** Use 2 cans (1 lb. each) apricots, drained, in place of apples. Use ⅔ cup sugar.

## STRAWBERRY-RHUBARB PUFF

*Pictured below.*

**3 cups cut-up rhubarb**
**1 pt. strawberries, cut up**
**1½ to 2 cups sugar**
**½ cup water**
**2 cups Gold Medal Flour**

**3 tsp. baking powder**
**1 tsp. salt**
**2 tbsp. sugar**
**⅓ cup vegetable oil**
**⅔ cup milk**

Heat oven to 450° (hot). Mix rhubarb, strawberries, sugar, and water in 9″ sq. pan. Cook 5 min. Measure flour by dip-level-pour method. Mix flour, baking powder, salt, and 2 tbsp. sugar. Stir in oil and milk only until dry ingredients are moistened. Drop by spoonfuls onto hot fruit, making 9 biscuits. Make a hole in top of each biscuit and put a little butter, sugar, and cinnamon in each. Bake 20 to 25 min. Serve warm with cream or whipped cream. *9 servings.*

**Winter Strawberry-Rhubarb Puff:** Follow recipe above —except use 1 pkg. (1 lb.) frozen rhubarb, thawed, and 1 pkg. (10 oz.) frozen strawberries, thawed, in place of the fresh fruit. Use only ½ cup sugar with fruit. Omit ½ cup water.

## FRUIT COCKTAIL DESSERT

**1 cup Gold Medal Flour**
**1 cup sugar**
**1 tsp. soda**
**dash of salt**
**1 egg, beaten**

**1 can (1 lb.) fruit cocktail, drained**
**¾ cup brown sugar (packed)**
**½ cup chopped nuts**

Heat oven to 350° (mod.). Measure flour by dip-level-pour method. Mix flour, sugar, soda, salt, and egg. Add fruit and blend well. Turn into ungreased 8″ sq. pan. In small bowl, mix brown sugar and nuts; sprinkle on top of fruit mixture in pan. Bake 50 min. Serve warm with whipped cream. *6 to 8 servings.*

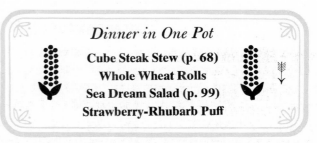

*Dinner in One Pot*
**Cube Steak Stew (p. 68)**
**Whole Wheat Rolls**
**Sea Dream Salad (p. 99)**
**Strawberry-Rhubarb Puff**

See next page for identification. ⟫→

## EASY GINGER COOKIES

Spicy-wonderful ginger cookies are quickly made with our gingerbread mix—try these variations.

**Ginger Cutouts:** Add ⅓ cup lukewarm water to gingerbread mix. Blend until smooth. Chill 1 to 2 hr. Roll ⅛″ thick. Cut with floured cooky cutter (gingerbread men or other shapes). Bake on lightly greased baking sheet 8 to 10 min. at 375°. *Makes 3 doz.*

**Gingersnaps:** Blend gingerbread mix with ⅓ cup shortening or vegetable oil and ½ cup milk. Beat vigorously ½ min. Drop rounded teaspoonfuls 3″ apart on ungreased baking sheet. Sprinkle with sugar. Bake at 375° 8 to 10 min. *Makes about 4 doz.*

**Ginger Drop Cookies:** Mix gingerbread mix with ½ cup lukewarm water until smooth. Chill. Drop by teaspoonfuls onto lightly greased baking sheet. Bake at 375° 10 to 12 min. *Makes about 3 doz.*

**Orange-Nut Ginger Bars:** Mix gingerbread mix and ¾ cup lukewarm water. Beat 2 min., medium speed on mixer or 300 strokes by hand. Fold in grated rind of 1 orange (about 1 tbsp.) and 1 cup chopped nuts. Pour into two well-greased 9″ sq. pans. Bake at 350° 12 to 15 min. While still warm frost with ⅔ recipe Orange Butter Icing (p. 133). Cut into bars. *Makes 4 doz.*

**Ginger Creams:** Add ½ cup lukewarm water to gingerbread mix. Blend until smooth. Mix in 1 cup canned pumpkin. Chill. Drop with teaspoon onto lightly greased baking sheet. Bake at 375° 10 to 12 min. Frost tops with ½ recipe Browned Butter Icing (p. 133). *Makes about 4 doz.*

**Ginger-Applesauce Bars:** Mix 1 cup applesauce and ¼ cup lukewarm water with gingerbread mix. Beat 2 min., medium speed on mixer or 300 strokes by hand. Add ½ cup raisins and ½ cup finely chopped nuts. Spread in greased and floured jelly roll pan, 15½x-10½x1″. Bake at 350° 12 to 15 min. Cool. Dust with confectioners' sugar. *Makes 36.*

## DATE BARS

Tempting bars with luscious date filling between crusts of honey, oats, and coconut are easy to make with our date bar mix. Store cooled bars in your cooky jar. And there is a wide variety of other ways you can use this mix.

**Almond Date Bars:** Add ¾ tsp. almond flavoring to date filling just before spreading over crumbly mixture.

**Apricot Date Bars:** Add ½ cup finely cut dried apricots to date filling mixture before adding water.

**Chocolate Chip Date Bars:** Add ½ cup semi-sweet chocolate pieces to crumb mixture before spreading bottom layer in pan.

**Pineapple Date Bars:** Combine ¼ cup hot water and 1 can (9 oz.) crushed pineapple, well drained, with date filling mix. Spread over crumbly mixture.

**Walnut Date Bars:** Add ½ cup chopped walnuts to date filling mixture before covering bottom crust.

**Date Bar Drop Cookies:** Heat oven to 400° (mod. hot). Mix date filling mix and ¼ cup hot water. Add crumbly mixture and 1 egg; mix thoroughly. Drop rounded teaspoonfuls about 2″ apart onto lightly greased baking sheet. Bake 8 to 10 min. Cool on wire rack. *Makes about 2½ doz.*

**Mincemeat Date Bars:** Heat oven to 400° (mod. hot). Combine crumbly mixture and date filling mix with 1 egg, ¼ cup hot water, ½ cup chopped nuts, and 1 cup mincemeat. Spread in greased oblong pan, 13x9½x2″. Bake 20 to 25 min. Frost while warm with Thin Icing: mix 1½ cups sifted confectioners' sugar, 3 tbsp. cream, ½ tsp. vanilla, and ½ tsp. almond flavoring. Cut into bars. *Makes 4 doz.*

**Brownie Date Bars:** Make batter for fudgy brownies using our brownie mix and spread in greased oblong pan, 13x9½x2″. Mix well both date and crumb mixture from a pkg. of our date bar mix, ½ cup hot water, and 1 egg. Spread evenly over brownie batter. Bake 40 to 45 min. Cool; cut into bars. *Makes 30.*

**Identification for picture, pp. 50-51.**

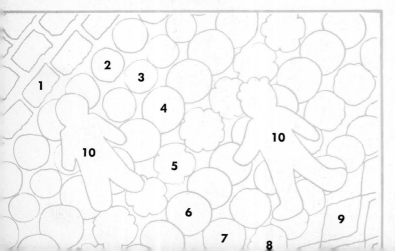

# BROWNIES

Follow the simple directions on our brownie mix pkg., then try these scrumptious variations.

**Peanut Butter Brownies:** Omit chopped nuts and add 3 tbsp. chunk-style peanut butter before baking.

**Double Fudge Brownies:** Add ½ cup semi-sweet mint chocolate pieces to batter for cake-like brownies.

**Coconut Brownies:** Use 1 cup coconut instead of nuts.

**Chocolate Peppermint Brownies:** As soon as brownies are removed from oven, place about 16 chocolate peppermint patties on top. Return to oven for a few minutes to soften patties. Spread over top with spatula as they melt.

**Cherry Brownies:** Add ¼ cup (about 16) chopped maraschino cherries, well drained, to batter.

**Brownie Confections:** Bake brownies. Brown ¼ cup soft butter to a delicate brown. Blend with 2 cups sifted confectioners' sugar. Stir in 2 tbsp. cream and 1 tsp. vanilla until smooth. Spread on brownies. Melt 1 sq. unsweetened chocolate (1 oz.) and 1 tbsp. butter. Cool; spread very thin coating over confectioners' sugar mixture. When toppings are set, cut in 1″ squares or bars. *(Pictured below.)*

# Homey, Hearty, Happy Lunches

Cream of Carrot Soup (p. 25)
Cheese Crackers
Tossed Green Salad
Chocolate Chip Cookies (p.120)

Cheeseburger Casserole (p. 37)
Sliced Tomato Salad
Ice Cream
Gingersnaps (p. 52)

Corn-Tomato Chowder (p. 23)
Saltines
Peanut Butter Brownies (p. 53)

French-toasted Hash Sandwiches (p. 31)
Corn Chips
Cherry or Raspberry Parfait (p. 46)

Chicken Salad on Lettuce (p. 43)
Rye Bread and Butter Sandwiches
Raspberry Sherbet

Ham Sandwiches with Mustard
Green and Gold Salad (p. 40)
Apple Crisp (p. 48)

Macaroni-Beef Sauté (p. 32)
Corn Muffins
Cole Slaw
Fruit Ambrosia (p. 46)

Welsh Rarebit (p. 37)
on Sesame Seed Crackers
Lettuce Wedges with Dressing
Pineapple Date Bars (p. 52)

# Lunchtime Stand-bys

*Don't "forget to remember" these old-time luncheon favorites that are every bit as good and easy today.*

Chili Con Carne
Crisp Crackers          Dill Pickles

Potato Salad
Cold Cuts          Rye Bread

Asparagus on Toast
Cheese Sauce
Crisp Bacon

Potato-Egg Scramble (p. 37)
Carrot Sticks
Fruit Sauce

Corned Beef Hash
Poached Eggs
Tomato Wedges

*Lunch-box meals by the millions go to school and work every day. Varied, appetizing lunches are more satisfying for the lunch carrier and more interesting for you, the packer.*

## A FOUR-STAR LUNCH

**Nourishing:** Remember it is a meal, not just a snack. Always include a protein food; include about ⅓ of the daily food needs.

**Appetizing:** Vary lunches with both soft and crisp foods, both sweet and tart, both hot and cold (if possible).

**Tasty:** Use well-seasoned sandwich fillings. Include pickles, olives, or relishes.

**Planned for Carrying:** See suggestions at right. Avoid cut fruits that discolor, leaky sandwich fillings. Leave crusts on sandwiches to prevent drying. Wrap strong-flavored foods such as green onions and radishes in aluminum foil.

### A Four-Star Lunch Box:

|  |  |
|---|---|
| Attractive | Easy to Clean |
| Durable | Supplied with a Vacuum Bottle |

## STUFFED MEAT ROLLS

Split 2 frankfurter buns in half lengthwise; spread generously with butter. Spread Egg and Olive Filling (below) down center of 2 thin slices bologna, salami, or ham. Roll up and place on bottom half of each bun. Cover with top of bun. Fasten with toothpicks. Wrap in plastic wrap or waxed paper. *Makes 2 sandwiches.*

**Egg and Olive Filling:** Mix 1 chopped hard-cooked egg, 1 tbsp. finely chopped ripe or stuffed olive, 1 tsp. drained pickle relish or piccalilli, and 1 tsp. prepared mustard.

*Take-to-School Lunch*

**Vegetable Soup**
**Stuffed Meat Roll**
**Celery Sticks**
**Graham Cracker Sandwich**
**(filled with favorite frosting)**
**Milk**

## FOODS THAT CARRY WELL

**Soup:** Have soup good and hot before pouring into vacuum bottle. Broth soups travel best.

**Sandwiches:** Sandwich-making hints on p. 26. Filling suggestions on pp. 26-27. Omit lettuce—it wilts. Keep several fillings on hand for variety.

**Relishes:** Pickles, celery, carrot sticks, radishes, olives.

**Beverages:** Milk, buttermilk, hot chocolate, tomato juice, coffee, lemonade, tea, fruit juice.

**Fruit:** Dates, raisins, prunes, dried apricots. Fresh apples, pears, peaches, bananas, oranges, grapes.

**Cookies or Cake:** Bake cupcakes in paper cups to keep moist longer. Split frosted cake squares and arrange so frosting is between, like a sandwich filling. Wrap two drop cookies, bottoms together.

**Pies:** Fruit turnovers are easy to eat. Pack pieces of fruit pie in plastic wedge-shaped boxes.

*Lunch for a Hard-Working Man*

**Tomato Soup**
**Cheese, Meat, and Salad Sandwich**
**Potato Chips**      **Pickle**
**Banana**      **Cherry Turnover**

## MEAT, CHEESE, AND SALAD SANDWICH

| | |
|---|---|
| 2 slices white or whole wheat bread | 1 slice Swiss or Cheddar cheese |
| 1 slice boiled ham, minced luncheon meat, or bologna | 3 thin tomato slices<br>2 leaves lettuce, washed |

Spread 1 slice bread with butter, the other with prepared mustard. Fill with meat and cheese. Wrap in plastic wrap or waxed paper to hold freshness. Arrange tomato slices between lettuce leaves and wrap in second sandwich-size package. At lunchtime, unwrap both parts, open sandwich and slip salad filling between bread and meat. *Makes 1 sandwich.*

### *Teen Special*

**Thick Slice of Cold Meat Loaf
in Hamburger Bun**

**Shoestring Potatoes      Stuffed Celery**

**Sugar 'n Spice Cupcake (p. 130)**

**Apple      Hot Chocolate**

### *Weight-Watcher's Lunch Box*

**Open-face Turkey Sandwich**

**Cabbage and Carrot Salad**

**Baked Custard**

**Apple, Peach, or Green Grapes**

**One Sugar Cooky**

### *Box Lunch for a Business Girl*

**Hot Bouillon**

**Salmon Salad Sandwich (p. 27)**

**Peeled Orange**

**Date Cake (p. 125)**

### *Man's Stick-to-the-Ribs Lunch*

**Cream of Chicken Soup**

**Two Corned Beef-Swiss Cheese Sandwiches**

**Assorted Relishes**

**Cherry Pie**

**Orange       Apple**

# Dinner

Every day homemakers ponder the question, "What shall we have for dinner?" From your letters and calls we know that you want something quick—to save precious hours for family fun and community activities; something nutritious—to keep your family healthy; and something colorful—to catch your family's eye. This section includes quick, nutritious, and colorful recipes to keep your family well fed and happy for many a dinner to come.

Today's popular convenience foods make it so easy to serve "almost immediate" dinners. When you use frozen, refrigerated, and canned foods, brown 'n serve rolls, and packaged mixes, you are taking advantage of the work of hundreds of "silent servants" outside your home. Bring your personal touch to these convenience foods by adding special seasonings and by arranging them attractively for serving.

The pages that follow are filled with ways to prepare all kinds of meat, fish, and poultry, and for vegetables to go with them. There are quick ideas for salads and breads, too. You will find dinners-in-a-dish, leftover brighteners, and all-in-the-oven meals, plus festive foods for company and cook-out foods for summer. And for those who want to end the meal with something sweet, there are inviting cakes and delectable desserts.

Tempting dinner menus have been included, too. Even if you don't use each menu just as it's planned, we hope you will glean ideas for new combinations of foods and flavors from them.

# A "Party Start" for Dinner

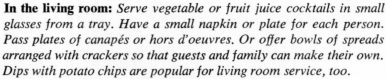

**In the living room:** *Serve vegetable or fruit juice cocktails in small glasses from a tray. Have a small napkin or plate for each person. Pass plates of canapés or hors d'oeuvres. Or offer bowls of spreads arranged with crackers so that guests and family can make their own. Dips with potato chips are popular for living room service, too.*

**At the dining table:** *Serve an appetizer soup, sea food cocktail, a special salad, or a small plate of hors d'oeuvres. Have the appetizer in place when guests come to the table.*

### QUICK CRANBERRY PUNCH

*Refreshing, ruby red.*

Reconstitute 1 can (6 oz.) frozen lemonade concentrate in large pitcher. Add 2 bottles (1 pt. each) cranberry cocktail and enough ice to chill. Just before serving, stir in 2 bottles (7 oz. each) ginger ale. *10 to 12 servings.*

### CIDER PUNCH

Combine 2 cups orange juice, 1 cup lemon juice, and 4 cups apple cider with 1 cup sifted confectioners' sugar; stir until dissolved. Pour over ice cubes. Garnish with mint leaves. *12 servings.*

### GRAPE JUICE CRUSH

*Pictured at right.*

| | |
|---|---|
| **2 cups grape juice** | **½ cup sugar** |
| **1 cup orange juice** | **2 cups ice water** |
| **¼ cup lemon juice** | **1 qt. chilled ginger ale** |

Mix fruit juices. Stir in sugar and water until sugar is dissolved. Add ginger ale. Serve immediately in glasses partially filled with cracked ice. *12 servings.*

*EASY COCKTAIL SNACKS—Crackers in variety, bacon-flavored or with sesame seeds, for example . . . Green or ripe olives . . . Pretzels . . . Potato chips, plain or flavored . . . Corn chips . . . Cheese sticks . . . Popcorn . . . Salted nuts.*

### TOMATO COCKTAILS

**Tomato Bouillon:** Combine equal amounts of tomato juice and bouillon (dilute canned bouillon or use cubes with boiling water). Serve hot.

**Tomato-Sauerkraut Cocktail:** Combine 2 parts tomato juice and 1 part sauerkraut juice. Serve hot or cold.

**Tomato-Clam Juice:** Combine equal amounts of clam juice and tomato juice; season to taste with onion, salt, and pepper. Serve hot.

## HA' PENNY SNACKS

*Golden cheese wafers. See picture, p. 63.*

| | |
|---|---|
| ¼ lb. butter (1 stick) | ½ tsp. salt |
| ½ lb. Cheddar cheese, grated | 1 cup Gold Medal Flour |
| ½ pkg. dehydrated onion soup mix | |

Let butter and cheese come to room temperature; mix thoroughly. Measure flour by dip-level-pour method. Add remaining ingredients and blend. Shape into 2 or 3 rolls, 1" in diameter. Wrap in waxed paper; chill. Heat oven to 375° (quick mod.). Slice roll into slices ¼" thick. Bake on ungreased baking sheet 10 to 12 min., or until slightly browned on edges. *Makes 6 to 8 doz.*

## DEVILS ON HORSEBACK

Fill pitted cooked large prunes with pimiento-stuffed olives or almonds around which anchovy fillets have been wound. Wrap a half slice of bacon around each stuffed prune. Broil 3" from heat for 2 to 3 min.

## CHEESE AND MEAT STACK-UPS

Soften 1 pkg. (3 oz.) cream cheese with fork. Beat in 2 tsp. prepared horse-radish. Slice 1 can (12 oz.) luncheon meat into 12 slices. Spread cheese mixture over 8 of the slices. Put together, sandwich-style, using 2 spread slices and 1 plain for each "sandwich." Cut each into 8 squares. Serve on toothpicks. *Makes 32.*

## OLIVE CHEESE BALLS

| | |
|---|---|
| ½ lb. grated processed sharp Cheddar cheese | ½ cup melted butter |
| 1¼ cups Gold Medal Flour | 1 jar (2 oz.) small stuffed olives (about 3 doz.) |

Measure flour by dip-level-pour method. Work cheese and flour together until crumbly. Add butter and stir well with fork. Mold one teaspoonful of cheese dough around each olive. Place balls 2" apart on ungreased baking sheet. Refrigerate 1 hr. or more. Heat oven to 400° (mod. hot). Bake 15 to 20 min. Serve hot. *Makes 3 to 4 doz.*

## FRUIT KABOBS

Assemble one piece each of 4 or 5 different fruits on wooden or bamboo skewers: a strawberry, a Bing cherry, a watermelon ball, and a pineapple chunk, for example. For individual service, stand 3 kabobs in a narrow wedge of honeydew melon. For a large party, stand kabobs in a scooped-out watermelon.

## FRESH VEGETABLE RELISHES

*One of the best, easiest, and most attractive of dinner appetizers.*

Prepare a variety of vegetable relishes (below), using perfect vegetables. Keep crisp in ice water or in refrigerator until serving time. Arrange in a large bowl filled with crushed ice. Delicious with a cheese dip like Piquant Dip (p. 64).

**Broccoli Buds and Cauliflowerets:** Break head of raw broccoli or cauliflower into bite-size flowerets.

**Celery Hearts:** Save coarse outer stalks for soup. Peel root end. Then quarter; slice quarters lengthwise, leaving some heart with each piece.

**Cucumber Petals:** Run a sharp-tined fork down the length of an unpeeled cucumber. Cut very thin slices crosswise.

**Lake Louise Poppies (Carrot Curls):** Slice carrots lengthwise, paper-thin, with vegetable slicer. Roll up and fasten with toothpicks. Crisp in ice water until curled.

**Radishes:** Scrub, leaving on a couple of green leaves.

**Spring or Green Onions:** Trim off green stalks, leaving about 2". Cut off root ends and remove loose skin. Wrap in damp cloth; chill.

**Turnip or Carrot Sticks in Olive Rings:** Cut sticks of peeled white turnip or carrot. Chill. Draw through canned pitted ripe olives.

## PIZZA APPETIZERS

Heat oven to 425° (hot). Using our refrigerated pizza, pat and stretch the dough into 12x10" rectangle on lightly greased baking sheet. Spoon on tomato sauce and add your favorite meat and cheese toppings. Bake 20 to 25 min. Cut into bite-size squares with kitchen shears or pastry wheel. *Makes about 60.*

## SIMPLE CANAPÉ SPREADS

**Savory Cream Cheese Spread:** Soften 1 pkg. (3 oz.) cream cheese with just enough milk or cream to spread. Season to taste with salt, freshly ground pepper, paprika, lemon juice, and onion juice or minced chives. Blend in ½ tsp. Worcestershire sauce and 2 tbsp. chili sauce, catsup, or chopped pimiento-stuffed olives.

**Sea Food Spread:** Mash canned or cooked crabmeat, shrimp, lobster, salmon, or tuna; moisten with mayonnaise; add a few drops lemon juice and minced parsley.

**Deviled Ham Spread:** Mash deviled ham with a little horse-radish, grated onion, and coarse black pepper to taste.

**Chicken or Turkey Spread:** Chop cooked chicken or turkey finely; add mayonnaise to moisten. Season to taste with salt and pepper; add a little finely chopped celery or almonds.

**Mushroom Spread:** Sauté chopped mushrooms in butter. Season with salt, Worcestershire sauce, and onion salt. Spread on canapé bases. Heat under broiler just before serving.

## CANAPÉ BASES

**Bread:** Cut thin slices into fingers, rounds, or any small shape you wish. Toast or quickly brown in butter on one side only. These may be made ahead of time. Spread topping on untoasted side.

**Canapé Bases from a Package:**

Crisp crackers

Toasted English muffin wedges

Melba toast

Brown 'n serve rolls, split crosswise.

## FESTIVE CANAPÉS

**Shrimp Circles:** Cut about 6 bread slices into 15 or 16 rounds, using a 1¾″ cutter. Toast, if desired; butter. Place a thin cucumber slice on each round, top with a dab of mayonnaise, a small cooked or canned shrimp, and a few capers.

**Hot Cheese Puffs:** Beat 2 egg whites until stiff. Fold in ½ tsp. baking powder, ¼ tsp. salt, ¼ tsp. paprika, and 1 cup grated sharp Cheddar or Swiss cheese. Spread ¼″ thick on toast canapé bases. Broil about 5 min. *Makes 12.*

**Sardine Canapés:** Soften 1 pkg. (8 oz.) cream cheese. Blend in 6 drops Tabasco, ¼ cup chili sauce, 1 tbsp. lemon juice (1 lemon), 1 tsp. olive juice, 20 small stuffed olives, chopped, and a dash of garlic salt. Spread on oblong crackers; top each with a whole sardine and a thin slice of stuffed olive.

## SEA FOOD COCKTAILS

**Shrimp, Oyster, or Clam Cocktail:** For each serving, use 6 chilled cleaned canned or cooked shrimp or fresh or frozen raw oysters or raw hard-shell clams. Place in lettuce-lined cocktail or sherbet glasses. Garnish with parsley and lemon wedge. Pass Cocktail Sauce (below).

**Crabmeat, Tuna, or Lobster Cocktail:** For each serving, use ⅓ cup chilled, flaked, canned or cooked crabmeat, tuna, or lobster combined with 1 tbsp. minced celery; chill. Arrange in lettuce-lined cocktail or sherbet glasses. Garnish with parsley and lemon wedges. Serve with Cocktail Sauce (below).

## COCKTAIL SAUCE

| | |
|---|---|
| ¾ cup catsup | ½ tsp. salt |
| ¼ cup lemon juice | 6 drops Tabasco |
| 3 tbsp. minced celery | dash cayenne pepper |

Combine; chill. Serve with sea food. *Makes 1 cup.*

See next page for identification. ⟫⟫⟶

## TEMPTING TUNA DIP

1 pkg. (3 oz.) cream
  cheese, softened
1 cup commercial sour
  cream
1 can (6½ or 7 oz.) tuna,
  drained and flaked
¼ cup stuffed olives,
  chopped

2 tbsp. chopped chives
2 tsp. prepared horse-
  radish
1 tsp. Worcestershire
  sauce
¼ tsp. salt

Blend cream cheese and sour cream until fluffy. Add remaining ingredients. Blend gently but thoroughly. Chill 2 hr. to blend flavors. Serve as dip for vegetable relishes, crackers, or chips. *Makes 2 cups.*

## GUACAMOLE

2 avocados
½ medium onion,
  minced
1 tbsp. vinegar

salt and pepper to taste
chopped green chili
  pepper to taste
1 very ripe tomato, peeled

Beat first 5 ingredients together with electric mixer on medium speed until smooth. Chop tomato finely with knife; fold into mixture. Serve as a dip; especially good with corn chips.

## CALIFORNIA ONION DIP

Stir contents of 1 pkg. (1½ oz.) dehydrated onion soup mix into 2 cups commercial sour cream. Refrigerate several hours or overnight, until flavors blend. *Makes about 2 cups.*

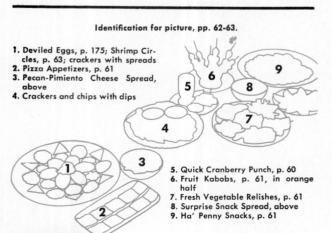

**Identification for picture, pp. 62-63.**

1. Deviled Eggs, p. 175; Shrimp Circles, p. 63; crackers with spreads
2. Pizza Appetizers, p. 61
3. Pecan-Pimiento Cheese Spread, above
4. Crackers and chips with dips
5. Quick Cranberry Punch, p. 60
6. Fruit Kabobs, p. 61, in orange half
7. Fresh Vegetable Relishes, p. 61
8. Surprise Snack Spread, above
9. Ha' Penny Snacks, p. 61

## SURPRISE SNACK SPREAD

*Its reddish color will brighten the appetizer tray.*

1 can (8 oz.) tomato
  sauce
1 tsp. instant minced
  onion
1½ cups grated Cheddar
  cheese

1 pkg. (4 oz.) dried
  beef, minced
¼ cup butter
1 egg, well beaten

Combine tomato and onion in pan. Cook over low heat 10 min. Add cheese, dried beef, and butter; continue to cook over low heat, stirring frequently, until well blended. Gradually stir half of hot mixture into beaten egg. Blend into hot mixture in pan. Boil 1 min., stirring constantly. Cool. Store, covered, in refrigerator. Soften in room before using. Spread on Melba toast or other canapé bases. *Makes 2 cups.*

## PECAN-PIMIENTO CHEESE SPREAD

1 lb. sharp cheese
⅔ to ¾ cup salad
  dressing or mayonnaise
¼ cup chopped pecans

2 tbsp. chopped onion,
  chives, or dried
  green onion
1 tbsp. finely chopped
  pimiento

Grate cheese; bring to room temperature. Add rest of ingredients and blend well. If too thick to spread, thin to desired consistency with more dressing. *Makes about 2¾ cups.*

## PIQUANT DIP

½ cup cottage cheese
1 cup commercial sour
  cream
1 hard-cooked egg,
  finely chopped
¼ cup minced green
  pepper
1 tbsp. catsup

1½ tsp. prepared
  horse-radish
1 tsp. Worcestershire
  sauce
½ small clove garlic,
  minced
½ tsp. dry mustard
½ tsp. salt

Mix cottage cheese and sour cream. Stir in remaining ingredients. Cover and chill 2 hr. to blend flavors. Serve as a dip for crackers, chips, or vegetable relishes. *Makes 1½ cups.*

# 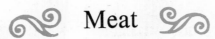 Meat

*There are many good and easy ways to cook your meat for dinner, but all methods fall into one of two classes: cooking without added moisture—for tender cuts; cooking with added liquid—for less tender cuts.*

| DRY HEAT METHODS *(for tender cuts)* | | BEEF | PORK | LAMB | VEAL |
|---|---|---|---|---|---|
| **Roasting** | 1. Season with salt and pepper.<br>2. Place fat side up, on rack in roasting pan.<br>3. Do not add water, do not cover.<br>4. Roast at 325° (except fresh pork—350°) until done. | Ribs<br>Rump (high quality)<br>Sirloin tip<br>Meat loaf | Loin<br>Leg<br>Spareribs<br>Ham<br>Picnic<br>Ham loaf | Leg<br>Shoulder | Leg<br>Shoulder<br>Loin<br>Meat loaf |
| **Broiling** | 1. Set oven for broiling.<br>2. Broil 2 to 3″ from heat until top is brown.<br>3. Season with salt and pepper.<br>4. Turn and broil until done.<br>5. Season and serve at once. | Steaks—rib, loin, T-bone, porter-house, strip<br>Ground | Ham and picnic slices<br>Bacon | Chops—shoulder, rib, loin<br>Ground<br>Kidney<br>Leg steaks | Liver |
| **Pan-Broiling** | 1. Place meat in heavy skillet. Cook slowly.<br>3. Do not add fat or water; do not cover.<br>3. Turn occasionally to brown and cook meat evenly.<br>4. Pour off fat as it accumulates.<br>5. Cook until done (do not over-cook); season and serve. | Same as for Broiling | Same as for Broiling | Same as for Broiling | Same as for Broiling |
| **Pan-Frying** | 1. Brown on both sides in small amount of hot fat.<br>2. Season with salt and pepper.<br>3. Do not cover.<br>4. Cook over medium heat until done, turning occasionally. | Same steaks as for broiling, only thinner<br>Liver | Thin chops<br>Tenderloin<br>Smoked ham slice<br>Bacon | Chops—shoulder, rib, loin<br>Ground<br>Liver | Chops<br>Liver<br>Steaks or cutlets<br>Ground |
| **MOIST HEAT METHODS** *(for less tender cuts)* | | **BEEF** | **PORK** | **LAMB** | **VEAL** |
| **Braising** | 1. Brown on all sides in fat in heavy pan.<br>2. Season with salt and pepper.<br>3. Add small amount of liquid, if necessary.<br>4. Cover tightly; cook at low temperature until tender. | Pot roasts<br>Short ribs<br>Steak—round or flank<br>Stew meat<br>Liver<br>Oxtails | Shoulder steaks<br>Chops<br>Cutlets<br>Spareribs<br>Liver<br>Heart | Neck slices<br>Shanks<br>Stew meat<br>Riblets<br>Breast<br>Heart | Breast<br>Shoulder<br>Chops<br>Steaks or cutlets<br>Stew meat<br>Liver |
| **Cooking in Liquid** | 1. Brown on all sides in own fat or other fat.<br>2. Season with salt and pepper.<br>3. Add liquid; cover kettle and cook below boiling until tender. | "Boiling beef"<br>Corned beef<br>Tongue | Fresh or cured—hocks, spareribs, picnic, butt | Shanks | Tongue<br>Heart<br>Sweet-breads |

## ROAST BEEF

*For carving instructions, see p. 81.*

**Standing rib roast**
**Choose: Rolled rib roast**
**Rump (high quality)**

Heat oven to 325° (slow mod.). Season meat with salt and pepper. Place fat-side-up on rack in open pan. Do not add water; do not cover; do not baste. Roast 18 to 20 min. per lb. for rare, 22 to 25 min. per lb. for medium, 27 to 30 min. per lb. for well done. Allow the longer time for smaller roasts. Add 10 min. per lb. for rolled roast.

*All-American Favorite*
(Pictured on p. 58.)
**Roast Standing Rib of Beef**
**Baked Potatoes (p. 92)**
**Carrots with Green Onions**
**Apple-Grape-Celery Salad (p. 96)**
**Allegretti Devils Food Cake**

## EVERYDAY POT ROAST

| | |
|---|---|
| **3- to 4-lb. beef chuck** | **6 to 8 carrots** |
| **⅓ cup horse-radish** | **6 to 8 pieces celery** |
| **salt and pepper** | **3 potatoes, cut in** |
| **6 to 8 small onions** | **half** |

Brown meat well on all sides in hot fat. Spread with horse-radish. Season with salt and pepper. Add a little water; cover and cook slowly 2 to 2½ hr., adding more water if necessary. Add vegetables and continue cooking 1 hr. Serve with Kettle Gravy (p. 83). *6 servings.*

## MINUTE OR CUBE STEAKS

Dip 4 to 6 minute or cube steaks in flour. Place in hot skillet in which just enough fat to keep meat from sticking has been melted. Pan-fry on one side 2 to 6 min. Turn and pan-fry other side 2 to 6 min. Remove to hot platter, sprinkle with salt and pepper; spread with butter, if desired. *4 to 6 servings.*

## BROILED STEAK

*For carving instructions, see p. 81.*

**Rib, Club, Tenderloin (filet mignon),**
**Choose: T-bone, Porterhouse, Sirloin,**
**Ground, Top round**

Place meat on rack in broiler pan, then place under broiler so top is 2″ from heat. With door closed on gas range, door slightly ajar on electric range, broil, turning once, until meat is done as desired. Season with salt and pepper and serve at once on hot platter.

| | 1″ thick | 2″ thick |
|---|---|---|
| **Rare:** | 5 min. each side | 16 min. each side |
| **Medium:** | 6 min. each side | 18 min. each side |
| **Well done:** | 8 min. each side | 20 min. each side |

## PAN-BROILED STEAK

Use steaks 1″ thick or thinner. (Oven-broil or charcoal-grill steaks over 1″ thick.) Heat heavy skillet, rubbing it with suet. Place steak in hot skillet and cook slowly. Do not add fat or water; do not cover. Cook about the same amount of time as for Broiled Steak (above). Pour off excess fat during cooking.

## STEAK CONTINENTAL

| | |
|---|---|
| **2-lb. flank steak or** | **3 tsp. soy sauce** |
| **¾″ thick round steak** | **1 tbsp. tomato paste** |
| **1 clove garlic,** | **1 tbsp. vegetable oil** |
| **quartered** | **½ tsp. pepper** |
| **1 tbsp. salt** | **½ tsp. oregano leaves** |

Score flank steak or trim all fat from round steak. Mash garlic with salt; add soy sauce, tomato paste, oil, pepper, and oregano. Mix well and rub into steak. Wrap in waxed paper and let stand in refrigerator 5 to 6 hr. or overnight. Broil 5 to 8 min. on each side, or to desired degree of doneness. *4 to 6 servings.*

## FLANK STEAK ROLL

Have a 1½-lb. flank steak scored. Season with salt and pepper. Spread with 1 qt. Bread Stuffing (p. 82). Starting from the long side, roll meat up like jelly roll; tie with string. Brown in hot fat; add 1 cup water. Cover tightly and cook slowly over low heat or in 350° (mod.) oven about 2 hr. Slice to serve. *6 servings.*

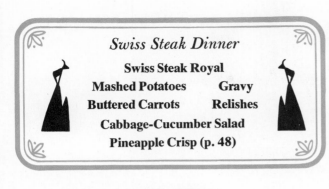

### Swiss Steak Dinner

Swiss Steak Royal

Mashed Potatoes    Gravy

Buttered Carrots    Relishes

Cabbage-Cucumber Salad

Pineapple Crisp (p. 48)

## SWISS STEAK

*The secret is thorough browning and slow cooking.*

| | |
|---|---|
| 1½- to 2-lb. round steak, cut 1″ thick | ½ tsp. seasoned salt or ¼ tsp. celery salt, ⅛ tsp. garlic salt, and ⅛ tsp. onion salt |
| ¼ cup Gold Medal Flour | |
| 3 tbsp. fat | |
| 1½ tsp. salt | 1 large onion, sliced |
| ¼ tsp. pepper | 1 cup water |

Dredge meat with flour; brown in hot fat over medium heat. Sprinkle with seasonings. Add onion and ½ cup liquid. Cover; simmer 1½ hr., until tender. Add second ½ cup liquid during cooking. *6 servings.*

**City Steak:** Make Swiss Steak (above)—except use 1 cup commercial sour cream and 1 can (4 oz.) mushrooms instead of other liquid.

**Swiss Steak Royal:** Make Swiss Steak (above)—except add 1 tsp. dry mustard to flour used for dredging steak. Add 1 clove garlic, grated, with liquid.

## NEW ENGLAND BOILED DINNER

| | |
|---|---|
| 3-lb. corned brisket of beef | 12 small or 6 medium onions |
| 6 carrots, quartered | 6 potatoes, quartered |
| 2 turnips, cubed | 1 head cabbage, cut in wedges |

Cut meat in serving-size pieces; cover with water. Bring to boil and cook slowly 3 hr. Add carrots, turnips, onions, and potatoes. Cook 15 min. Add cabbage, cook another 10 min. Arrange vegetables around meat on platter. Pass horse-radish. *6 servings.*

**Ham Boiled Dinner:** Use 3-lb. smoked ham, shank end, in place of corned beef in New England Boiled Dinner (above).

## BEEF STEAK PIE WITH POTATO CRUST

| | |
|---|---|
| 1 lb. round steak, cut in 1″ cubes | ¼ tsp. pepper |
| | dash each thyme and garlic salt |
| 3 tbsp. fat | |
| 3 small onions, peeled and thinly sliced | 2 cups water |
| | 3 medium potatoes, pared and thinly sliced |
| 3 tbsp. flour | |
| 1½ tsp. salt | |

Heat oven to 350° (mod.). Dredge meat in flour. Place in skillet with fat. Brown meat until very brown and crusty, about 15 min. per side. Add onions and cook until golden brown, about 10 min. Put in 2-qt. baking dish. Sprinkle with flour and seasonings; pour water over top. Bake 45 min. to 1 hr., until meat is tender. Remove from oven; increase oven temperature to 450° (hot). Place potatoes on top and sprinkle with salt and paprika. Return to oven and bake about 30 min., until potatoes are browned and tender. *4 to 6 servings.*

## OVEN-BARBECUED STEAKS

| | |
|---|---|
| 3-lb. round steak, cut ¾″ thick | 1 tbsp. brown sugar |
| | 1 tbsp. prepared mustard |
| 2 tbsp. vegetable oil | 1 tbsp. Worcestershire sauce |
| ½ cup chopped onions | |
| ¾ cup catsup | ½ tsp. salt |
| ½ cup vinegar | ⅛ tsp. black pepper |
| ¾ cup water | |

Heat oven to 350° (mod.). Cut steak into 10 equal portions. Pour oil into skillet. Brown each piece of steak on both sides. Transfer steaks to a roasting pan. Add onions to oil in skillet and brown lightly. Add rest of ingredients to make a barbecue sauce and simmer 5 min. Pour sauce over steaks in pan. Cover. Bake 2 hr., or until meat is fork tender. *10 servings.*

## GOOD BROWN STEW

2 lb. boneless beef
  chuck, cut in 1" cubes
4 cups hot water
1 tsp. lemon juice
1 tsp. Worcestershire
  sauce
1 clove garlic, minced
1 medium onion, sliced

1 small bay leaf
2 tsp. salt
¼ tsp. pepper
pinch allspice
1 tsp. sugar
6 carrots, quartered
8 small onions
3 potatoes, peeled and
  cut in eighths

Brown meat thoroughly in 1 to 2 tbsp. fat in large heavy kettle. Add remaining ingredients—except carrots, whole onions, and potatoes; simmer 1 hr. 45 min., adding water if necessary. Add carrots, onions, and potatoes and cook about 30 min., until vegetables are tender. Thicken liquid, if desired, for gravy. *6 servings.*

## CUBE STEAK STEW

4 cube steaks, cut in
  2x½" strips
3 tbsp. flour
1½ tsp. salt
¼ tsp. pepper
½ tsp. monosodium
  glutamate
3 tbsp. fat
1 large onion, thinly
  sliced
4 medium potatoes,
  peeled and cubed

1 clove garlic, minced
1 tsp. salt
1 can (1 lb. 4 oz.)
  tomatoes (2½ cups)
1 can (8 oz.) tomato
  sauce
1 pkg. (10 oz.) frozen
  peas
½ medium green pepper,
  seeded and cut into
  ¼" strips

Dredge meat in mixture of flour, salt, pepper, and monosodium glutamate. Melt fat in large heavy kettle; brown meat on all sides. Add onion, potatoes, garlic, salt, tomatoes, and tomato sauce. Heat to boil; lower heat and simmer, stirring occasionally, about 30 min., or until meat and vegetables are almost tender. Add peas and green pepper. Heat to boil; lower heat and cook 5 min. longer, until peas are tender but pepper is still crisp. *6 servings.*

**Note:** *For thicker stew, blend 2 tbsp. flour with ⅓ cup water and stir into stew. Cook, stirring occasionally, until thickened.*

## MARIE'S BOILED MEAT BALLS

*The old-fashioned goodness of German meat balls, yet so easy to prepare.*

⅓ lb. each ground veal,
  pork, and beef
1 egg, slightly beaten
1 tsp. salt
¼ tsp. pepper
1 medium onion, finely
  chopped

½ envelope dehydrated
  onion soup mix
  (about ¼ cup)
1 medium bay leaf,
  broken
½ to 1 tsp. salt
3 cups boiling water
¼ cup Gold Medal Flour
½ cup cold water

Mix first five ingredients thoroughly; shape into balls the size of walnuts. Add onion soup mix, bay leaf, and salt to boiling water. Drop meat balls into boiling water; reduce heat and simmer, covered, ½ hr. Combine flour and cold water. Add to simmering meat stock. Bring to boil; boil 1 min., uncovered, or until gravy is slightly thickened. Serve with mashed potatoes, noodles, or rice. *Makes 15 to 18 meat balls, 6 to 8 servings.*

## BAKED MEAT BALLS

*They brown as they bake. Serve them with spaghetti sauce or with Easy Mushroom Sauce (p. 103).*

2 eggs
½ cup milk
1 tbsp. instant
  minced onion

3 slices bread, cubed
2 tsp. salt
¼ tsp. pepper
2 lb. ground beef

Heat oven to 350° (mod.). Beat eggs and milk. Stir in onion, bread, and seasonings. Add beef and mix well. Shape ¼ cup mixture into ball; shape the rest approximately the same size. Place in shallow pan. Bake 30 to 40 min. *Makes about 18 meat balls.*

## DOUBLE-QUICK CHEESEBURGER SKILLET

Heat oven to 500° (hot). Combine 1 lb. ground beef, 2 tbsp. instant minced onion, 1 tsp. garlic powder, and salt and pepper to taste. Spread half the meat in a lightly greased heavy 8″ skillet. Lay 5 slices Cheddar cheese over meat. Spread rest of meat over cheese. Sprinkle with salt and pepper. Bake 10 min. Turn oven to broil; broil 5 min., or until top is nicely browned. Spoon off excess fat. Cut in wedges to serve. *4 servings.*

## HAMBURGER STROGANOFF

| | |
|---|---|
| ½ cup minced onion | 1 lb. fresh mushrooms |
| 1 clove garlic, minced | or 1 can (6 oz.) |
| ¼ cup butter | sliced mushrooms, |
| 1 lb. ground beef | drained |
| 2 tbsp. flour | 1 can (10½ oz.) cream |
| 1 tsp. salt | of chicken soup, |
| ¼ tsp. pepper | undiluted |
| | 1 cup commercial sour |
| | cream |

Sauté onion and garlic in butter over medium heat. Add meat and brown. Add flour, salt, pepper, and mushrooms. Cook 5 min. Add soup; simmer, uncovered, 10 min. Stir in sour cream. Heat through. Serve with noodles or rice. *4 to 6 servings.*

## BUDGET BEEF NOODLE CASSEROLE

| | |
|---|---|
| 1 lb. ground beef | ¼ cup chopped onion |
| ½ tsp. salt | ½ cup diced smoked |
| 1 tsp. beef extract | cheese |
| 1 egg, beaten | 1½ cups cooked noodles |
| 1 can (8 oz.) tomato | 2 tsp. Worcestershire |
| sauce | sauce |
| | ¼ cup crushed soda |
| | crackers |

Heat oven to 350° (mod.). Combine all ingredients and pat into well-greased 1½-qt. baking dish. Bake 30 min. covered and 20 to 30 min. uncovered. *6 to 8 servings.*

## BRAISED SHORT RIBS

| | |
|---|---|
| 2 lb. lean short ribs, | 2 tsp. salt |
| cut in serving-size | ½ tsp. pepper |
| pieces | 2 tbsp. shortening |
| ⅓ cup Gold Medal | ½ cup hot water |
| Flour | 2 tsp. horse-radish |

Roll meat in flour blended with seasonings. Brown well in shortening, using large heavy skillet or Dutch oven. Reserve enough fat to barely cover the bottom of the kettle. Add water and horse-radish. Cover tightly and simmer on top of range about 2½ hr., or until tender. Add more water if needed. *4 servings.*

**Short Ribs with Vegetables:** Braise short ribs (above) 2 hr. Add 6 small carrots, 3 medium onions, and 9 short strips of celery. Cook 30 to 40 min. longer.

## CREAMED DRIED BEEF

| | |
|---|---|
| 4 oz. dried beef, | ¼ cup Gold Medal Flour |
| shredded | ⅛ tsp. pepper |
| ¼ cup butter | 2 cups milk |

If dried beef is very salty, cover with hot water, bring to boil and then drain. Sauté beef in butter until edges curl; then blend in flour and pepper; let bubble. Gradually add milk; bring to boil, stirring constantly. Boil 1 min. Serve on toast, crisp noodles, baked potatoes, or hot popovers. *4 servings.*

*Cold Weather Dinner*

**Short Ribs with Vegetables**

**Mashed Potatoes      Kettle Gravy (p. 83)**

**Spinach**

**Butterfly Salad (p. 41)**

**Victoria Sandwich (p. 128)**

## HAMBURGERS IN CHEESE SAUCE

2 lb. ground beef

2 tsp. salt

¼ tsp. pepper

12 large, very thin onion slices

1 can (10½ oz.) cream of celery soup

1 tsp. dry mustard

½ tsp. Worcestershire sauce

¼ cup chili sauce

1½ cups grated sharp Cheddar cheese

12 hamburger buns, split

Heat oven to 350° (mod.). Lightly form beef into 12 patties, sprinkling both sides with salt and pepper. Place in two baking pans, 13x9½x2″. Top each with a slice of onion. Bake 20 min. While hamburgers are baking, combine soup, seasonings, and cheese in pan. Cook over medium heat, stirring constantly, until cheese melts. Set aside. When hamburgers are done, pour off excess juice, add cheese sauce, and bake 10 min. more. Toast split buns on baking sheet in oven at the same time. Serve hamburgers between toasted bun halves. *12 servings.*

## BEEFBURGER SPECIALS

1 lb. ground beef

3 tbsp. catsup

2 tsp. prepared mustard

1½ tsp. horse-radish

1 small onion, finely chopped

1 tsp. salt

½ cup soft bread crumbs

¼ cup milk

1½ tsp. Worcester-shire sauce

Combine all ingredients. Shape into 4 large (½″ thick) or 8 small (¼″ thick) patties. Broil on pan 3″ below source of heat, about 6 min. on each side for the large patties (4 min. for smaller ones), or until browned outside and medium done inside. *4 servings.*

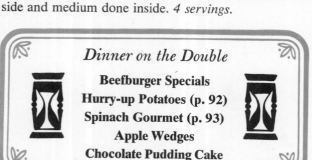

*Dinner on the Double*

**Beefburger Specials**

**Hurry-up Potatoes (p. 92)**

**Spinach Gourmet (p. 93)**

**Apple Wedges**

**Chocolate Pudding Cake**

## DOUBLE-QUICK MEAT LOAF AND GRAVY DUET

2 lb. ground beef

1 packet (1½ oz.) dehy-drated onion soup mix

1 can (10½ oz.) cream of mushroom soup

Heat oven to 350° (mod.). On a 22 to 24″ strip of heavy-duty aluminum foil, mix beef and onion soup mix thoroughly, being careful not to tear foil. Form into loaf and pour undiluted cream of mushroom soup over loaf. Wrap loosely in foil. Place on baking sheet. As this loaf bakes, the meat juices combine with the mushroom soup to make a wonderful brown gravy to serve over rice, noodles, or potatoes. Bake 1 hr. and 20 min. *6 to 8 servings.*

## FAVORITE MEAT LOAF

3 slices soft bread

1 cup milk

1 egg, beaten

1 lb. ground beef

¼ lb. ground pork

¼ lb. ground veal

¼ cup minced onion

1¼ tsp. salt

¼ tsp. each pepper, dry mustard, sage, celery salt, and garlic salt

1 tbsp. Worcestershire sauce

Heat oven to 350° (mod.). Tear bread in pieces into large mixing bowl; add remaining ingredients and mix thoroughly. Form lightly into loaf and place in shallow baking pan. If desired, spread 3 tbsp. catsup or chili sauce over top of loaf before baking. Bake 1½ hr. *8 servings.*

**Barbecued Beefies:** Shape Favorite Meat Loaf (above) into 8 individual loaves (3x2x1″); place in shallow baking pan. Top each with a thin slice of onion. Pour Texas Barbecue Sauce (p. 154) or bottled barbecue sauce over loaves; baste often during baking.

**Cheese Ribbon Meat Loaf:** Make Favorite Meat Loaf (above) and pat out half of meat mixture in greased loaf pan, 9x5x3″. Combine 1 egg white, slightly beaten, and 1 tbsp. water; lightly toss with 2 medium slices soft bread, torn into tiny pieces, and ¼ lb. grated Cheddar or crumbled Bleu cheese. Cover meat with cheese mixture; top with rest of meat. Bake 1½ hr. *(Pictured on p. 100.)*

## ROAST PORK

*Try this with Roast Onions (p. 91). For carving in-structions, see p. 81.*

**Pork loin (loin end or center cut)**

**Choose: Fresh pork shoulder**
**(butt, picnic, or fresh ham)**

Heat oven to 350° (mod.). If using loin, have back-bone cut loose or removed. Season with salt and pepper. Place fat-side-up in roasting pan. Do not add water; do not cover; do not baste. Roast 35 to 40 min. per lb., until meat thermometer registers 185°. For uses for leftover pork, see p. 157.

## BRAISED PORK CHOPS

**Pork loin**

**Choose: Shoulder chops**

**Pork steak**

Trim excess fat. Brown chops slowly in heavy skillet. Cover tightly and cook until tender, 25 to 30 min., adding a small amount of liquid, if desired.

## STUFFING-TOPPED PORK CHOPS

| | |
|---|---|
| **6 pork chops (¾″ thick)** | **1¼ tsp. salt** |
| **½ cup water** | **½ to 1 tsp. dried sage** |
| **2 tbsp. butter** | **½ tsp. poultry** |
| **¼ cup chopped celery** | **seasoning** |
| **2 tbsp. finely minced** | **¼ tsp. pepper** |
| **onion** | **1 can (8 oz.) cream-** |
| **2 cups soft bread crumbs** | **style corn (1 cup)** |

Heat oven to 350° (mod.). Brown chops. Remove chops to baking pan, 13x9½x2″; add water and cover pan tightly with aluminum foil. Bake 1 hr. Prepare stuffing: melt butter in small skillet, add minced celery and onion, and sauté; add to bread cubes along with seasonings. Toss with corn. Spoon stuffing over chops. Bake ½ hr. longer uncovered. *6 servings.*

## MEXICAN PORK CHOPS

| | |
|---|---|
| **4 lean pork chops,** | **1 can (1 lb. 13 oz.)** |
| **1″ thick** | **tomatoes** |
| **4 thin slices onion** | **½ to 1 tsp. salt** |
| **¼ cup uncooked rice** | |
| **(not instant)** | |

Trim any excess fat from chops. Season chops well on both sides with salt and pepper. Brown on both sides in lightly greased hot skillet. Top each chop with a slice of onion, 1 tbsp. rice, and cover with whole tomatoes. Add any remaining tomatoes and juice to skillet. Season with salt. Cover tightly and simmer over low heat or bake in foil-covered baking dish, 11½x7½x1½″, in 350° (mod.) oven 1½ hr., or until tender. *4 servings.*

## BREADED PORK TENDERLOIN

Flatten 1 lb. pork tenderloin patties. Season; dip in beat-en egg and bread crumbs. Fry in hot fat until golden brown on both sides. Reduce heat; add a small amount of water, cover tightly and braise until tender, about 30 min. Serve hot with a tomato sauce. *4 servings.*

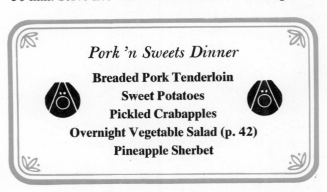

*Pork 'n Sweets Dinner*

**Breaded Pork Tenderloin**
**Sweet Potatoes**
**Pickled Crabapples**
**Overnight Vegetable Salad (p. 42)**
**Pineapple Sherbet**

## PORK CHOPS AND APPLES

| | |
|---|---|
| **6 pork chops** | **¼ cup brown sugar** |
| **3 or 4 unpeeled apples,** | **(packed)** |
| **cored and sliced** | **½ tsp. cinnamon** |
| | **2 tbsp. butter** |

Heat oven to 400° (mod. hot). Brown chops on all sides in hot fat. Place apple slices in greased baking dish. Sprinkle with sugar and cinnamon; dot with butter. Top with chops. Cover; bake 1½ hr. *6 servings.*

## BARBECUED SPARERIBS

| | |
|---|---|
| 3 to 4 lb. spareribs, cut in serving pieces | 3 tbsp. Worcestershire sauce |
| 1 lemon, sliced | 1 tsp. chili powder |
| 1 large onion, sliced | 1 tsp. salt |
| 1 cup catsup | 2 dashes of Tabasco |
| | 1 cup water |

Heat oven to 450° (hot). Place ribs in baking pan, meaty side up. On each piece place a slice of lemon and onion. Roast 30 min. Combine remaining ingredients; pour over ribs. Reduce heat to 350° (mod.) and bake 1½ hr. more. Baste 2 or 3 times while baking. *4 servings.*

## SWEET-LEMON SPARERIBS

| | |
|---|---|
| 3 lb. spareribs, cut in serving pieces | 3 tbsp. catsup |
| 1 can (6 oz.) frozen concentrated lemonade | 1 to 2 tsp. vinegar, if desired |
| 2 cans water | 3 tbsp. brown sugar (packed) |
| 3 tbsp. soy sauce | 2 tbsp. cold water |
| ½ tsp. salt | 3 tbsp. cornstarch |

Place spareribs in skillet with water to cover; bring to boil, cover and simmer 1 hr. Pour off water. Combine lemonade and 2 cans water. Add soy sauce, salt, catsup, vinegar, and sugar. Pour ⅔ cup of this mixture over ribs; cover and cook over medium heat 1 hr., or until ribs are tender, adding more of the lemonade mixture, if necessary. Remove ribs and pour excess fat from skillet. Add remaining sauce. Blend water into cornstarch and stir into sauce in skillet. Cook and stir until sauce is thickened. Serve sauce separately to be poured over ribs. *4 servings.*

## BAKED SPARERIBS

Heat oven to 350° (mod.). Cut ribs in 2- or 3-rib portions. Brown over low heat in roasting pan. Season with salt and pepper. Top with onion slices, if desired. Add small amount of water or tomato juice. Cover and bake 1½ to 2 hr. Allow ¾ to 1 lb. of ribs per person.

**Stuffed Spareribs:** Have ribs in 2 strips; brown as above. Place Bread Stuffing (p. 82) between pieces, meaty-side-out. Bake as above.

## MOCK CHICKEN LEGS

Tender chunks of pork and veal arranged on skewers to resemble chicken legs, crumb-coated and ready to cook, are available at many meat dealers. Bake in moderate oven or braise over low heat 1 hr.

## TENDERLOIN PATTIES SUPREME

| | |
|---|---|
| 6 pork tenderloin patties (1″ thick) | ⅓ cup lemon-lime carbonated beverage |
| 6 onion slices (¼″ thick) | 1 tsp. Worcestershire sauce |
| ¼ cup catsup | ⅛ tsp. chili powder |

Heat oven to 350° (mod.). Salt patties generously on both sides. Place in 9″ sq. baking dish. Top each with a slice of onion. Mix remaining ingredients and pour over meat. Cover and bake 1½ hr. Uncover and bake 30 min. longer. Watch carefully to prevent scorching. *6 servings.*

## SPARERIBS AND SAUERKRAUT

Brown 4 lb. spareribs in Dutch oven. Season with salt and pepper. Add small amount of water; cover and cook slowly 1 hr. Remove ribs and place 1 can (1 lb. 13 oz.) sauerkraut mixed with ¼ cup brown sugar and 2 apples, chopped, in Dutch oven. Top with ribs and cook, covered, 30 min., or until ribs are done and flavors are blended. *4 servings.*

## BAKED HAM

To bake uncooked ham, heat oven to 325° (slow mod.). Roast whole ham 18 to 20 min. per lb., half ham 22 to 25 min. per lb. (Half ham is best for small families; butt end of ham is meatier.)

Prepare ready-to-eat precooked or canned ham according to can or pkg. directions.

Boned hams, though a bit more expensive, have little waste and are easy to carve.

For ham flavor on a budget, choose a picnic, uncooked or fully cooked; it's pork shoulder cured like ham.

## ORANGE-GLAZED BAKED HAM

Bake ham (above). About 30 min. before ham is done, score fat in diamond design and insert a whole clove in each diamond. Mix 1 can (6 oz.) thawed frozen concentrated orange juice, ¼ cup brown sugar, and a pinch each of ground cloves and ground cinnamon. Pour half this mixture over ham. Bake 30 min., basting occasionally with remaining orange mixture.

For orange sauce to serve with ham: remove ham to platter, pour off grease; add water to pan and cook with orange glaze until sauce consistency.

## BAKED HAM SLICE

Cut slashes in edge of 1″ thick center-cut slice of ham. Sprinkle with 1 tsp. dry mustard and ¼ cup brown sugar. Place in heavy skillet or baking pan. Pour on milk at side of ham slice until it barely reaches top. Bake, uncovered, in 350° (mod.) oven 1¼ hr.

## BROILED HAM SLICE

Select 1″ thick center-cut ham slice. Slash edges to prevent curling. Broil 10 min. 3″ from heat. Turn and broil 5 min. on second side. Spread with prepared mustard, cranberry sauce, or currant jelly. Broil 5 min. more. If using ready-to-eat ham, broil 5 min. on each side.

## HAM WITH SPINACH STUFFING

| | |
|---|---|
| 1 pkg. (10 oz.) frozen chopped spinach | ¼ tsp. salt |
| | ⅛ tsp. pepper |
| ¼ cup diced celery | 2 slices (½ lb. each) precooked ham, ¼ to ½″ thick |
| 1 can (3 oz.) chopped mushrooms, drained | |
| 2 tbsp. chopped onion | 1 tbsp. butter, melted |
| 2 tbsp. vegetable oil | Horse-radish Sauce (p. 103) |

Heat oven to 350° (mod.). Cook spinach as directed on pkg.; drain. Sauté other vegetables in oil until transparent. Add to spinach. Add salt and pepper. Place 1 ham slice in a shallow baking dish; spread with spinach mixture. Top with remaining ham slice. Brush with butter. Cover and bake 15 min.; uncover and bake 15 min. more. Serve with Horse-radish Sauce. *4 to 6 servings.*

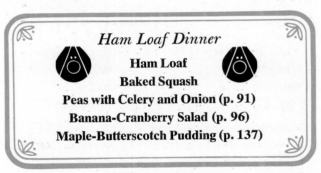

*Ham Loaf Dinner*

**Ham Loaf**

**Baked Squash**

**Peas with Celery and Onion (p. 91)**

**Banana-Cranberry Salad (p. 96)**

**Maple-Butterscotch Pudding (p. 137)**

## HAM LOAF

| | |
|---|---|
| 1½ lb. smoked ham, ground | 2 eggs, beaten |
| | 1 cup milk |
| ½ lb. fresh pork, ground | 1 cup fine bread crumbs |
| | ¼ tsp. pepper |

Heat oven to 350° (mod.). Grease loaf pan, 9x5x3″. Mix ingredients thoroughly and pack into pan. Bake 1¼ hr., or until done. *8 servings.*

## HAM 'N LIMAS

Cook 1 pkg. frozen baby Lima beans until tender. Meanwhile, place 1 center-cut ham slice, ¾″ thick, in shallow pan. Broil 5 min. on each side 3″ from heat. Arrange beans over ham; sprinkle with 1 cup grated Cheddar cheese (¼ lb.); broil until cheese melts and bubbles. Serve immediately. *4 to 6 servings.*

## ROAST VEAL

**Choose: Rib, Loin, Leg, Breast,
Rolled shoulder or rump**

Sprinkle with salt and pepper. Place fat-side-up in roasting pan. If roast lacks covering of fat, cover with salt pork or fat bacon. Do not add water; do not cover. Roast at 325° (slow mod.) 25 to 30 min. per lb.

## BARBECUED VEAL ROAST

| | |
|---|---|
| **4-lb. rolled shoulder of veal** | **1 tbsp. sugar** |
| **¾ cup catsup** | **1 tsp. dry mustard** |
| **½ cup water** | **1 tbsp. Worcestershire sauce** |
| **3 tbsp. vinegar** | **¼ tsp. Tabasco** |
| **1½ tsp. celery seeds** | |

Heat oven to 350° (mod.). Rub roast well with salt and pepper. Roast 2 hr. Combine remaining ingredients and pour over roast; bake 1 to 1½ hr. longer, basting occasionally with sauce while roasting. If sauce evaporates before end of baking time, add a little water. Save sauce from pan and serve with meat. *8 servings.*

## BREADED VEAL CUTLETS

Dip veal cutlets, chops, or steaks in flour or corn meal, then in beaten egg mixed with a little water, then in fine cracker or dry bread crumbs. Brown on both sides in hot fat. Season with salt and pepper. Add a small amount of water, cream, or diluted cream soup; cover tightly. Cook slowly 45 to 60 min. on top of range or in oven at 325° (slow mod.).

## SCHNITZEL SURPRISE

Lay a thin slice of cooked ham and a thin slice of Cheddar cheese on 4 veal cutlets. Top with 4 more cutlets. Dip cutlets in beaten egg, then in dry bread crumbs. Brown in hot fat, then bake in 325° (slow) oven 1 hr. Garnish with tomato.

## VEAL STEW

*A beautiful and appetizing dinner in a dish: tender veal cubes, rich tomato sauce, fluffy Corn Meal Dumplings.*

| | |
|---|---|
| **2 medium slices salt pork** | **dash of pepper** |
| **1½ lb. veal stew meat, cut into 1″ cubes** | **1 cup diced potatoes** |
| **4 cups tomato juice** | **½ cup diced celery** |
| **1 tsp. salt** | **½ cup chopped onion** |
| **2 to 3 dashes Tabasco** | **Corn Meal Dumplings (below)** |

Using Dutch oven or 10″ skillet, fry salt pork until crisp; set pork aside. Brown veal in pork fat over low heat about ½ hr. Remove excess fat. Crumble salt pork and add along with tomato juice and seasonings to veal. Cover and simmer 1 hr. Add vegetables; cover and simmer 30 min. more. Add more tomato juice if necessary. Finish cooking with Corn Meal Dumplings. *6 to 8 servings.*

**Corn Meal Dumplings:** Combine 1½ cups Bisquick, ½ cup yellow corn meal, and 2 tsp. dried parsley flakes. Add ¾ cup milk all at once and stir only until blended. Drop rounded tablespoonfuls of dumpling batter onto hot stew. Cook 10 min. uncovered. Cover tightly and steam 10 min. more.

## JANETTE'S VEAL

*Poppy Seed Noodles are the perfect accompaniment for any meat cooked in a rich sauce or gravy.*

| | |
|---|---|
| **2 lb. veal, cut in 1″ pieces** | **⅛ tsp. pepper** |
| **⅓ cup Gold Medal Flour** | **3 tbsp. hot fat** |
| **2 tsp. paprika** | **1 clove garlic, minced** |
| **1 tbsp. salt** | **2 cups sweet or commercial sour cream** |
| | **Poppy Seed Noodles (below)** |

Heat oven to 350° (mod.). Dredge meat in flour mixed with seasonings; brown in hot fat with garlic. Add cream; cover and bake 1 hr. (Cream may curdle.) Serve in circle of Poppy Seed Noodles. *6 to 8 servings.*

**Poppy Seed Noodles:** Cook 5 to 6 oz. noodles as directed on pkg. Drain. Melt 3 tbsp. butter. Add 1 tbsp. poppy seeds and, if desired, ½ cup blanched almonds. Add drained noodles and toss.

## ROAST LAMB

*For carving instructions, see p. 81.*

**Choose: Leg (full leg or short)**
**Shoulder (bone-in or rolled)**

Heat oven to 325° (slow mod.). Place roast, fat-side-up, on rack in roasting pan. Do not cover; do not add water. Roast 30 to 35 min. per lb. Increase time 5 min. per lb. for rolled roast.

|  | Weight | Roasting Time |
|---|---|---|
| Leg (medium) | 6 lb. | 3 hr. |
| (well done) | 6 lb. | 3½ hr. |
| Crown | 5 lb. | 3¾ hr. |
| Shoulder (bone-in) | 4 lb. | 2¼ hr. |
| Shoulder (cushion) | 4 lb. | 2½ hr. |
| Shoulder (rolled) | 4 lb. | 2½ hr. |

For additional seasoning, cut gashes in leg and stuff with dry mustard and clove of garlic.

## BROILED LAMB CHOPS AND STEAKS

**Rib chops**
**Choose: Shoulder chops**
**Leg steaks**

Remove skin covering from fat. Slash edges of fat. Broil 1" thick chops and steaks 3" from heat. Broil rib or loin chops 6 to 7 min. on each side; broil shoulder chops or leg steaks 8 min. on each side. Serve with mint jelly.

**Broiled Lamb Patties:** Season ground lamb with minced onion, salt, and pepper. Shape into 1" thick patties. Broil 3" from heat 10 min. on each side.

## LAMB AND CARROT MEAT BALLS

| | |
|---|---|
| ¾ lb. ground lamb | ⅛ tsp. pepper |
| 1½ cups ground or grated carrots | 2 tbsp. hot fat |
| 1 medium onion, grated | ¼ cup Gold Medal Flour |
| 1 egg | 1½ cups hot water |
| 2 tsp. salt | ½ tsp. basil, if desired |

Mix lamb, carrots, onion, egg, salt, and pepper. Shape into 12 balls. Sauté until brown in hot fat. Remove from heat. Blend in flour; stir in water. Add basil. Cover skillet and simmer 30 to 40 min. *4 to 6 servings.*

## LAMB STEW

| | |
|---|---|
| 2 lb. boneless lamb shoulder, 2" cubes | 3 medium carrots, cut in 1" pieces |
| 2 tbsp. fat | 1 medium onion, sliced |
| 2 cups hot water | 1 medium potato, diced |
| 2 tsp. salt | 1 cup fresh or frozen peas |
| ¼ tsp. pepper | Parsley Dumplings (below) |
| 1 small bay leaf | |

Brown meat in hot fat over medium heat in Dutch oven. Add water and seasonings. Simmer, covered, 2 hr., adding more water if needed. Add carrots, onion, and potato; simmer 20 min. Add peas. Thicken stew and top with Parsley Dumplings. *6 servings.*

**Parsley Dumplings:** Add ¾ cup milk and ¼ cup chopped parsley to 2 cups Bisquick. Mix thoroughly with fork. Drop by spoonfuls onto boiling stew. Cook over low heat, 10 min. uncovered and 10 min. covered; liquid should just bubble gently. Serve stew topped with Dumplings.

## SAVORY LAMB

| | |
|---|---|
| 2 lb. boneless lamb, cut in 1" cubes | ¾ cup chopped onion (1 medium) |
| ¼ cup Gold Medal Flour | 1 cup sliced celery (3 stalks) |
| 1½ tsp. salt | ½ cup green pepper, cut in 1" squares |
| ¼ tsp. pepper | Raisin Curried Rice (below) |
| 2 tbsp. fat | |
| 1 cup water | |
| ½ tsp. mace | |

Dredge meat in mixture of flour, salt, and pepper. Brown slowly in fat about 20 min. Pour off all fat. Sprinkle any remaining seasoned flour over lamb; add water, mace, and onion. Cover tightly and simmer 45 min. Skim excess fat from top. Add more water, if necessary. Add celery and green pepper; simmer 45 min., or until meat is tender. Serve over Raisin Curried Rice. *6 servings.*

**Raisin Curried Rice:** Combine 1 cup rice (not instant), ½ cup raisins, 1 tsp. salt, 1½ tsp. curry powder, and 4 cups boiling water. Cover and simmer 20 to 25 min., until rice is tender. Drain—don't rinse. *Makes 4 cups.*

## SAUSAGE

Choose sausage in bulk, in ready-to-slice rolls, or shaped in patties, ready to cook. Or choose sausage links, uncooked or partially cooked. Check sausage labels for cooking directions and serving suggestions. Bologna, liverwurst, and salami, also members of the sausage family, are usually served cold.

## POLISH OR COUNTRY SAUSAGE

Simmer, covered, in a little water 10 min. Drain and brown evenly 10 min. Serve with hominy, sauerkraut, or scalloped potatoes.

## CREOLE SCONE PIE

| | |
|---|---|
| 1 lb. bulk pork sausage | ⅛ tsp. pepper |
| ¼ cup chopped green pepper | 1 cup cooked tomatoes |
| ¼ cup chopped onion | 2 cups cooked corn or green beans |
| ¼ cup Gold Medal Flour | Scone Shell (below) |

Brown sausage in large skillet; add green pepper and onion; cook until soft. Drain off excess fat reserving ¼ cup. Stir flour, salt, and pepper into the ¼ cup fat in skillet. Blend in tomatoes; cook until smooth and thick, stirring occasionally. Add vegetables and heat through. Pour into hot baked Scone Shells; cut in wedges to serve. *6 servings.*

**Scone Shell:** Heat oven to 425° (hot). Stir 1½ cups Gold Medal Flour, 2 tsp. baking powder, and 1 tsp. salt together; cut in ⅓ cup soft shortening. Stir in 1 egg, beaten, and ⅓ cup milk. Round up and roll out larger than inverted 9″ pie pan. Place in pie pan. Build up fluted edge; prick sides and bottom well with fork to prevent puffing. Bake 15 min.

## CHEESE-STUFFED FRANKS

Split frankfurters lengthwise almost through. Place ¼″ stick of sharp cheese in each. Wrap each frank spirally with strip of bacon, fastening with toothpick at each end. Starting with split-side-down, broil until bacon is crisp.

## FRANKFURTERS

**Simmered:** Drop in boiling water; reduce heat, cook 5 to 8 min.
**Grilled:** Heat slowly in hot fat, turning to brown.
**Broiled:** Rub with butter or oil; broil 3″ from heat, turning to brown.

Do not pierce with fork during cooking. Serve with baked beans, with hot potato salad, or in hot dog buns.

## FRANKFURTER CREOLE

| | |
|---|---|
| 2 tbsp. shortening | 1 can (8 oz.) tomato sauce |
| 1 large onion, thinly sliced | 1 to 2 tsp. chili powder |
| ½ green pepper, cut in narrow strips | 1 tsp. sugar |
| ½ cup thinly sliced celery | ½ tsp. salt |
| 1 can (1 lb. 4 oz.) tomatoes (2½ cups) | 8 to 10 frankfurters |

Heat shortening in large skillet. Sauté onion, green pepper, and celery in shortening over low heat for 5 min., or until vegetables are tender but not brown. Add tomatoes, tomato sauce, chili powder, sugar, and salt. Mix thoroughly and simmer 10 min., uncovered. Drain sausages and cut them in thirds. Add to tomato mixture and heat. Serve on fluffy white rice or spaghetti. *6 to 8 servings.*

**Note:** *2 cans (4 oz. each) Vienna sausages may be substituted for frankfurters.*

## DOUBLE-QUICK FRANK 'N CORN SUPPER

| | |
|---|---|
| 6 frankfurters | 1 tbsp. butter |
| 2 tbsp. chopped onion | 1 can (1 lb.) cream-style corn |
| ¼ cup chopped green pepper | |

Cut frankfurters into ½″ pieces. Brown franks, onion, and pepper in butter. Add corn; heat through. *4 servings.*

### CRISPY FRIED LIVER

Trim skin and membrane from 1 lb. baby beef liver. Leave in serving-size pieces or cut in strips, 4x¾". Dip in Bisquick, then in milk, and again in Bisquick. Fry in hot fat over medium heat until crispy brown, about 5 min.; turn and fry on other side. Season with salt and pepper. *4 servings.*

**Liver with Bacon:** Fry bacon first; remove and keep warm while frying liver.

**Liver with Onions:** Fry liver; remove and keep warm. Put sliced onion rings into fat; cover and steam until soft. Uncover and cook until golden brown.

### LIVER AND BACON PATTIES

| | |
|---|---|
| **4 slices bacon** | **1 tsp. salt** |
| **1 lb. sliced beef liver** | **⅛ tsp. pepper** |
| **1 small onion** | **1 to 1½ cups crushed Wheaties** |
| **1 egg, slightly beaten** | **3 tbsp. fat** |

Fry bacon until lightly browned; remove from pan. Brown liver on both sides. Grind together bacon, liver, and onion. Add egg, salt, and pepper. Mix well. Shape into 6 patties. Coat with crushed Wheaties and brown in hot fat. *4 to 6 servings.*

### LIVER CREOLE

| | |
|---|---|
| **4 slices bacon, diced** | **1 can (1 lb.) tomatoes** |
| **1 lb. calves or baby beef liver** | **⅛ tsp. cayenne pepper** |
| **3 tbsp. flour** | **½ tsp. chili powder** |
| **⅓ cup diced green pepper** | **1½ tsp. salt** |

Fry bacon until crisp. Remove bacon and all but 3 tbsp. fat. Dredge liver in flour and brown in drippings. Put bacon and other ingredients over liver. Cover and simmer 45 min. *4 servings.*

### STUFFED VEAL HEART

Trim small cords and vessels from veal heart. Fill cavity with 1 cup well-seasoned Bread Stuffing (p. 82). Tie with string. Brown in hot fat. Add ½ cup hot water; cover tightly and simmer 1½ hr. *2 to 3 servings.*

### TONGUE

Choose baby beef, veal, or lamb tongue. To fresh tongue add 1 tbsp. salt, 1 small onion, a few whole black peppercorns, and 1 bay leaf. Cover tongue with cold water. Bring to boil; reduce heat and simmer until tender, about 1 hr. per lb. Remove from water; cool slightly and trim off bone and gristle and remove skin. Slice. Serve with Horse-radish Sauce or Mustard Cream Sauce (p. 103). *3-lb. beef tongue serves 6 to 8.*

**Smoked Tongue:** Select smoked beef tongue. Cook as directed above, omitting seasonings. It tastes much like ham when served with Raisin Sauce (p. 103).

### BROILED LAMB KIDNEYS

Cut 8 lamb kidneys and 8 strips of bacon in half. Wrap half a strip of bacon around each kidney half and secure with toothpick. Broil 3" from heat until bacon is crisp, 15 to 20 min., turning once. *4 servings.*

### MIXED GRILL

| | |
|---|---|
| **6 lamb chops, cut 1-rib thick** | **6 pork sausages or 6 slices of bacon** |
| **6 chicken livers** | **6 large mushroom caps** |

Place chops, livers, and sausages or bacon on broiler rack. Broil 3" from heat 5 min. Season chops and liver with salt and pepper. Turn meat with tongs. Broil 5 min. more. Add mushrooms, rounded-side-up; brush with butter. Broil 5 min. more. Serve immediately. *6 servings.*

## ROAST CHICKEN, TURKEY, DUCKLING, OR GOOSE

Select roasting chicken, turkey, duckling, or goose. Allow ½ to ¾ lb. ready-to-cook weight per serving. Remove any pinfeathers and wash. Pat dry.

Make 1 cup Bread Stuffing (p. 82) for each ready-to-cook pound of fowl. Stuffing may be made ahead of time, but place it in fowl just before roasting. Stuff body and neck cavities lightly; never pack stuffing in.

Place skewers across opening and lace together with string. Tie leg ends to tail. Many turkeys are cut in such a way that the leg ends can be tucked under a band of skin, thus closing the cavity. Skewer neck skin to back. Fold wings across back with tips touching. Rub skin with unsalted fat.

Heat oven to 325° (375° for chicken). Place fowl, breast up, on rack in shallow roasting pan. Do not sear. Do not add water. Do not cover. When bird has browned as much as you wish, place over the breast tent-fashion a piece of heavy-duty aluminum foil.

Roast until done (leg joint should move readily). See chart of roasting times (below).

## ROAST ROCK CORNISH GAME HENS

Thaw 12- to 15-oz. frozen game hens. Wash and pat dry. Heat oven to 425° (hot). Rub cavities of thawed hens with salt and pepper. If desired, stuff with 1½ to 2 tbsp. Bread Stuffing (p. 82). Place breast-side-up in roasting pan. Brush hens with unsalted fat. Roast about 1 hr., or until fork tender, brushing hens with fat 2 or 3 times during roasting. Serve immediately.

## ROASTING TURKEY IN ALUMINUM FOIL

*This method shortens roasting time; also prevents spattering the oven. Turkey is really steam-roasted and will be a light golden brown.*

Prepare turkey for roasting. Place bird on aluminum foil; wrap snugly. Seal securely to prevent drippings from escaping into the pan. Place foil-wrapped turkey, breast up, in bottom of a shallow pan. Place in 450° (very hot) oven and roast to within 15 to 20 min. of total roasting time given in the timetable (below). Remove from oven. Quickly fold foil away from bird to edges of pan. Return to oven and continue roasting until done (leg joint moves readily).

| *Ready-to-Cook Weight | Oven Temperature | **Total Cooking Time |
|---|---|---|
| **Turkey** | | |
| 4 to 6 lb. | 325° | 3 to 3¾ hr. |
| 6 to 8 lb. | 325° | 3¾ to 4½ hr. |
| 8 to 12 lb. | 325° | 4 to 5 hr. |
| 12 to 16 lb. | 325° | 5 to 6 hr. |
| 16 to 20 lb. | 325° | 6 to 7½ hr. |
| 20 to 24 lb. | 325° | 7½ to 9 hr. |
| **Chicken** | | |
| 4 to 5 lb. | 375° | 1½ to 1¾ hr. |
| over 5 lb. | 375° | 1¾ to 2 hr. |
| **Goose** | | |
| 6 to 8 lb. | 325° | 3 to 3½ hr. |
| 10 to 12 lb. | 325° | 3¾ to 4¼ hr. |
| **Duckling** | | |
| 4 to 6 lb. | 325° | 1½ to 2 hr. |

*Stuffed weight of a bird is about the same weight before it is drawn.
**For well done, add 5 to 10 min. per lb.

| Ready-to-Cook Weight | Oven Temperature | Total Roasting Time |
|---|---|---|
| 8 to 10 lb. | 450° | 2¼ to 2½ hr. |
| 10 to 12 lb. | 450° | 2¾ to 3 hr. |
| 14 to 16 lb. | 450° | 3 to 3¼ hr. |
| 18 to 20 lb. | 450° | 3¼ to 3½ hr. |
| 22 to 24 lb. | 450° | 3¼ to 3¾ hr. |

## BROILED CHICKEN

Select broiler-fryer chickens, 1½ to 2½ lb. Have chickens split, quartered, or cut in pieces. Season, using about 1 tsp. salt and ¼ tsp. pepper per chicken. Brush well with melted fat. Arrange in bottom of broiling pan—not on rack—so that chicken is kept moist in the juices. For easy cleaning, line pan with aluminum foil. For halves, bring wing tip onto back under shoulder joint.

Start broiling skin-side-up. Broil 25 to 30 min. on each side, turning once and brushing with fat several times. Broil total of 50 to 60 min., until chicken is tender. For gas oven: broil at 375° (quick mod.) but do not set on broil; for electric oven: set oven at broil, broiling as far from source of heat as possible—at least 7″. *2 to 4 servings.*

*Family Choice*

**Fried Chicken**

**Scalloped Potatoes**          **Asparagus**

**Pineapple-Bing Cherry Salad (p. 96)**

**Chocolate Sundaes**

## FRIED CHICKEN

| | |
|---|---|
| **½ cup Gold Medal Flour** | **¼ tsp. paprika** |
| **1 tsp. salt** | **2½-to 3-lb. frying chicken, cut in pieces** |
| **¼ tsp. pepper** | |

Mix flour, salt, pepper, and paprika in paper bag. Shake 3 or 4 pieces of chicken at a time in bag to coat thoroughly. Starting with meaty pieces, place chicken in heavy skillet in hot vegetable oil, ½ to 1″ deep. Cover; cook 10 to 15 min. over medium heat. Remove cover, reduce heat, and keep turning chicken until all pieces are uniformly browned, 20 to 25 min. Drain on absorbent paper. *4 servings.*

## CHIPPER CHICKEN

| | |
|---|---|
| **1 medium bag potato chips** | **1 tsp. salt** |
| **¼ cup butter** | **⅛ tsp. pepper** |
| **1 tsp. garlic salt** | **2- to 3-lb. broiler-fryer, cut in pieces** |

Heat oven to 350° (mod.). Crush potato chips finely. Melt butter in frying pan and add seasonings. Roll chicken in seasoned butter, then in chips. Place chicken in oblong pan, 13x9½x2″. Bake 1½ hr. *4 servings.*

## OVEN-FRIED CHICKEN

| | |
|---|---|
| **½ cup Gold Medal Flour** | **2 tsp. paprika** |
| **1 tsp. salt** | **½ cup shortening (half butter)** |
| **¼ tsp. pepper** | **2- to 3-lb. frying chicken, cut in pieces** |

Heat oven to 425° (hot). Mix flour, salt, pepper, and paprika in paper bag. Put shortening in oblong pan, 13x9½x2″, and set in oven to melt. Shake 3 or 4 pieces of chicken at a time in bag to coat thoroughly. Place chicken, skin-side-down, in single layer in hot shortening. Bake 30 min. Turn skin-side-up and bake another 30 min., or until chicken is tender. *4 servings.*

**For Gravy:** Add 2 tbsp. flour (saved from dredgings) to drippings in pan. Bring to boil. Add about 1½ cups hot water. Boil 1 min.

## WESTERN RANCH DINNER

Follow recipe for Oven-fried Chicken (above)—except bake chicken 45 min., then turn. Make Biscuits (p. 44). Push chicken to one side in pan; place biscuits in single layer on other side. Drain 1 can (1 lb. 13 oz.) Cling peach halves. Place a whole clove in each half and place on top of chicken. Bake another 15 min., or until biscuits are lightly browned.

## PARMESAN FRIED CHICKEN

Follow recipe for Oven-fried Chicken (above)—except after coating with seasoned flour, dip chicken in mixture of 2 eggs beaten with 3 tbsp. milk. Roll egg-coated chicken pieces in mixture of ⅔ cup grated Parmesan cheese and ⅓ cup fine dry bread crumbs. Bake.

## CHICKEN DINNER PIE

Heat oven to 425° (hot). Make Pastry (below) and divide in half. Roll one half; fit in 9" pie pan and trim, leaving 1" overhanging edge. Roll other half into rectangle, 14x9", cut into twelve ½" strips. Blend Filling and Sauce (below). Spoon into pie pan. Twist strips of pastry across filling in crisscross pattern (about 1¼" apart). Trim; turn overhanging edge over strips, seal, and flute. Bake 35 to 40 min., or until lightly browned. *6 servings.*

**Pastry:** Measure 1½ cups Gold Medal Flour by dip-level-pour method. Mix flour and ¾ tsp. salt. Cut in ½ cup lard (or ½ cup plus 2 tbsp. hydrogenated shortening). Sprinkle with 3 tbsp. water; mix with fork. Round into ball.

**Filling:** Mix 2¼ cups cubed cooked chicken, ½ cup slivered cooked carrots, ½ cup frozen peas, thawed, 1 can (8 oz.) onions, halved, 1 tsp. salt, and ⅛ tsp. each pepper and thyme.

**Sauce:** Make 1 cup Medium Cream Sauce (p. 103)—except use ½ cup each chicken broth and thin cream.

## CHICKEN MARENGO

| | |
|---|---|
| 6 chicken breasts or thighs (3 lb.) | 1 tbsp. salt *(omelude)* |
| ¼ cup Gold Medal Flour | 1 tsp. dried basil — *use pesto* |
| ¼ cup butter | ½ cup water |
| 3 small onions, finely chopped | 1 can (8 oz.) tomato sauce |
| 1 clove garlic, minced | ¼ lb. fresh mushrooms, sliced, or 1 can (6 oz.) sliced mushrooms |
| 3 tbsp. snipped parsley or 1 tbsp. dried parsley flakes | |

*needs more*

*also parm. cheese*

Coat chicken pieces with flour. Melt butter in large skillet; place chicken, skin-side-down, in skillet and brown; turn and brown other side. Add onions, garlic, parsley, salt, basil, water, and tomato sauce. Cover tightly and simmer 50 to 60 min., or until chicken is tender. Remove cover; move chicken to one side, add mushrooms, and simmer 5 min. more. If necessary, add more water to sauce mixture at this time for desired consistency. *6 servings.*

*\* CUT CHICKEN INTO BITE-SIZE PIECES*

## STEWED CHICKEN

| | |
|---|---|
| 4- to 5-lb. stewing hen | 1 slice onion (2 slices if older hen) |
| 1 sprig parsley | |
| 1 celery stalk with leaves, cut up | 2 tsp. salt |
| 1 carrot, sliced | ½ tsp. pepper |

Clean and cut up chicken. Place in kettle with just enough boiling water to cover; add remaining ingredients. Cover. Simmer gently until tender, 2 to 3 hr. Add more water, if necessary. Let cool in stock. Remove meat from bones in pieces as large as possible to use in chicken dishes. *A 5-lb. chicken gives 4 cups of cut-up cooked chicken and 3 to 4 cups of chicken stock.*

**Stewed Chicken with Dumplings:** Make dumplings by adding ¾ cup milk to 2 cups Bisquick; mix thoroughly with fork. Make 10 to 12 dumplings by dropping batter by tablespoonfuls onto boiling Stewed Chicken (above). Cook, uncovered, 10 min.; cover and continue cooking 10 min. *Makes 8 servings.*

## CHICKEN À LA KING

| | |
|---|---|
| ⅓ cup mushrooms (2-oz. can) | 1 cup chicken broth |
| ¼ cup chopped green pepper | 1 cup cream (20% butterfat) |
| ¼ cup butter | 1 cup diced cooked chicken |
| ¼ cup Gold Medal Flour | ¼ cup chopped pimiento |
| ½ tsp. salt | |
| ⅛ tsp. pepper | |

Sauté mushrooms and green pepper in butter. Blend in flour and seasonings. Cook over low heat, stirring until mixture is smooth and bubbly. Remove from heat. Slowly stir in broth and cream. Bring to boil over low heat, stirring constantly. Boil 1 min. Add chicken and pimiento. Continue cooking until meat is heated through. Serve hot in patty shells, pastry cases, biscuit rings, or timbale cases; or over toast points, noodles, or fluffy rice. *4 servings.*

# Carving Cues

*Three things to make the carver's job easier:* **Well-cooked meat.** *Not under-done or overdone. Then allow meat to rest 15 min. before carving. Place on platter in positions shown in sketches.* **A sharp knife.** *Use it only for carving.* **Space for carving.** *Avoid crowding the platter with other foods or garnishes.*

### PORK LOIN ROAST

Your meat retailer will separate backbone from ribs. Backbone can then be removed after roasting.

**1.** Place roast on platter so rib bones face you. They are your guide for slicing. **2.** Insert fork firmly in top of roast. Cut close against both sides of each rib, so that you will have alternately one slice with bone and one without.

### ROAST LEG OF LAMB

**1.** Place leg of lamb with shank bone to the right and meaty section on far side. **2.** Insert fork firmly in larger end of leg and cut 2 or 3 slices on near side or where bone is nearest surface. **3.** Turn roast so it rests on surface just cut. Insert fork in left of roast; starting at shank end, slice down to leg bone until aitchbone is reached. **4.** With fork still in place, run knife along leg bone releasing all the slices.

### BLADE POT ROAST

The long, slow cooking process of moist heat softens tissues attached to bone so bone can be slipped out easily when roast is done.

**1.** Hold pot roast firmly with fork inserted at left. Separate a section by running knife between 2 muscles, and close to bone if bone has not been removed. **2.** If desired, turn section on side and cut in slices across grain.

### PORTERHOUSE STEAK

A steak is carved *with* the grain because the meat fibers are tender and relatively short.

**1.** Insert fork at left and cut close around bone. Lift bone to side of platter out of way. **2.** Cut across full width of steak, making wedge-shaped portions widest at far side. Each serving will thus have a piece of tenderloin and large muscle. **3.** Serve flank end last if additional servings are needed.

### STANDING RIB ROAST

Your meat retailer will separate backbone from ribs. Then backbone can be removed in the kitchen after roasting.

**1.** Insert fork firmly between 2 top ribs. From the far outside edge slice across the grain toward the ribs. **2.** Release each slice by cutting close along the rib with the knife tip. **3.** After each cut, lift slice to side of platter.

### ROLLED RIB ROAST

Place larger cut surface down.

**1.** Slice across grain toward the fork from the far right side. **2.** As each slice is carved, lift it to side of platter. Remove each cord only as it is approached.

### BAKED WHOLE HAM

Shank end should be to carver's right.

**1.** Find the side nearest the bone and cut 3 or 4 slices. **2.** Turn ham so it rests on surface just cut. Hold ham firmly with fork and cut small wedge from shank end. Keep fork in place to steady ham and cut thin slices down to leg bone. **3.** Release slices by cutting along bone at right angles to slices.

### BAKED HALF HAM

**1.** Remove cushion section, turn ham on cut side and make slices beginning at large end. **2.** For more servings, separate from shank by cutting through joint. Remove bone, turn and slice.

### CHICKEN OR TURKEY

Place chicken or turkey with leg at right of carver.

**1.** Cut leg from body, first bending it back with left hand. Sever and lift to plate. **2.** Sever thigh from drumstick. Slice meat from leg. **3.** Then with fork astride breast, cut down sharply on joint joining wing to body. **4.** Cut thin slices of breast where wing was, working up to breast bone.

## BREAD STUFFING

*Use 1 cup of stuffing for each pound of the ready-to-cook weight. The recipe below is for a 4-lb. bird.*

| | |
|---|---|
| ⅓ cup butter | 1 tsp. salt |
| ¼ cup finely minced onion | ¼ tsp. pepper |
| 4 cups (1 qt.) coarse or fine bread crumbs or cubes | 1 tsp. dried sage, thyme, or marjoram |
| ½ cup chopped celery (stalks and leaves) | poultry seasoning (to taste) |

Melt butter in large heavy skillet. Add onion and cook until yellow, stirring occasionally. Stir in some of bread crumbs. Heat, stirring to prevent excessive browning. Turn into deep bowl. Mix in remaining ingredients lightly. For dry stuffing, add little or no liquid. For moist stuffing, mix in lightly with fork just enough hot water or broth to moisten dry crumbs. Cool and place stuffing in bird when ready to bake. *Makes 1 qt. stuffing.*

**Mushroom Stuffing:** Add sautéed chopped mushrooms (3- or 4-oz. can).

**Giblet Stuffing:** Add the cooked giblets, chopped.

**Corn Bread Stuffing:** Use crumbled corn bread or corn muffins for half the bread.

**Sausage Stuffing:** Add ⅓ lb. bulk pork sausage, crumbled and browned, for each quart. Omit salt; use sausage fat as part of fat.

**Oyster Stuffing:** Add 1 cup chopped drained oysters.

### STUFFING TIPS

A 1-lb. loaf of bread makes 8 cups of crumbs.

Pack stuffing loosely—it swells.

Stuffing may be made ahead of time but should be stuffed in poultry just before roasting.

For dry, crusty stuffing (a favorite with some), spread an extra amount in shallow pan and bake the last 30 min. of roasting.

## MUSHROOM-WILD RICE STUFFING

| | |
|---|---|
| ½ lb. sliced mushrooms (or 4-oz. can) | ½ cup chopped celery |
| ¼ cup butter | 2 cups cooked wild rice |
| ¼ cup minced onion | ¾ tsp. salt |
| 1 tbsp. minced parsley | dash of pepper |

Sauté mushrooms in butter 5 min. Remove mushrooms, add onion, parsley, and celery; cook until onions are yellow. Add rice, salt, pepper, and mushrooms. *Enough to stuff a 4- to 5-lb. chicken.*

**Note:** *Brown or white rice may be substituted for part of the wild rice.*

*TO SAVE TIME AND WORK* — Use *packaged herb-seasoned stuffing and prepare as directed on pkg.*

## STUFFING BALLS

*An exciting new quick bread with the spicy flavor of stuffing.*

| | |
|---|---|
| 2 cups Bisquick | ⅔ cup milk |
| 1 tsp. poultry seasoning | 2 cups soft bread crumbs |
| 1 tsp. instant chopped onion | |
| 1 tsp. dried celery flakes | ¼ cup butter, melted |
| 1 tsp. parsley flakes | whole cranberry sauce |

Heat oven to 400° (mod. hot). Put Bisquick and herbs in mixing bowl. Add milk all at once. Stir with fork into a soft dough. Beat 15 strokes. It will be stiff, but sticky. Toss bread crumbs in melted butter. Drop Bisquick mixture by tablespoonfuls into buttered crumbs and gently roll until covered. Place on greased baking sheet. With back of spoon, make a deep indentation in each ball. Bake 12 to 15 min. Before serving, place a spoonful of whole cranberry sauce in each indentation. Serve with poultry or roast pork. *Makes 12 balls.*

## PAN GRAVY

*Pan Gravy is rich with the natural meat fats left in the pan after cooking roasts, steaks, chops, and roasted or fried chicken.*

| THIN | MEDIUM | THICK |
|---|---|---|
| 1 tbsp. fat | 2 tbsp. fat | 3 tbsp. fat |
| 1 tbsp. flour | 2 tbsp. flour | 3 tbsp. flour |
| 1 cup liquid* | 1 cup liquid* | 1 cup liquid* |

*water, meat stock, or bouillon-cube broth

Remove meat or poultry to warm place. Pour off fat; measure amount needed back into pan. Add level tablespoonfuls of flour. Use equal amounts of flour and fat. Stir fat and flour together until smooth, then cook over low heat, stirring steadily until it's bubbly and brown. Take from heat, stir in liquid slowly. Always measure liquid—too much weakens flavor. Return pan to heat, stirring and scraping in the rich drippings. Boil 1 min., season and serve. *Makes 1 cup.*

**Creamy Gravy:** Use milk for half of liquid in Pan Gravy (above).

**Easy Mushroom Gravy:** Brown 1 can ( 2 oz.) mushrooms, drained, in fat before adding flour in making Pan Gravy (above). Use mushroom liquid as part of liquid. Blend in ½ tsp. Worcestershire sauce.

**A Good Way to Extend a Small Amount of Gravy:** Combine equal amounts of gravy and cream of mushroom soup. Heat. If too thick, thin with a tablespoon or two of water.

*IN A HURRY?—Try canned beef or chicken gravy; heat and add favorite seasonings to taste.*

## KETTLE GRAVY

*Kettle Gravy is made from the liquid in which pot roasts and stews have been simmered. Remember, the less liquid you use, the richer the flavor of the broth will be.*

| THIN | MEDIUM | THICK |
|---|---|---|
| 1 cup meat broth | 1 cup meat broth | 1 cup meat broth |
| ¼ cup cold water | ¼ cup cold water | ¼ cup cold water |
| 1 tbsp. flour | 2 tbsp. flour | 3 tbsp. flour |

Remove meat; keep warm. Skim excess fat from meat broth and store for future use. Pour off broth; measure amount needed and return to kettle.

Shake water and flour together in covered jar. For a smooth mixture, always put the water in first and the flour on top. Stir flour and water slowly into hot broth. Bring to boil. Cook 1 min., until thickened. Season and serve. *Makes 1 cup.*

## BROWN ONION SAUCE

*When you are serving meat loaf or a broiled meat and the men in the house want gravy, try this flavorful sauce.*

| | |
|---|---|
| 3 tbsp. butter | 1½ tsp. Worcestershire sauce |
| 3 tbsp. flour | |
| 1 can (13 oz.) French-style onion soup | 1 tsp. gravy flavoring (such as Kitchen Bouquet) |

Melt butter in small saucepan. Stir in flour; add soup gradually. Cook over low heat, stirring constantly, until sauce is smooth and thickened. Add flavorings. *Makes 2 cups.*

**Note:** *Dehydrated onion soup may be substituted for canned onion soup by adding ½ pkg. of the soup mix to 2 cups boiling water and cooking as directed on pkg.*

*Easy Fish Dinner*

**Pan-fried Fish**
**Potatoes Anna (p. 92)**
**Green Beans Hong Kong (p. 86)**
**Lemon Spice Surprise (p. 130)**

## PAN-FRIED FISH

*For small game fish, such as trout, perch, sunfish, or crappies.*

Sprinkle fish with salt and pepper. Dip in flour or corn meal. Pan-fry in hot skillet with fat ⅛″ deep (part butter gives superb flavor) over medium heat until golden brown. Turn carefully and brown other side, about 10 min. in all. Drain. Serve hot.

## BROILED FISH

*For fillets, small whole fish, or steaks. See picture of broiled halibut steak, pp. 146-147.*

Dip 4 or 6 fish fillets in oil. Sprinkle with salt and paprika. Place skin-side-down on greased broiler pan or baking pan in oven at 500° (very hot). Broil 2 to 3″ from heat for 3 min. Remove and pour over 2 to 4 tbsp. chicken broth (or bouillon cube dissolved in water). Return to 450° oven for 10 min. Pour 1 tbsp. lemon juice and ¼ cup melted butter over fillets just before serving. *4 servings.*

## BAKED FISH

*Suitable for any size or cut.*

Heat oven to 350° (mod.). Place fish on aluminum foil in shallow baking pan or in greased shallow pan. Sprinkle with salt, pepper, and melted butter. Bake 20 min. for fillets, 30 min. for steaks, 15 min. per lb. for whole fish. Serve with tartar sauce.

## GOLDEN FISH PUFFS

| | |
|---|---|
| 1 pkg. (1 lb.) frozen pike fillets, thawed | ¼ cup mayonnaise |
| ⅛ tsp. salt | ¼ tsp. dill seeds |
| 1 egg white | ¼ tsp. onion juice |

Heat oven to 425° (hot). Place fillets in greased 9″ sq. baking dish. Season with salt and pepper. Add salt to egg white and whip until stiff but not dry. Fold in mayonnaise, dill seeds, and onion juice. Spoon onto fillets. Bake about 12 min., or until fish flakes easily and top is puffed and brown. *4 servings.*

## SALMON LOAF

| | |
|---|---|
| 2 cans (1 lb. each) salmon | 2 tbsp. lemon juice |
| 2 eggs | 2 tsp. chopped onion |
| milk | ¼ tsp. salt |
| 3 cups coarse cracker crumbs | ¼ tsp. pepper |

Heat oven to 350° (mod.). Flake salmon; remove bones and skin. Blend in eggs. Stir in liquid from salmon plus enough milk to make 1½ cups. Add remaining ingredients. Spoon lightly into greased loaf pan, 9x5x3″. Bake 45 min. Garnish with lemon wedges. *8 servings.*

## DOUBLE-QUICK CRISPY FISH STICKS

*Especially good with creamed mixed vegetables.*

| | |
|---|---|
| 1 pkg. (8 oz.) frozen fish sticks | 1 tsp. barbecue seasoning |
| ¼ cup tomato-flavored French dressing | 1 tbsp. lemon juice |
| | ½ tsp. prepared mustard |

Spread fish sticks in a shallow pan lined with aluminum foil. Brush well with a mixture of dressing, seasoning, lemon juice, and mustard. Bake according to pkg. directions for oven-baked fish sticks. Turn and brush with dressing mixture again during last half of baking time. *4 servings.*

## SHRIMP CREOLE

| | |
|---|---|
| 2 tbsp. butter | ⅛ tsp. cayenne pepper |
| ½ cup minced onion | 1 tsp. salt |
| 1 bay leaf, crushed | 1 can (6 oz.) tomato |
| ¼ cup diced celery | paste |
| 1 tsp. minced parsley | 2½ cups water |
| ½ cup chopped green pepper | 2 cups seasoned cooked shrimp (14-oz. can) |

Melt butter over low heat. Add onion and cook until yellow. Blend in remaining ingredients except shrimp. Cook slowly, stirring occasionally, about 30 min. Stir in shrimp. Serve on hot cooked rice. *6 servings.*

## FRENCH FRIED SHRIMP

Peel shells from 2 lb. fresh shrimp, leaving last section and tail intact. Cut slit through center back without severing either end; remove black line. Dry shrimp thoroughly; coat generously with unseasoned flour. Dip into Golden Fry Batter (below), letting excess drip off. Fry in hot vegetable oil (375°) 3 to 4″ deep until golden brown. Drain on absorbent paper. Serve immediately with tartar sauce or soy sauce. *4 to 6 servings.*

**Golden Fry Batter:** Blend ½ cup vegetable oil and 1 cup Gold Medal Flour. Add 1 egg and 1½ cups milk. Beat with rotary beater until smooth; batter is thin.

## SEA FOOD NEWBURG

| | |
|---|---|
| ¼ cup butter | 2 cups cooked sea food |
| ¼ cup Gold Medal Flour | (lobster, crab, shrimp, or combination) in large pieces |
| ½ tsp. salt | |
| ¼ tsp. pepper | 1 tbsp. sherry flavoring |
| 2 cups milk | or lemon juice |
| 2 egg yolks, beaten | |

Melt butter over low heat in heavy saucepan. Blend in flour and seasonings. Cook over low heat, stirring until mixture is smooth and bubbly. Remove from heat; stir in milk gradually. Bring to boil, stirring constantly. Boil 1 min. Stir half of hot sauce into egg yolks; then blend into remaining sauce. Just before serving, stir in sea food and sherry flavoring. Serve hot in Popovers (p. 119) or patty shells. *6 to 8 servings.*

## BROILED LOBSTER TAILS

Buy a 6- to 8-oz. lobster tail for each serving. Thaw frozen tails; cut away thin undershell with kitchen scissors. To keep tails from curling while they broil, bend each backward toward shell to crack or insert skewer lengthwise between shell and meat. Place on rack in broiler with shell side up about 3″ below heat; broil 5 min. Turn flesh side up; brush with melted butter, sprinkle with paprika, and broil 6 to 8 min. longer. Serve with melted butter and lemon wedges.

## HAZEL'S BAKED FISH

| | |
|---|---|
| 1 pkg. (1 lb.) frozen pike fillets, thawed | 1 can (8 oz.) tomato sauce |
| 3 tbsp. butter | 1 cup buttered croutons |
| 4 to 6 thin onion slices or ½ cup chopped green onions | ¼ cup Parmesan cheese |

Heat oven to 350° (mod.). Cut fillets into serving pieces. Melt butter in oblong baking dish and dip fish in butter, placing skin-side-down. Season to taste. Place an onion slice on each piece of fish. Cover with tomato sauce, sprinkle with croutons, and top with cheese. Bake 30 to 35 min. *4 servings.*

**Note:** *In place of the tomato sauce, 1 can tomato soup diluted with ¼ cup water or 1 can (1 lb. 4 oz.) tomatoes, using only enough of the liquid to moisten the fish, may be used.*

*Good 'n Hearty Dinner*

**Hazel's Baked Fish**
**Corn on the Cob**
**Fresh Spinach Salad (p. 95)**
**Butter Dips (p. 118)**
**Peach Pie (p. 143)**

*Vegetable cookery has become ever so easy today, with the new methods of vegetable harvesting and shipping. You can buy garden-ripe vegetables the year 'round, often cleaned and packaged in clear cellophane bags that help retain the foods' freshness. Or you may buy vegetables quick-frozen or canned in new, improved ways. Choose the kind that best fits your time and purpose.*

## COOKING FRESH VEGETABLES

Wash all vegetables thoroughly before cooking. Cook with only enough salted water (½ tsp. salt to 1 cup water, ¼ to 1″ deep, depending on size and kind of saucepan) to prevent scorching. Add more water if necessary. Quickly bring water to boil; reduce heat and begin to count cooking time. Cook only until crisp-tender. If vegetables are cooked correctly, there will not be an excessive amount of liquid. Rather than drain off extra liquid, cook it down by removing cover from vegetables the last few minutes of cooking.

## HEATING CANNED VEGETABLES

Drain off liquid into saucepan. Boil quickly to reduce amount to half. Add vegetables and heat quickly; do not boil. Season.

## COOKING FROZEN VEGETABLES

Follow directions on package. As a rule, do not thaw before cooking.

### ASPARAGUS

**How to Cook:** Break off tough ends as far down as snaps easily. Remove scales if sandy or tough. Leave stalks whole or cut into pieces. Tie whole stalks in bunches with string and cook upright in narrow deep pan or coffeepot. If cut up, cook pieces from lower stems first, add tips the last 5 to 8 min. Cook, covered, in 1″ boiling salted water: whole asparagus, 10 to 20 min.; 1″ pieces, 10 to 15 min.; tips, 5 to 8 min.

**Ways to Serve**

Add butter, salt, and pepper.

Top with melted butter to which a few drops of lemon juice, minced chives, grated nutmeg, or prepared mustard have been added.

Serve on toast topped with creamed dried beef, ham, or chicken.

Top with Mock Hollandaise Sauce (p. 104).

Sprinkle with slivered almonds.

### BEANS—GREEN, WAX, OR SNAP

**How to Cook:** Snap off ends. Leave whole, cut French-style into lengthwise strips, or cut crosswise into 1″ lengths. If desired, add a clove of garlic or a bit of onion while cooking. Cook, covered, in ½ to 1″ boiling salted water: whole beans, 15 to 20 min.; cut, 15 to 20 min.; French-cut, 10 min.

**Ways to Serve**

Add butter, salt, pepper, and savory, if desired.

Toss cooked French-style beans with butter, onion, lime or lemon juice, salt, and pepper.

Add crumbled bacon bits and a little bacon fat to cooked beans.

Combine canned beans with mushroom soup, top with fried onion rings; heat in 375° oven 20 min.

### GREEN BEANS HONG KONG

Cut 3 slices of bacon in quarters. Sauté until slightly crisp. Drain off all but 2 tsp. of bacon drippings. Add 1½ tbsp. chopped onion and 1 clove garlic, chopped. Cook 2 min. Drain 1 can (1 lb.) French-style green beans. Add drained beans and 1 tbsp. soy sauce to bacon mixture. Toss until beans are heated. *4 servings.*

## BEANS—LIMA

**How to Cook:** Snap pods open; remove beans. Or cut thin strip from inner edge of pod with knife; push beans out. Cook, covered, in ½ to 1″ boiling salted water 20 to 30 min.

**Ways to Serve**

Add butter, salt, pepper, and a dash of nutmeg, if desired.

Combine with corn, whole-kernel or cream-style, and garnish with pimiento.

To 3 cups cooked Lima beans add 1 can condensed pepper pot or tomato soup. Heat.

Combine 1 pkg. frozen Lima beans with cream, salt, and pepper. Bake, covered, at 350° (mod.) 1 hr.

Sauté 1 can (4 oz.) mushrooms, drained, in 1½ tbsp. butter. Toss with 1 pkg. frozen Lima beans, cooked as directed.

### LIMA BEANS IN SOUR CREAM

| | |
|---|---|
| 2 cups hot cooked Lima beans | 2 tbsp. butter |
| 2 tbsp. finely chopped onion | ½ cup commercial sour cream |
| 2 tbsp. minced pimiento | |

While beans are cooking, sauté onion and pimiento in butter. Drain beans; add onion, pimiento, and sour cream. Season to taste with salt and pepper; heat through. *6 servings.*

### SAVORY BABY GREEN LIMAS

| | |
|---|---|
| 1 pkg. frozen baby Lima beans (2 cups fresh) | ¼ tsp. salt |
| 1 tsp. dry mustard | 2 tbsp. butter, melted |
| 1 tsp. sugar | 1 tsp. lemon juice |

Cook beans as directed on pkg. with mustard, sugar, and salt. Drain. Mix in butter and lemon juice. Serve immediately garnished with a half slice of lemon. *4 servings.*

## BEETS

**How to Cook:** Cut off all but 2″ of tops. Save tops. Leave whole with root ends. Boil until tender; drain. Run cold water over beets and slip off skins and root ends. For quick cooking, pare; then dice or slice. Cook, covered, in boiling salted water to cover (with a little vinegar added to preserve color): young whole beets 30 to 45 min.; sliced, 10 to 20 min.

**Ways to Serve**

Add butter, salt, pepper, and basil, savory, or caraway, if desired.

Sprinkle with minced chives or parsley.

### HARVARD BEETS

| | |
|---|---|
| 1 tbsp. cornstarch | ⅔ cup liquid (beet juice plus water) |
| 1 tbsp. plus 1 tsp. sugar | ¼ cup vinegar |
| ¾ tsp. salt | 1 can (1 lb.) cubed or sliced beets, drained |
| dash of pepper | |

Mix cornstarch, sugar, salt, and pepper. Slowly blend in liquid and vinegar. Bring to boil over medium heat; boil 1 min. Add beets and heat. *4 servings.*

## BROCCOLI

**How to Cook:** Remove large leaves and ends of tough stalk parts. If thick, make 3 to 4 gashes through each stem so stems will cook as quickly as bud tops. Set upright in pan. Cook, covered, in 1″ boiling salted water 10 to 15 min.

**Ways to Serve**

Add butter, salt, and pepper.

Top with Mock Hollandaise Sauce (p. 104).

Add oregano and lemon juice.

Sprinkle top with grated cheese.

### ITALIAN BROCCOLI

Cook 1 pkg. frozen broccoli until almost tender. Drain. Sauté until delicately browned in 3 tbsp. hot olive oil. Sprinkle with 2 tbsp. Parmesan cheese. *4 to 5 servings.*

## BRUSSELS SPROUTS

**How to Cook:** Remove discolored leaves and stem ends. Leave whole. Cook, covered, in ½ to 1" boiling salted water 8 to 10 min.

**Ways to Serve**

Add butter, salt, and pepper.

Combine with onions, peas, beans, or celery.

Sprinkle with a little nutmeg. If desired, add a little diced crisp bacon or a few chopped toasted almonds.

### SAUTÉED BRUSSELS SPROUTS

| | |
|---|---|
| **2 pkg. (10 oz. each) fro-zen Brussels sprouts** | **1 bay leaf** |
| **1 small onion, chopped** | **2 whole cloves** |
| | **¼ cup butter** |

Place Brussels sprouts, onion, bay leaf, and cloves in 1 cup boiling salted water. When water boils again, turn heat low and simmer about 5 min., until Brussels sprouts are tender. Drain, remove bay leaf and cloves; add sprouts to butter which has been melted in skillet. Sauté over low heat, shaking pan frequently until they are delicately browned. Do not break the sprouts. Serve very hot. *8 servings.*

## CABBAGE

**How to Cook:** Remove wilted outside leaves. Shred or cut in wedges. Remove most of core. Cook, covered, in ½ to 1" boiling salted water: 2" wedges, 10 to 15 min.; shredded, 5 to 8 min. For red cabbage, add a little lemon juice or vinegar to keep color bright.

**Ways to Serve**

Add butter, salt, and pepper.

Blend with well-seasoned cream, Cream or Cheese Sauce (p. 103).

Mix shredded cabbage with corn; sprinkle with crisp bacon bits.

Sprinkle with buttered toast crumbs or caraway seeds.

## PANNED CABBAGE

Blend 2 tbsp. fat, 1 tsp. beef extract, and ⅛ tsp. salt in skillet and heat. Add 3 cups shredded cabbage. Cover tightly and cook over very low heat until tender, about 10 min. *4 servings.*

## BOHEMIAN CABBAGE

| | |
|---|---|
| **5 to 6 cups finely shredded cabbage (1 medium head)** | **¼ tsp. pepper** |
| **¼ cup water** | **½ tsp. caraway seeds** |
| **1 tbsp. minced onion** | **½ cup commercial sour cream** |
| **1 tsp. salt** | |

Mix all ingredients except sour cream in pan or skillet. Cover, steam 5 min. Add sour cream; heat through. *6 servings.*

## CRISP 10-MINUTE CABBAGE

| | |
|---|---|
| **1½ cups milk** | **1½ tbsp. butter** |
| **4 cups shredded cabbage** | **1 tsp. salt** |
| **1½ tbsp. flour** | **⅛ tsp. pepper** |

Heat milk and add cabbage. Simmer about 5 min. Mix flour and butter; stir in a little of the hot milk. Stir this mixture into the cabbage and cook 4 to 5 min., or until thickened, stirring constantly. Season with salt and pepper. Serve hot. *4 servings.*

## SWEET-SOUR RED CABBAGE

| | |
|---|---|
| **5 cups shredded red cabbage (1 head)** | **½ cup water** |
| **4 slices bacon, diced** | **⅓ cup vinegar** |
| **2 tbsp. brown sugar** | **1 tsp. salt** |
| **2 tbsp. flour** | **⅛ tsp. pepper** |
| | **1 small onion, sliced** |

Cook cabbage in 2 cups salted water (1 tsp. salt) in covered pan 5 to 8 min., or until crisp-tender. Drain. Fry bacon; remove bacon and half of bacon fat. Add sugar and flour to remaining fat; blend. Add water, vinegar, seasonings, and onion; cook until thick, 5 min. Add bacon and cabbage; heat through. Garnish with more diced bacon. *6 servings.*

## CARROTS

**How to Cook:** Remove tops; scrub, pare thinly, or scrape. Leave whole, grate coarsely, or cut into "coins" (round slices), diagonal slices, strips, or cubes. Cook, covered, in ½ to 1″ boiling salted water: large whole carrots, 20 to 30 min.; young, 15 to 20 min.; sliced, 10 to 20 min.; shredded, 5 min. Add a pinch of sugar or a bit of orange peel for extra flavor.

**Ways to Serve**

Add butter, salt, and chopped chives.

Add butter, brown sugar, prepared mustard, and salt to sliced cooked carrots.

Mix cooked shredded carrots with mashed potatoes.

Sprinkle grated raw carrots with ginger, salt, pepper, and enough water to moisten. Bake 30 min. in 350° (mod.) oven.

### CARROTS AU GRATIN

| | |
|---|---|
| **3 cups diced carrots** | **⅛ to ¼ tsp. pepper** |
| **6 soda crackers, crushed (¼ cup)** | **2 tbsp. melted butter** |
| **1 tsp. onion salt** | **½ cup grated sharp cheese** |
| **¼ cup chopped green pepper** | |

Heat oven to 425° (hot). Cook carrots in ½″ boiling salted water 10 min. Combine crackers, onion salt, green pepper, and pepper. Alternate layers of carrots and crumb mixture in greased 1-qt. baking dish. If any carrot liquid is left, spoon over top. Pour butter over and sprinkle with cheese. Bake 15 to 20 min., or until cheese melts. *6 servings.*

### SKILLET CARROTS

*Cook other vegetables in season (green beans, summer squashes, mushrooms, onions, or sliced celery) this easy way. Add your favorite herbs or lemon juice to make them more interesting.*

Pour 1 tbsp. vegetable oil in 9 or 10″ skillet. Add 1 lb. (2 cups) cut-up carrots and stir over heat 1 or 2 min. Add boiling water to half the depth of vegetables and ¾ tsp. salt. Cover and simmer 10 to 15 min., or until tender. Uncover; add herbs and extra seasoning and continue cooking until water boils away. *4 servings.*

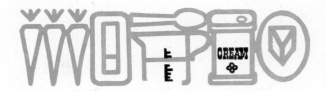

### CARROTS IN CREAM

*Corn, green beans, peas, and cut-up asparagus are also delicious cooked in cream.*

| | |
|---|---|
| **2 cups hot cooked sliced carrots** | **½ cup cream (20% butterfat)** |
| **1 tbsp. butter** | **salt and pepper to taste** |

Add butter, cream, salt, and pepper to carrots just before serving. Reheat, but do not let boil. Serve in custard cups or ramekins. *4 to 6 servings.*

### GLAZED CARROTS

Slice 3 medium carrots lengthwise. Cook (left); drain and save liquid. Heat ¼ cup sugar, 1 tbsp. butter, and carrot liquid in skillet. Add carrots and heat 8 to 10 min., until glazed. *2 to 3 servings.*

## CAULIFLOWER

**How to Cook:** Remove leaves. Leave whole, cutting out center core, or separate into flowerets. Remove any discoloration with knife. Cook, covered, in ½ to 1″ boiling salted water: whole cauliflower, 20 to 30 min.; flowerets, 8 to 15 min.

**Ways to Serve**

Add butter, salt, and pepper.

Top with Mushroom, Cheese, Egg, or Curry Sauce (p. 103), or Lemon Butter Sauce (p. 104).

Sprinkle with grated cheese; broil until cheese melts.

Stick salted almonds or peanuts into whole cooked head. Serve with Cream Sauce (p. 103).

### CAULIFLOWER WITH CHEESE SAUCE

Heat oven to 350° (mod.). Pour 2 cups Medium Cream Sauce (p. 103) over 1 head cooked cauliflower (whole or in flowerets) in baking dish. Sprinkle with ½ to 1 cup grated sharp cheese. Bake 20 min., or until cheese melts and sauce is bubbly. *4 servings.*

## CELERY

**How to Cook:** Remove any leaves and coarse strings. Reserve "hearts" to serve raw. Slice outer stalks into 1½ to 2″ pieces. Cook, covered, in 1″ boiling salted water 15 to 20 min. Add bouillon cube for extra flavor.

**Ways to Serve**

Add butter, salt, and pepper.

Top with Cream, Egg, or Cheese Sauce (p. 103), or Mock Hollandaise Sauce (p. 104).

Combine with cooked cauliflowerets or peas.

## PAN BRAISED CELERY

Remove root ends from celery. Slice celery thinly to make 3 cups. Melt 1 to 2 tbsp. butter in a skillet. Cook, covered, until celery sizzles; reduce heat. Braise 4 to 5 min. Add a few drops of water if necessary. Cook only until crisp-tender. Season with salt and pepper to taste. *3 to 4 servings.*

## CREOLE CELERY

½ cup chopped onion
½ cup chopped green pepper
2 tbsp. butter

2 to 2½ cups cooked tomatoes
2 cups diced celery
1 tsp. salt

Sauté onion and green pepper in butter about 5 min. Add tomatoes, celery, and salt. Cover; simmer 20 to 25 min., or until celery is tender. *6 to 8 servings.*

 ## CORN

**How to Cook:** Remove husks, silk, and blemishes just before cooking. Best when eaten as soon after picking as possible. Boil 5 to 8 min. in enough unsalted water to cover. (Salt toughens corn.)

**Ways to Serve**

Add butter, salt, and pepper.

Combine fresh corn, cut from ears, or whole-kernel corn with baby green Limas as succotash.

Combine canned cream-style and whole-kernel corn.

Combine equal amounts of drained canned whole-kernel corn and canned tomatoes in baking dish; season with green pepper, salt, and pepper; sprinkle with cracker crumbs and grated cheese; bake 30 min.

## SCALLOPED CORN

1 can (1 lb.) cream-style corn (2 cups)
1 egg, slightly beaten
½ cup milk
½ cup cracker or bread crumbs

¼ cup chopped onion
¼ cup chopped green pepper or 2 tbsp. chopped pimiento
1 tbsp. butter
salt and pepper

Heat oven to 350° (mod.). Combine all ingredients. Pour into 1-qt. baking dish. Bake 35 min. *4 servings.*

**Scalloped Corn and Ham:** Make Scalloped Corn (above)—except add 1 cup diced cooked ham.

**Cheese Scalloped Corn:** Make Scalloped Corn (above)—except add ¼ cup grated Cheddar cheese.

## CORN SESAME SAUTÉ

3 tbsp. vegetable oil
2 cloves garlic, finely chopped
2 to 4 tbsp. sesame seeds
1 can (12 oz.) corn with sweet peppers, drained (1½ cups)

¼ tsp. basil
½ tsp. salt
¼ tsp. pepper
¼ cup chopped parsley
¼ cup grated Parmesan cheese

Add oil to skillet and sauté garlic and sesame seeds in oil until lightly browned. Add corn, basil, salt, and pepper; blend. Cook until corn is thoroughly warmed. Garnish with parsley. Pass cheese. *4 to 5 servings.*

 ## EGGPLANT

**How to Cook:** Slice, cube, or cut into strips. Paring is not necessary unless skin is tough. Cut when ready to cook, as it discolors. Cook, covered, in ½″ boiling salted water 10 to 15 min. Or season with salt and pepper; dip in flour or dry bread or cracker crumbs, then in beaten egg, then crumbs again; sauté in hot fat 5 to 10 min. Or brush with butter and broil 5 min.

**Ways to Serve**

Combine cubed eggplant with sautéed tomatoes or onions or green pepper.

Sprinkle fried eggplant with minced chives, parsley, or grated Parmesan cheese.

## ONIONS

**How to Cook:** Peel under running water (prevents tears). Leave whole, slice, or quarter, depending on size. Cook, covered, in 1 to 2″ boiling salted water: small whole onions, 15 to 25 min.; large whole, 30 to 40 min.; sliced, 10 min. Bake large whole onions at 350° 50 to 60 min.

**Ways to Serve**

Buttered, with salt and pepper.

Combine with cooked carrot sticks and green beans.

### ONIONS AU GRATIN

Cook 2 cups peeled whole white onions (above) or use 1 can (1 lb.). Prepare 1 cup Cheese Sauce (p. 103). Pour over the drained cooked onions. *4 to 6 servings.*

### FRIED ONION RINGS

Allowing ½ onion per serving, cut large Bermuda or Spanish onions in ⅓ to ¼″ thick slices. Separate into rings. Dry thoroughly; coat generously with flour. Using tongs, dip rings into Thin Fritter Batter (below), letting excess drip off. Fry a few at a time in ½ to 1″ deep hot fat or oil about 2 min., or until golden. Drain.

**Thin Fritter Batter:** Stir 1 cup Gold Medal Flour, 1 tsp. baking powder, and ½ tsp. salt together in bowl. Mix 1 egg, 1 cup milk, and ¼ cup vegetable oil. Add to dry ingredients. Beat until smooth.

### ROAST ONIONS

Peel medium-sized onions and cut in half. Arrange around roast beef or roast pork, or in a buttered baking dish. Sprinkle with salt, paprika, and brown sugar. Bake in 325° oven during the last 1½ hr. of roasting time for meat. If baked in buttered baking dish, roast 1 to 1½ hr., or until of desired softness.

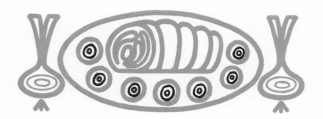

## PARSNIPS

**How to Cook:** Pare or scrub with brush. Leave whole or cut in halves, quarters, slices, or cubes. Remove cores from larger parsnips. A little sugar in water improves flavor. Cook, covered, in 1″ boiling salted water: whole parsnips, 20 to 40 min.; pieces, 8 to 20 min. or bake at 350° 30 to 45 min.

**Ways to Serve**

Boil and mash; combine with whipped cream and nutmeg.

Add salt and pepper; sprinkle with minced parsley.

### BUTTER BROWN PARSNIPS

Cook parsnips and drain thoroughly. For 5 parsnips melt ⅓ cup butter or shortening in skillet. Brown on all sides, watching carefully and turning frequently. (Parsnips scorch easily because of their high sugar content.) Serve hot. *5 servings.*

## PEAS

**How to Cook:** Shell just before cooking. Add 1 tsp. sugar and a few pods or leaf of lettuce to water for additional flavor. Cook, covered, in 1″ boiling salted water 8 to 15 min.

**Ways to Serve**

Buttered, with salt and pepper.

With sautéed mushrooms.

Add sautéed diced bacon, salt, and pepper.

Add minced fresh mint to new peas while cooking.

Add 1 or 2 tbsp. of green mint jelly to cooked peas just before serving (omit butter).

### PEAS WITH CELERY AND ONION

| | |
|---|---|
| 1 cup celery, sliced diagonally | ⅓ cup thinly sliced onion |
| 2 pkg. (10 oz. each) frozen peas | butter |

Add celery to ½ cup boiling salted water and cook 3 min. Add peas and onion; return to boil rapidly. Cook 5 min., or until peas are tender. Remove from heat. Drain and add butter. *6 servings.*

##  POTATOES—WHITE

**How to Cook:** Scrub with brush; remove eyes. Leave skins on whenever possible or pare thinly. Leave whole or cut in large pieces or slices. Cook, covered, in 1″ boiling salted water: whole potatoes, 30 to 35 min.; cut, 20 to 25 min. To bake: rub skins with fat for soft skins; prick a few holes with fork (for steam to escape). Bake at 375° 1 hr.; at 350°, 1½ hr.

**Ways to Serve**

Buttered, with salt and pepper.

With gravy, Cream Sauce (p. 103), or sour cream.

Mash and add butter, salt, pepper, and hot milk. Whip vigorously until light and fluffy.

### HURRY-UP POTATOES

Wash and pare 2 medium potatoes. Cut crosswise in ⅛″ slices. Brush broiler rack with a little melted shortening and arrange potatoes on rack. Brush tops with more melted shortening. Sprinkle with ¾ tsp. salt. Broil until tender, 6 to 10 min. *2 to 3 servings.*

### POTATOES ANNA

Melt 2 tbsp. butter in heavy skillet. Arrange thinly sliced raw potatoes in 2 or 3 layers. Sprinkle each layer with salt and pepper; dot generously with butter. Cover; steam 15 min. Uncover; cook until tender and crispy brown on the bottom. Invert on serving plate.

### IRENE'S SCALLOPED POTATOES

| | |
|---|---|
| 3 to 4 cups thinly sliced or coarsely grated raw potatoes | 1 tbsp. minced onion |
| | 2 to 4 tbsp. butter |
| | 1¼ cups milk, heated |

Heat oven to 350° (mod.). Arrange potatoes in layers in 1½-qt. baking dish. Sprinkle each layer with onion, salt, and pepper; dot with butter. Add hot milk. Bake, uncovered, about 1¼ hr. *4 servings.*

*IN A HURRY? Try our instant mashed potatoes, scalloped potato mix, and au gratin potato mix. Frozen potato products are mighty handy, too.*

##  POTATOES—SWEET OR YAMS

**How to Cook:** Without paring, boil 30 to 35 min. When tender, drain and slip off skins. To bake: scrub, then dry; rub with a little vegetable oil. Bake (large) at 350° 50 to 60 min.

**Ways to Serve**

Mash with butter, salt, and pepper; add flavor with orange juice, crushed pineapple, or chopped dates.

Serve mashed, garnished with chopped pecans or toasted coconut.

### SKILLET CANDIED SWEET POTATOES

Mix 1 cup brown sugar, ¼ cup butter, ¼ cup water, and ½ tsp. salt in heavy skillet; cook until mixture boils. Add 6 cooked sweet potatoes or yams and cook slowly, turning occasionally, about 20 min., or until potatoes have a caramel-like glaze. *6 servings.*

### SWEET POTATO BALLS

Combine cooked mashed sweet potatoes, butter, salt, and pepper. Drop ⅓ to ½ cup at a time onto crushed cereal flakes which have been spread over waxed paper. Place each ball on pineapple slice in buttered pan. Top with maraschino cherry. Heat at 350° 20 min. Serve hot.

### APPLESAUCE SWEET POTATOES

| | |
|---|---|
| 1 can (1 lb. 1 oz.) sweet potatoes, drained | ⅓ cup brown sugar |
| ½ tsp. salt | ½ tsp. cinnamon |
| 1 can (8 oz.) applesauce | 3 tbsp. chopped nuts |
| | 2 tbsp. butter |

Heat oven to 375° (quick mod.). Put sweet potatoes in shallow baking dish; sprinkle with salt. Spoon applesauce over sweet potatoes. Combine sugar and cinnamon; sprinkle nuts over top. Dot with butter. Bake 45 min. *6 servings.*

**RUTABAGAS AND TURNIPS**

**How to Cook Rutabagas:** Pare, slice, dice, or cut into strips. Cook, covered, in 1″ boiling salted water 25 to 40 min. A little sugar in water improves flavor.

**How to Cook Turnips:** Remove tops (save greens). Pare, slice, dice, or cut into strips. Cook, covered, in 1″ boiling salted water: whole turnips, 20 to 30 min.; sliced or diced, 15 to 20 min.

## RUTABAGA WITH SOUR CREAM

Heat oven to 350° (mod.). Mix 1½ lb. rutabaga, cooked and cubed, with salt and pepper to taste and ¼ cup chopped onion in 1½-qt. baking dish. Bake 15 min. Stir in ½ to 1 cup commercial sour cream; bake 15 min. more. *4 to 6 servings.*

 **SPINACH**

**How to Cook:** Cut off any root ends and damaged leaves. Wash thoroughly. Cook 5 to 15 min., using only the water that clings to the leaves after washing. To preserve color, cook uncovered first 5 min.

**Ways to Serve**

Add butter, salt, and pepper; or a dash of lemon juice or vinegar; or prepared horse-radish.

Top with Cream or Egg Sauce (p. 103).

Sprinkle with sieved or sliced hard-cooked egg, or chopped toasted almonds or peanuts, or sautéed mushrooms, or crisp bacon bits.

## SPINACH GOURMET

1 pkg. (10 oz.) frozen chopped spinach
1 can (3½ oz.) tiny button mushrooms
1 tsp. minced onion
1 tsp. minced garlic
1 tsp. salt
dash of pepper
2 tbsp. butter
⅓ cup commercial sour cream
1 to 2 tbsp. cream or milk

Cook spinach according to pkg. directions, omitting salt. Drain well. Combine spinach with mushrooms, onion, garlic, salt, pepper, and butter. Thin sour cream with cream; add to spinach mixture and heat just to boil. Serve immediately. *4 servings.*

 **SQUASHES—SUMMER**

**How to Cook:** Remove stem and blossom ends. Remove large seeds (except in zucchini) and coarse fiber, if any. Leave whole, slice, or dice. Paring is not necessary. Boil whole squashes 30 to 60 min.; cut, 10 to 15 min. Or bake at 350° (whole) 30 to 60 min.

**Ways to Serve**

With butter, salt, and pepper.

Add Worcestershire sauce and onion, lemon juice, or minced parsley or chives.

Top with Mock Hollandaise Sauce (p. 104), Tomato Sauce (p. 103), catsup, or chili sauce.

## SQUASHES—WINTER

**How to Cook:** Hubbard: pare, if desired; remove seeds and fibers, cut into serving pieces. Acorn: do not pare; remove seeds, brush with butter and seasonings before, during, and after baking. Bake at 375° 40 to 60 min. Bake halves of acorn squash cut-side-down, turn after half of baking time. Bake covered for moist top, uncovered for crusty top. Or boil 25 to 30 min.

**Ways to Serve**

Add butter, salt, and pepper.

Mashed, served with a little whipped cream, sugar, and nutmeg; or with brown sugar and butter.

 **TOMATOES**

**How to Cook:** Peel, if desired. Leave whole or cut in slices or quarters. Cover pan, add no water; add a bay leaf, if desired. Simmer 8 to 10 min. Or cut into slices, dip in flour, and sauté in butter. Or cut halves or thick slices, brush with butter, and broil 3 to 5 min.

**Ways to Serve**

Add minced onion, parsley, or sweet basil.

Sprinkle with toasted bread crumbs or croutons browned in lightly flavored garlic butter.

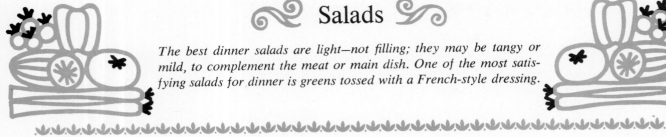

# Salads

*The best dinner salads are light—not filling; they may be tangy or mild, to complement the meat or main dish. One of the most satisfying salads for dinner is greens tossed with a French-style dressing.*

## BEST TOSSED SALAD

*A tangy delight with Classic French Dressing.*

| | |
|---|---|
| 1 large head lettuce | ½ small bag spinach |
| 1 bunch leaf lettuce | (2 cups) |
| ½ small bunch endive | Classic French Dressing |
| (about 1 cup) | (below) |

Keep greens dry and cold. Use choice parts, discarding stems and cores. Tear greens into bite-size pieces. Just before serving, toss with Classic French Dressing. *6 to 8 servings.*

## CLASSIC FRENCH DRESSING

| | |
|---|---|
| ¼ cup olive oil or vegetable oil | 1 small clove garlic, pressed or minced |
| 2 tbsp. wine or tarragon vinegar | ⅛ to ¼ tsp. fresh ground pepper |
| 1½ tsp. salt | ⅛ to ¼ tsp. monosodium glutamate |

Toss salad greens with oil until leaves glisten. Add vinegar combined with rest of ingredients. Toss again. Serve immediately.

## HOW TO BE FAMOUS FOR YOUR TOSSED SALADS

**Use a Variety of Greens**

Bibb lettuce

Romaine

Curly endive

Water cress

Leaf lettuce

Escarole

Spinach

**Add One or More of These for Flavor and Color**

Green onions or scallions

Radishes

Green peppers

Leeks

Celery

*Tomatoes

Cucumbers

Cauliflowerets

*Tomatoes dilute dressing, so place them at side of salad after serving.*

**Occasionally Try Unusual Additions**

Sliced water chestnuts

Tiny croutons browned in garlic butter

Artichoke hearts

Parmesan or Roquefort cheese

Crisp bacon

Palm hearts

Sliced mushrooms

Ripe olives

Anchovies

## GREEN AND WHITE SALAD

1 head lettuce
½ bunch endive
½ small head cauliflower
1 can (8 oz.) artichoke hearts
12 ripe olives, cut up

¼ cup olive or vegetable oil
2 tbsp. tarragon vinegar
1 tsp. salt
1 clove garlic, minced
12 shakes monosodium glutamate

Tear greens into bite-size pieces. Break cauliflower in small pieces; cut artichoke hearts in half, olives in slices. Toss together. Add oil and toss until greens are coated. Add rest of ingredients and toss again. *4 to 6 servings.*

## FRESH SPINACH SALAD

½ lb. washed, dried spinach, torn in bite-size pieces (4 cups)
1 small Bermuda onion, sliced

¼ cup diced celery
4 hard-cooked eggs, sliced
Classic Garlic Dressing (right)

Toss vegetables and eggs together. Chill. Before serving, toss with Classic Garlic Dressing. *8 servings.*

## CAESAR'S SALAD

**In advance:** Cover ½ clove garlic with 2 tbsp. vegetable oil; let stand. Also, prepare 2 cups croutons (cut bread into cubes, toast in oven). Place 3 qt. dry, cold, crisp salad greens in large bowl. Add ½ cup each vegetable oil, grated Parmesan cheese, and crumbled Bleu cheese. Salt and pepper to taste. Break 1 raw egg over greens. Squeeze juice of 2 lemons (4 to 6 tbsp.) over egg. Toss well.

**Just before serving:** Remove garlic from vegetable oil; combine oil and croutons and sprinkle over top of salad. *8 servings.*

## ITALIAN MUSHROOM AND LIMA BEAN SALAD

1 pkg. (10 oz.) frozen Lima beans
8 sliced fresh mushrooms or 1 can (4 oz.) sliced mushrooms, drained
4 green onions, sliced (3 to 4 tbsp.)

1 tbsp. chopped fresh parsley or 1 tsp. dry parsley flakes
½ tsp. oregano
Classic Garlic Dressing (below)

Cook beans until tender as directed on pkg. Drain, rinse under cold running water, and drain thoroughly again. Toss with remaining ingredients. Heap into large dish lined with crisp salad greens. Garnish with chopped tops of green onions or thinly sliced onion rings. Chill in refrigerator 1 to 2 hr. *4 to 6 servings.*

**Classic Garlic Dressing:** Shake together in small jar 2 tbsp. vegetable oil, 1 tbsp. vinegar, ¾ tsp. salt, dash each ground black pepper, and monosodium glutamate, and 1 small clove garlic, crushed.

## ZUCCHINI TOSSED SALAD

½ head lettuce, torn into bite-size pieces
½ head romaine, torn into bite-size pieces
2 medium zucchini, thinly sliced
1 cup sliced radishes

3 green onions, sliced (about 2 tbsp.)
1 oz. Bleu cheese, crumbled (about 2 tbsp.)
Classic French Dressing (p. 94)

Toss lettuce, romaine, zucchini, radishes, onions, and cheese. Then toss with Classic French Dressing. *6 to 8 servings.*

## FRUIT SALAD COMBINATIONS

**Apple-Grape-Celery Salad:** Diced apple, Tokay grapes (halved and seeded) or green seedless grapes, diced celery, and chopped nuts with Fruit Salad Mayonnaise (p. 102).

**Orange-Grapefruit-Avocado-Pomegranate Salad:** Orange and grapefruit sections, avocado slices, pomegranate seeds, or sliced strawberries. Garnish with water cress, if desired. Serve with a fruit dressing.

**Melon-Cherry-Plum-Grape Salad:** Melon wedges (cantaloupe or honeydew), Bing cherries, plum slices, and/or green seedless grapes with fruit dressing.

**Ambrosia Salad:** Combine cut-up orange sections, diced apple, and banana slices with Fruit Salad Mayonnaise (p. 102). Top with plain or toasted coconut.

**Peach-Grape Salad:** Diced fresh peaches and green seedless grapes with Vanilla Mayonnaise Topping (p. 102).

**Pineapple-Strawberry-Cream Cheese Salad:** Diced fresh pineapple and strawberries with cream cheese balls rolled in chopped nuts.

**Pineapple-Bing Cherry Salad:** Chill 1 can (14 oz.) pineapple chunks and 1 can (14 oz.) Bing cherries. Drain and add ¼ cup chopped pecans, ½ cup whipping cream, whipped, and 1 tbsp. mayonnaise. Serve on lettuce. *6 servings.*

**Apple-Avocado-Celery Salad:** Diced red apple, diced avocado, and sliced celery with Sour Cream Mayonnaise (p. 102).

**Pineapple-Cherry-Cream Cheese Salad:** Place slice of chilled pineapple on bed of greens. Put cream cheese ball in the center. Surround with 5 Bing cherries in which seeds have been replaced with almonds. Serve with Fruit Salad Mayonnaise (p. 102).

**Banana-Cranberry Salad:** Two long slices of banana centered with cubes of jellied cranberry sauce and chopped nuts. Sweet French Dressing (p. 102).

**Pear-Cranberry Salad:** Top canned pear halves with Cranberry-Orange Relish (p. 105); serve one pear half per person on fresh greens. *(Pictured on p. 160.)*

**Orange-Onion Salad:** Remove skin and membrane of 2 or 3 oranges. Cut in ¼″ thick slices. Slice 1 Bermuda onion paper-thin. Alternate slices of orange and onion on curly endive or lettuce. Serve with French Dressing (p. 102). *6 servings.*

## WALDORF SALAD

| | |
|---|---|
| 2 cups diced unpeeled apples | ¼ to ½ cup broken unsalted nuts |
| 1 cup diced celery | ½ cup mayonnaise (or use 4 to 6 tbsp. thinned with cream) |

Toss apples, celery, and nuts with mayonnaise. Serve in lettuce cups. Top each serving with a maraschino cherry. *4 servings.*

**Pear Waldorf Salad:** Substitute 1 cup diced fresh pears for 1 cup of the apples.

**Date Waldorf Salad:** Substitute ½ cup cut-up dates for ½ cup of the apples.

**Cranberry Waldorf Salad:** Serve on a slice of chilled jellied cranberries.

## VEGETABLE SALAD COMBINATIONS

Cooked asparagus tips on thick tomato slices, sprinkled with grated cheese.

Shredded cabbage, grated carrots, chopped green pepper, and chopped green onion tossed with Frenchaise Dressing (p. 102).

Chilled cooked okra pods and sliced celery with French dressing and spiked with a little horse-radish.

Red kidney beans, cooked cut green beans, chopped green pepper, and chopped onion tossed with oil and vinegar, salt, pepper, and sugar; then chilled.

Cooked beet chunks and coarsely chopped curly endive tossed with French dressing to which caraway seeds have been added.

Grated raw carrots and drained crushed pineapple mixed with raisins and mayonnaise.

## OLD-FASHIONED CABBAGE SLAW

1 tsp. salt

¼ tsp. pepper

½ tsp. dry mustard

½ to 1 tsp. celery seeds

2 tbsp. sugar

¼ cup chopped green pepper

1 tbsp. chopped red pepper or pimiento

½ tsp. grated onion

3 tbsp. vegetable oil

⅓ cup white vinegar

3 cups finely chopped cabbage (green or red or a combination)

Place ingredients in large bowl in order given. Mix well. Cover and chill thoroughly. Garnish with water cress and sliced stuffed olives just before serving, if desired. *4 servings.*

## ONION-CUCUMBER SALAD

1 cucumber

½ medium onion

½ cup vinegar

½ cup water

1½ to 2 tbsp. sugar

¼ tsp. salt

dash of pepper

Pull tines of fork firmly down length of cucumber, repeating around cucumber; thinly slice. Thinly slice onion, separating rings. Combine remaining ingredients. Pour over vegetables; marinate at least 1 hr. Drain to serve. *4 to 6 servings.*

*So Easy, So Good*

**Marie's Boiled Meat Balls**
**Mashed Potatoes**
**Succotash**
**Old-fashioned Cabbage Slaw**
**Fresh Berry Pie (p. 144)**

## TANGY TOMATO ASPIC

*See picture opposite.*

**1 pkg. (6 oz.) lemon-flavored gelatin**

**2½ cups boiling water**

**1 can (15 oz.) tomato sauce**

**3 tbsp. white vinegar**

**1 tsp. salt**

**1½ tsp. onion juice**

**dash each of Tabasco, pepper, ground cloves, and cayenne pepper**

Dissolve gelatin in water. Blend in remaining ingredients. Pour into 10 to 12 individual molds or a 6-cup ring mold. Chill until firm. Serve on greens with mayonnaise. *8 to 10 servings.*

**Aspic Ring with Sea Food Salad:** Fill center of aspic ring with your favorite sea food salad (p. 43).

**Aspic Cubes in Tossed Salad:** Toss cubes of aspic and torn lettuce with French dressing.

**Aspic with Artichoke Hearts or Hearts of Palm:** Serve aspic on greens with artichoke hearts or hearts of palm.

## SEA DREAM SALAD

**1 pkg. (6 oz.) lime-flavored gelatin**

**2 cups boiling water**

**4 medium cucumbers**

**2 onions, grated**

**1 tsp. salt**

**¼ tsp. cayenne pepper**

**1 cup mayonnaise**

Dissolve gelatin in water. Grate cucumbers and strain to get juice; reserve pulp. Add cucumber juice, onions, and seasonings to gelatin. Pour into 1-qt. ring mold. Chill until firm. Unmold on lettuce or endive. Add cucumber pulp to mayonnaise for dressing. Arrange tomato wedges around outside. *6 to 8 servings.*

*Light Company Supper*

**Tangy Tomato Aspic Ring with Sea Food Salad (p. 43)**

**Hot Popovers (p. 119)**

**Dutch Apple Pie (p. 143)**

## PACIFIC LIME MOLD

**1 pkg. (3 oz.) lime-flavored gelatin**

**1 cup boiling water**

**1 can (9 oz.) crushed pineapple**

**1 cup creamy cottage cheese**

**1 tsp. horse-radish**

**½ cup mayonnaise or ½ cup whipping cream, whipped**

**¼ cup chopped nuts**

Dissolve gelatin in water. Add juice from pineapple; chill until slightly thickened. Beat until frothy. Fold in remaining ingredients. Chill until set. *6 servings.*

## BEET AND HORSE-RADISH MOLD

**1 can (1 lb. 4 oz.) beets**

**3 tbsp. vinegar**

**1 pkg. (3 oz.) lemon-flavored gelatin**

**½ tsp. salt**

**2 tbsp. onion juice**

**2 tbsp. prepared horse-radish**

**¾ cup diced celery**

Drain liquid from beets; add water to make 1½ cups. Heat liquid and vinegar; add gelatin and dissolve. Add salt and onion juice; chill until partially set. Chop beets finely; stir into gelatin with horse-radish and celery. Pour into 8″ ring mold or individual molds. Chill until firm. Unmold on lettuce and top with mayonnaise. *6 to 8 servings.*

## PERFECTION SALAD

**1 pkg. (3 oz.) lemon-flavored gelatin**

**2 tbsp. lemon juice or vinegar**

**1 tsp. salt**

**1 cup finely shredded cabbage**

**1 cup finely diced celery**

**2 finely chopped pimientos**

**6 chopped sweet pickles**

**Cheese-Olive Dressing (below) or mayonnaise**

Prepare gelatin according to pkg. directions. Add lemon juice and salt. When partially set (mixture mounds off spoon), add remaining ingredients. Pour into 6 or 8 individual molds. Chill until firm. Unmold on individual plates. Garnish with endive or water cress. Top with mayonnaise or Cheese-Olive Dressing.

**Cheese-Olive Dressing:** Combine 1 pkg. (3 oz.) cream cheese, softened, and ¼ cup cream; beat until smooth. Fold in ¼ cup chopped ripe olives.

## DOUBLE-QUICK
## ORANGE GELATIN RING

| | |
|---|---|
| 1 pkg. (6 oz.) orange-flavored gelatin | 1 pt. orange sherbet |
| 2 cups boiling water | 1 can (11 oz.) mandarin oranges, drained |

Dissolve gelatin in water. Immediately add sherbet and stir until melted. Add oranges. Pour into 1½-qt. ring mold and chill until firm. Unmold on greens. *10 to 12 servings.*

## CRANBERRY-BANANA MOLD

| | |
|---|---|
| 1 pkg. (3 oz.) raspberry-flavored gelatin | 1 can (1 lb.) whole cranberry sauce |
| 1 cup boiling water | 2 medium bananas |
| | ½ cup chopped pecans |

Dissolve gelatin in water. Add cranberry sauce and stir until blended. Chill until partially thickened. Add sliced bananas and pecans. Spoon into molds; chill until firm. Serve on greens. *6 to 9 servings.*

## CHEESE DELIGHT

| | |
|---|---|
| 1 pkg. (3 oz.) lemon-flavored gelatin | 1 can (8½ oz.) crushed pineapple |
| 1 cup boiling water | 1 cup whipping cream, whipped |
| 1 cup grated cheese | |

Combine gelatin and water. Chill until slightly thickened. Fold in cheese, drained pineapple, and whipped cream. Pour into 1-qt. mold. Chill. *6 servings.*

---

*Easy Do-Ahead Dinner*

**Cheese Ribbon Meat Loaf (p. 70)**
**Buttered Italian Green Beans**
**Fruit Gelatin Mold**
**Old-fashioned Yeast Biscuits (p. 116)**
**Chiffon Cake with Cocoa Fluff (p. 135)**

---

## CREAMY ORANGE-PINEAPPLE SALAD

| | |
|---|---|
| 1 can (8½ oz.) crushed pineapple | 1 pkg. (3 oz.) cream cheese |
| 1 pkg. (3 oz.) orange-flavored gelatin | 1 cup whipping cream |
| | 1 carrot, grated (about ⅓ cup) |

Drain pineapple, reserving juice. Add water to juice to make 1 cup; heat to boil. Add boiling liquid to gelatin and cream cheese; beat with rotary beater until smooth. Cool, stirring occasionally. Whip cream. Fold cream, grated carrot, and pineapple into cooled gelatin. Pour into individual molds. Chill until firm. *8 to 12 servings.*

## FRUIT GELATIN MOLD

*See picture opposite.*

| | |
|---|---|
| 1 pkg. (3 oz.) lemon- or strawberry-flavored gelatin | 2 oranges, diced |
| 1 cup boiling water | 1 cup pineapple chunks, drained |
| 1 cup liquid (syrup from fruit plus cold water) | 1 banana, sliced |
| | 1 apple, diced |
| | ½ cup broken walnuts |

Dissolve gelatin in water. Add syrup and cold water; chill until partially set. Add fruits and nuts; chill until firm. Unmold on lettuce. Pass your choice of dressing. *6 servings.*

## CINNAMON APPLESAUCE SWIRL SALAD

*A light red salad to brighten any dinner plate; the perfect complement for pork or poultry.*

| | |
|---|---|
| ⅓ cup red cinnamon candies | 1 can (1 lb.) applesauce (2 cups) |
| 2 pkg. (3 oz. each) or 1 pkg. (6 oz.) lemon-flavored gelatin | 2 pkg. (3 oz. each) cream cheese |
| 2 cups boiling water | ¼ cup cream |
| | 2 tbsp. mayonnaise |

Dissolve candies and gelatin in water; stir in applesauce. Chill until partially set. Pour into 8″ sq. pan. Mix cheese, cream, and mayonnaise until smooth. Stir gently into jellied applesauce for swirled effect. Chill until firm. Serve squares on greens. *9 to 12 servings.*

## FRENCH DRESSING

1 cup olive oil, vegetable oil, or combination

¼ cup vinegar

¼ cup lemon juice

½ tsp. paprika

1 tsp. salt

½ tsp. dry mustard

Beat all ingredients with rotary beater or shake well in tightly covered jar. Keep in covered jar in refrigerator. Shake again to mix before using; it separates after standing. *Makes 1½ cups.*

**Sweet French Dressing:** To ½ cup French Dressing add 2 tbsp. confectioners' sugar or honey.

**Piquant French Dressing:** To ½ cup French Dressing add 2 tbsp. sugar, ½ tsp. each celery seeds and grated onion. Let 1 clove garlic, cut crosswise, stand in dressing 1 hr.

**Roquefort or Bleu Cheese Dressing:** Mash ¼ cup Roquefort or Bleu cheese with ⅛ tsp. Worcestershire sauce. Blend in ½ cup French Dressing.

**Garlic French Dressing:** Crush 1 clove garlic into fine paste. Mix in some freshly ground pepper and ½ cup French Dressing.

**Herb French Dressing:** To ½ cup French Dressing add 2 tsp. minced parsley, ⅛ tsp. powdered thyme, and ½ tsp. oregano.

## RANCHO ROQUEFORT DRESSING

*See picture below.*

1 cup commercial sour cream

2 green onions, cut fine

2 tbsp. mayonnaise

2 tbsp. lemon juice

½ cup Roquefort or Bleu cheese, crumbled

salt and pepper to taste

Blend all ingredients. Let ripen several hours before serving. Serve on lettuce wedges.

## MAYONNAISE

Mayonnaise is the best choice for sea food, poultry, meat, and cooked vegetable salads. It can be bought ready-made and is easily varied.

**Vanilla Mayonnaise Topping:** Just before serving, blend ½ cup softened vanilla ice cream with ¼ cup mayonnaise. Mix with fruit salad or pass at the table.

**Frenchaise Dressing:** Beat ¼ cup French Dressing into ½ cup mayonnaise.

**Fruit Salad Mayonnaise:** To ½ cup mayonnaise add ¼ cup whipping cream, whipped.

**Thousand Island Dressing:** To 1 cup mayonnaise add 2 tbsp. chili sauce, 1 tbsp. chopped dill pickle, 1 tsp. minced onion, and 1 hard-cooked egg, chopped.

**Sour Cream Mayonnaise:** Add ½ cup commercial sour cream to 1 cup mayonnaise; season.

## RUBY RED DRESSING

½ cup currant jelly

¼ cup vegetable oil

2 tbsp. lemon juice

dash of salt

few drops of onion juice

Beat jelly with fork until smooth. Add rest of ingredients and beat until smooth. *Makes ¾ cup.*

## LEMON OR LIME HONEY DRESSING

⅓ cup undiluted frozen concentrate for lemonade or limeade

⅓ cup honey

⅓ cup vegetable oil

1 tsp. celery or poppy seeds

Combine all ingredients. Beat with rotary beater until blended and smooth. Serve over fruit salads. *Makes 1 cup.*

## CREAM SAUCE

*The Thin Sauce is like coffee cream; for creamed vegetables and soup. The Medium Sauce is like thick cream; for creamed and scalloped dishes. The Thick Sauce is like batter; for croquettes and soufflés.*

| THIN | MEDIUM | THICK |
|------|--------|-------|
| 1 tbsp. butter | 2 tbsp. butter | ¼ cup butter |
| ½ to 1 tbsp. flour | 2 tbsp. flour | ¼ cup flour |
| ¼ tsp. salt | ¼ tsp. salt | ¼ tsp. salt |
| ⅛ tsp. pepper | ⅛ tsp. pepper | ⅛ tsp. pepper |
| 1 cup milk | 1 cup milk | 1 cup milk |

Melt butter over low heat in saucepan. Blend in flour and seasonings. Cook over low heat, stirring until mixture is smooth and bubbly. Remove from heat. Stir in milk. Bring to boil, stirring constantly. Boil 1 min. *Makes 1 cup sauce.*

**Velvet Sauce:** Make Medium Cream Sauce (above)—except use chicken, veal, or fish stock in place of milk. Add ⅛ tsp. nutmeg.

**Cheese Sauce:** Make Medium Cream Sauce (above)—except add ½ cup grated Cheddar cheese. Stir until cheese is melted.

**Mustard Cream Sauce:** Make Medium Cream Sauce (above)—except add 1 tbsp. prepared mustard.

**Horse-radish Sauce:** Make Medium Cream Sauce (above)—except add ⅓ cup bottled horse-radish, ¼ tsp. dry mustard, and a dash of paprika.

**Curry Sauce:** Make Medium Cream Sauce (above)—except sauté ½ tsp. curry powder in the butter before adding flour and other seasonings.

**Egg Sauce:** Make Medium Cream Sauce (above)—except add 2 diced hard-cooked eggs.

## ❀ SAUCES FOR MEATS AND FISH ❀

### TARTAR SAUCE

Combine 1 cup mayonnaise, 1 tsp. grated onion, 2 tbsp. minced dill pickle, 1 tbsp. minced parsley, and 2 tsp. cut-up pimiento. For sea food. *Makes 1 cup sauce.*

### RAISIN SAUCE

Mix ½ cup brown sugar (packed), 1 tsp. dry mustard, 2 tbsp. cornstarch; slowly add 2 tbsp. each vinegar and lemon juice, ¼ tsp. grated lemon rind, 1½ cups water, and ½ cup raisins. Stir over low heat until thick. Best with ham. *Makes 1½ cups sauce.*

### TOMATO SAUCE

Sauté 2 tbsp. chopped onion and 2 tbsp. chopped green pepper in 1 tbsp. butter until onion is transparent. Add 1 can (8 oz.) tomato sauce; season with salt and pepper. Heat over low heat. Excellent with both meat and fish. *Makes 1¼ cups sauce.*

### MILLIE'S MUSTARD SAUCE

Blend ⅓ cup sugar, ⅓ cup prepared mustard, ⅓ cup condensed tomato soup, ⅓ cup butter, 3 tbsp. vinegar and 1 egg yolk, slightly beaten, in saucepan. Boil 1 min., stirring constantly. Serve over baked ham, meat loaf, hamburgers, or frankfurters. *Makes 1¼ cups sauce.*

### EASY MUSHROOM SAUCE

Drain 1 can (2 oz.) sliced mushrooms and save juice. In medium skillet, sauté mushrooms and 1 tbsp. minced onion in 1 tbsp. butter until light brown. Add 1 can (10½ oz.) cream of mushroom soup, mushroom juice, and a few drops Worcestershire sauce. Cook over medium heat, stirring occasionally, until hot. For meats. *Makes 2 cups sauce.*

### CUCUMBER SAUCE

Add 1 cup finely diced cucumber, ½ tsp. minced onion, and 1 tbsp. prepared mustard to ½ cup mayonnaise. Season with salt, pepper, and paprika. Chill. Nice with ham or fish. *Makes 1¼ cups sauce.*

## ❀ SAUCES FOR VEGETABLES ❀

### CELERY CHEESE SAUCE

Mix 1 can (10½ oz.) cream of celery soup with ⅓ cup milk and ½ cup shredded sharp cheese (or use 1 pkg. (3 oz.) softened cream cheese plus 1 tbsp. minced chives). Cook over low heat, stirring occasionally, until cheese is melted and sauce has heated through. Serve over carrots, cauliflower, onions, potatoes, or broccoli. *Makes 1⅔ cups sauce.*

### QUICK COMPANY SAUCE

Whip ½ cup whipping cream. Fold in ½ cup mayonnaise and any one of the following:

¼ cup well-drained pickle relish (for corn and green beans)

¼ cup chopped, well-drained cucumber (for broccoli and tomatoes)

¼ cup chili sauce (for corn and Lima beans)

2 tbsp. prepared mustard and ¼ tsp. dill (for carrots and cauliflower)

Serve as a topping for hot vegetables as suggested above. *Makes 1¾ cups sauce.*

### LEMON BUTTER SAUCE

Heat ¼ cup butter; add 2 tbsp. lemon juice and 1 tsp. grated lemon rind. Keep hot.

### MOCK HOLLANDAISE SAUCE

*See picture at right.*

Blend 1 can (10½ oz.) cream of chicken soup, ¼ cup mayonnaise, and 1 tbsp. lemon juice. Cook over low heat, stirring occasionally, until sauce has heated through. Serve over cooked broccoli, carrots, or asparagus. *Makes 1½ cups sauce.*

*Dinner with Eye Appeal*

**Braised Pork Chops (p. 71)
with Red Cinnamon Apple Rings**

**Boiled Potatoes          Tossed Salad**

**Asparagus with Mock Hollandaise Sauce**

**Praline Coconut Cake (p. 132)**

## MEAT ACCOMPANIMENTS

**Whole Cranberry Sauce:** Boil 2 cups water and 2 cups sugar together 5 min. Add 4 cups cranberries. Boil, without stirring, until all skins pop, about 5 min. Cool. *Makes 4½ cups.*

**Tangy Pickled Beets:** Bring to boil 2 to 4 tbsp. vinegar, ½ cup liquid drained from 1 can (1 lb.) whole baby beets or sliced beets, 2 tbsp. sugar, 2 cloves, ½ tsp. salt, 3 peppercorns, and ¼ bay leaf. Pour over drained beets. Chill 6 to 8 hr. *Makes 2 cups.*

**Cranberry-Orange Relish:** Put rind and pulp of 1 large orange and 4 cups cranberries through food chopper. Mix in 2 cups sugar and let stand several hours.

**Red Cinnamon Apple Rings:** Make syrup of 1 cup water, 2 cups sugar, ⅓ cup red cinnamon candies, and a few drops red food coloring. Pare and core apples; slice into ½" rings. Cook apple rings in syrup until tender. Use as garnish for pork and poultry. *(See picture at left.)*

## CURRIED FRUIT BAKE

| | |
|---|---|
| 1 can (1 lb.) pear halves | 1 can (1 lb. 4 oz.) pineapple slices or chunks |
| 6 maraschino cherries | ⅓ cup butter, melted |
| 1 can (1 lb.) Cling peaches or apricot halves | ¾ cup brown sugar (packed) |
| | 4 tsp. curry powder |

Heat oven to 325° (slow mod.). Drain fruit and arrange in oblong pan, 13x9½x2". Pour mixture of remaining ingredients over fruit. Bake 15 min. Baste with drippings in pan; bake 15 min. more. Serve hot as meat accompaniment. *12 servings.*

*QUICK MEAT ACCOMPANIMENTS— You'll find a wide array of delicious canned and bottled relishes and sauces to serve with meats at your grocery store: chili sauce, corn relish, chow chow, etc.*

## SALMON SUPPER

*See picture below.*

3 tbsp. chopped onion

⅓ cup chopped green pepper

3 tbsp. fat

1 tsp. salt

¼ cup Gold Medal Flour

1 can (10½ oz.) cream of celery or mushroom soup

1½ cups milk

1 can (7 oz.) salmon, drained

1 cup cooked peas

1 tbsp. lemon juice

½ recipe Easy Biscuits (p. 44)

Heat oven to 450° (hot). Sauté onion and pepper in hot fat until onion is golden. Blend in salt and flour. Gradually stir in soup and milk. Bring to boil; boil 1 min. Add flaked salmon, peas, and lemon juice. Pour into oblong baking dish, 11½x7½x1½". Top with biscuits. Bake 10 to 12 min. *6 to 8 servings.*

## SHRIMP-CHICKEN CURRY

3 to 4 tbsp. butter

1 medium onion, diced

1 medium apple, peeled and diced

2 cans (10½ oz. each) chicken à la king

2 to 3 tsp. curry powder

1 can (4½ oz.) deveined shrimp, drained

2 tbsp. lemon juice

3 to 4 cups cooked rice (1 cup uncooked)

Sauté onion and apple in butter. Add chicken, curry powder, shrimp, and lemon juice; heat well. Serve over cooked rice with accompaniments of coconut, chutney, raisins, slivered salted almonds, chopped green pepper, and chopped hard-cooked eggs. *4 to 6 servings.*

*Meal in a Casserole*

**Salmon Supper**
**Lettuce Wedges with French Dressing**
**Fruit Parfaits (p. 46)**
**Caramel Nut Slices (p. 124)**

## CHINESE SHRIMP AND MUSHROOMS

⅓ cup vegetable oil
or ½ cup butter

1 lb. fresh shrimp
(shelled and cleaned)

2 cups bamboo shoots
or finely sliced
celery

1 can (6 oz.) sliced
mushrooms

1 tbsp. soy sauce

1 tsp. powdered ginger

1 tsp. salt

⅛ tsp. pepper

1 tbsp. cornstarch

½ cup beef or chicken
broth

3 to 4 cups cooked rice
(1 cup uncooked)

Heat oil in skillet. Add shrimp; fry, turning frequently, for about 10 min., or until shrimp are light pink. Remove shrimp, sauté bamboo shoots or celery and mushrooms; add soy sauce, ginger, salt, and pepper; cook 5 min., tossing mixture lightly. Add shrimp, cook another 5 min. Add cornstarch, mixed to a thin paste with a little cold water, and broth. Simmer 1 min. to thicken. Serve with cooked rice. *4 servings.*

## BAKED TUNA CHOW MEIN CASSEROLE

1 cup chopped celery

¼ cup chopped onion

2 tbsp. chopped green
pepper

1 tbsp. butter

1 can (10½ oz.) cream
of mushroom soup,
thinned with ¼ cup
milk and ¼ cup water

1 can (6½ or 7 oz.) tuna

1⅓ cups chow mein
noodles

¾ cup (4 oz.) salted
cashew nuts

¼ tsp. monosodium
glutamate

⅛ tsp. pepper

Heat oven to 350° (mod.). Sauté celery, onion, and green pepper in butter. Mix in thinned soup, tuna, 1 cup noodles, cashews, and seasonings. Pour into buttered 1½-qt. baking dish. Sprinkle with remaining ⅓ cup chow mein noodles. Bake 30 min. *4 to 6 servings.*

## TUNA-BROCCOLI CASSEROLE

Heat oven to 450° (hot). Split stalks from 1 pkg. (10 oz.) frozen broccoli; cook 3 min.; drain. Place in 1½-qt. baking dish. Cover with 1 can (7 oz.) tuna, flaked. Mix 1 can (10½ oz.) cream of mushroom soup and ½ soup can milk; pour over tuna. Sprinkle ½ cup crushed potato chips over top. Bake 15 min. *4 servings.*

## SCALLOPED TUNA

2 cans (6½ or 7 oz. each)
tuna, in large pieces

2 cups crushed potato
chips or cheese crackers

3 cups Medium Cream
Sauce (p. 103)

¾ cup sliced ripe
olives or sautéed
mushrooms

Heat oven to 350° (mod.). Arrange ingredients in alternate layers in buttered 1½-qt. baking dish. Finish with a sprinkle of chips. Bake 35 min. *6 servings.*

## TUNA PUFF CASSEROLE

1 can (6½ or 7 oz.) tuna

1 can (10½ oz.) cream
of mushroom soup

1 cup soft bread cubes

½ cup diced celery

1 tbsp. minced onion

¼ cup chopped ripe
olives

½ tsp. lemon juice

¼ tsp. Tabasco

¼ cup mayonnaise

4 eggs, separated

Heat oven to 325° (slow mod.). Drain and flake tuna. Blend ½ can of soup with tuna. Combine tuna-soup mixture with next 7 ingredients and egg yolks. Add another dash of Tabasco to egg whites. Beat until stiff, but not dry. Fold into tuna-soup mixture. Turn into 1½-qt. baking dish. Bake 35 to 40 min. Dilute remaining soup with ⅓ cup water. Heat and serve as sauce for casserole. *6 servings.*

## BUSY-DAY SHRIMP 'N PEAS

¾ lb. shrimp in the shell
or 1 pkg. (7 or 8 oz.)
frozen shelled shrimp

1 pkg. (10 oz.) frozen peas

1 can (10 oz.) frozen
cream of shrimp
soup, thawed

½ cup milk

2 tbsp. cheese spread

4 tsp. sherry flavoring

4 Toast Cups (below),
patty shells, or
biscuits

Cook shrimp and peas according to pkg. directions; drain. In saucepan, combine soup and milk; add shrimp and peas. Heat and stir just to simmering. Cook slowly about 5 min. Add cheese and sherry flavoring. Keep warm over very low heat. Serve in Toast Cups, patty shells, or over hot biscuits. *4 servings.*

**Toast Cups:** Cut crusts from thinly sliced bread. Brush generously with melted butter. Press into large muffin cups. Toast in 350° (mod.) oven 10 to 15 min.

## FRANKFURTER SUPPER DISH

*See picture opposite.*

6 frankfurters

1 pkg. (10 oz.)
   frozen green beans

1½ cups Medium
   Cream Sauce (p. 103)

½ tsp. Worcestershire
   sauce

¼ cup grated sharp
   cheese

½ cup buttered bread
   crumbs

Heat oven to 375° (quick mod.). Drop franks into boiling water and heat 5 to 6 min. Cut in 1″ pieces. Cook beans half the time directed on pkg. Make Cream Sauce, stirring in Worcestershire sauce. Stir beans and franks into Cream Sauce. Pour into greased 1½-qt. baking dish. Sprinkle with cheese and bread crumbs. Bake 30 min. *6 servings.*

### Budget-Wise Supper
**Frankfurter Supper Dish**
**Sliced Tomato Salad**
**Applesauce Gingerbread (p. 138)**

## EGGS FOO YUNG

1 medium green pepper,
   chopped

1 medium onion,
   chopped

1 can (4½ oz.)
   deveined shrimp,
   chopped

1 can (5 oz.) sliced water
   chestnuts, well drained

1 cup bean sprouts, well
   drained

2 to 3 tbsp. soy sauce

5 eggs

Hot Soy Sauce (below)

Heat just enough fat to cover bottom of skillet. Sauté green pepper and onion until tender. Stir in shrimp, vegetables, and soy sauce. Heat. Remove from heat. Beat eggs until thick, about 5 min. Blend shrimp mixture into eggs. Again heat fat to cover bottom of skillet. Using ladle or cup, pour egg mixture into skillet forming patties. When brown on one side, turn over. Serve with Hot Soy Sauce. *Makes 16 2½″ patties.*

**Hot Soy Sauce:** Make a paste of 2 tbsp. cornstarch and ¼ cup cold water. Stir into 2 cups boiling bouillon or consommé and 2 tbsp. soy sauce. Cook, stirring constantly, until thick and clear.

## DOUBLE-QUICK RAVIOLI CASSEROLE WITH SAUSAGE

1 can (3 oz.) sliced
   mushrooms, drained

2 cans (15½ oz. each)
   ravioli in tomato
   sauce

½ cup catsup

1 green pepper, diced

1 cup grated Cheddar
   cheese (¼ lb.)

1 pkg. (7½ oz.) brown 'n
   serve sausage links or
   patties

Heat oven to 350° (mod.). Combine mushrooms, ravioli, and catsup. Alternate layers of ravioli mixture with green pepper and cheese in greased 1½-qt. baking dish. Cover and bake 30 min. Brown sausage; drain well. Arrange sausage links spoke-fashion or overlap patties atop casserole; return to oven, uncovered, and bake 10 min. more. *8 servings.*

## CHICKEN-WILD RICE CASSEROLE

2 cups cut-up cooked
   chicken

1½ to 2 cups cooked wild
   rice (directions on pkg.)

¼ cup chopped green
   pepper

1 can (10½ oz.) cream
   of mushroom soup

½ soup can milk

salt and pepper

Heat oven to 350° (mod.). Mix all ingredients; place in greased 2-qt. baking dish. Bake 30 min. *6 servings.*

**Note:** *Cooked white or brown rice may be substituted for all or part of the wild rice.*

## PORK CHOP DINNER

4 pork chops, 1″ thick

1 tsp. salt

¼ tsp. pepper

¼ cup water

4 medium potatoes,
   halved

4 medium onions, halved

4 medium carrots, cut
   lengthwise

Trim excess fat from chops (use fat in skillet to brown chops). Brown chops slowly over medium heat, about 15 min. per side. Drain off excess grease. Season chops with salt and pepper. Add water, cover tightly, and simmer over medium low heat for 30 min. Place potatoes, onions, and carrots on top of chops and simmer an additional 30 to 40 min., or until vegetables are tender. *4 servings.*

## DOUBLE-QUICK CONQUISTADOR CHILI

1 can (15½ oz.) chili, without beans

3 tbsp. finely chopped onion

1 can (12 oz.) corn with sweet pepper, drained

½ cup grated Swiss or Cheddar cheese

Heat oven to 350° (mod.). Put chili into 8 or 9" baking dish. Top with onion and corn; sprinkle with cheese. Bake 15 to 20 min., until bubbly. *4 to 6 servings.*

## CHILI CON CARNE

Brown 1 lb. ground beef, ½ lb. bulk pork sausage, and 1 large onion, chopped; crumble meats with fork. Add 1 can (1 lb. 4 oz.) tomatoes, 1 can (1 lb. 4 oz.) kidney beans, 1 to 2 tbsp. chili powder, and ½ to 1 tsp. salt. Simmer 1 hour. *4 servings.*

*Note: For 6 servings, use 2 cans of kidney beans.*

## CHILI ENCHILADAS

*See picture opposite.*

Speedy Tortillas (below)

½ large Bermuda onion, chopped

½ lb. ground beef

1 can (15½ oz.) chili, without beans

¼ tsp. salt

dash of pepper

¼ tsp. crushed red pepper seeds

½ lb. cheese, grated

Heat oven to 350° (mod.). Sauté 2 tbsp. onion and ground beef in a little hot fat. Add chili, salt, pepper, and pepper seeds. Simmer, covered, 10 min. Brush tortillas on both sides with melted butter. Place 1 tbsp. chili mixture, 1 tsp. onion, and 1 tsp. grated cheese in center of each tortilla; roll up. Place filled tortillas in two rows in baking dish, 13x9½x2". Spoon remaining chili mixture over rolled tortillas, being careful to cover each tortilla to keep it soft. Sprinkle remaining chopped onion and cheese over chili. Bake, uncovered, 15 min., or until cheese melts. *4 servings.*

**Speedy Tortillas:** Mix 1 cup Bisquick and ¼ cup water. Knead about 1 min. on board lightly dusted with corn meal. Shape into 8 balls; flatten each ball into a 5" circle. Bake on ungreased griddle until slightly browned on both sides. Keep soft between towels.

## SOUTHERN CHILI BAKE

2 lb. lean ground beef

1½ tbsp. chili powder

½ tsp. monosodium glutamate

1 small clove garlic, crushed, or ⅛ tsp. garlic powder

1¼ tsp. salt

2 cans (8 oz. each) tomato sauce

½ cup chopped green pepper, if desired

Corn Bread Batter (p. 119)

Heat oven to 350° (mod.). Brown beef in 10" skillet over medium heat until pink color disappears. Drain off excess fat. Add seasonings and tomato sauce. Spread mixture evenly in 10" baking dish or skillet. Sprinkle with green pepper. Cover with Corn Bread Batter. Bake 30 to 35 min. *6 to 8 servings.*

## SPANISH SAUCE OVER BUTTERED HOMINY

1 to 2 tbsp. shortening

1 lb. ground beef

1 large onion, finely chopped

1 clove garlic, minced

1 tbsp. chili powder

1 tsp. salt

⅓ cup chopped ripe or stuffed green olives

1 can (1 lb. 13 oz.) tomatoes

¼ cup butter

1 can (1 lb. 13 oz.) or 2 cans (1 lb. each) hominy, drained

Melt shortening in heavy skillet; add ground beef, stirring with fork to break up. Add onion and garlic. Brown meat well. Add chili powder, salt, olives, and tomatoes; blend well. Simmer, uncovered, 1 hr. (At the end of this time, the mixture should be the consistency of a rich sauce with meat in it.) Melt the butter in a saucepan and heat hominy in it. Serve the meat sauce over hominy. *4 to 6 servings.*

**Note:** *Spanish Sauce may also be served over hot cooked rice, macaroni, or noodles.*

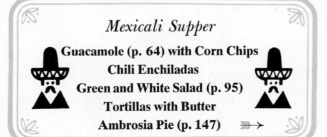

*Mexicali Supper*

Guacamole (p. 64) with Corn Chips

Chili Enchiladas

Green and White Salad (p. 95)

Tortillas with Butter

Ambrosia Pie (p. 147)

## TOPSY-TURVY PIE

| | |
|---|---|
| 1 lb. ground beef | ¼ cup water |
| ½ cup chopped onion | 1 tsp. salt |
| ¼ cup chopped green pepper | 1 tsp. chili powder |
| 1 can (8 oz.) tomato sauce | 1 can (4½ oz.) chopped ripe olives |
| | Biscuit Topping (below) |

Heat oven to 425° (hot). Brown meat in fat. When meat is half browned, add onion and green pepper. Cook, stirring frequently, until meat is well browned and onion is transparent. Add tomato sauce, water, seasonings, and olives; mix well. Pour into 9″ pie pan. Make Biscuit Topping. Roll to fit top of pie pan. Make slits in top; place over meat. Bake 15 to 20 min. Remove from oven and let stand a minute. Invert onto serving plate. Serve in wedges. *6 servings.*

**Biscuit Topping:** Mix 1 cup Bisquick and ⅓ cup cream or ¼ cup milk plus 2 tbsp. butter, melted. Beat 15 strokes On floured board, knead 8 to 10 times.

## CABBAGE PATCH STEW

| | |
|---|---|
| 1 lb. ground beef | 1 cup cooked tomatoes |
| 2 medium onions, sliced thin | 1 tsp. salt |
| 1 cup shredded cabbage | dash of pepper |
| ½ cup diced celery | 1 tsp. chili powder |
| 1 can (1 lb.) red kidney beans | 2 cups hot mashed potatoes |

Brown beef in hot fat over medium heat; add onions, cabbage, and celery; cook until yellow. Add water to cover (about 2 cups); simmer 15 min. Add beans, tomatoes, and seasonings; cook 15 to 25 min. Serve in bowls topped with spoonfuls of mashed potatoes. *6 servings.*

*TO SAVE TIME AND WORK — Use frozen chopped onion. So handy. No "onion" tears.*

### New Ideas Dinner

**Topsy-turvy Pie**
**Corn Sesame Sauté (p. 90)**
**Celery and Carrot Sticks**
**Chip Chocolate Orange Chiffon Cake (p. 132)**

## BEEF CHOW MEIN BAKE

| | |
|---|---|
| 1½ lb. ground round steak | 1 can (10½ oz.) cream of mushroom soup |
| 1½ cups chopped celery | 2 to 3 tbsp. soy sauce |
| 1 medium onion, finely chopped | 1 can (3½ oz.) chopped mushrooms |
| 1 can (10½ oz.) tomato soup | 2 cups chow mein noodles |
| | ½ cup cashew nuts |

Heat oven to 350° (mod.). Brown beef. Add celery and onion; sauté until transparent. Stir in tomato and mushroom soups, soy sauce, and mushrooms. Add 1½ cups noodles. Pour into 2-qt. baking dish. Bake, uncovered, 25 to 30 min. Sprinkle with remaining ½ cup noodles and cashew nuts. Bake, uncovered, an additional 10 min. Serve with hot fluffy rice. *8 servings.*

## STEAK SUPPER IN FOIL

| | |
|---|---|
| 1½ lb. chuck steak, 1″ thick | 4 stalks celery, cut in sticks |
| 1 envelope (1½ oz.) dehydrated onion soup mix | 2 to 3 medium potatoes, quartered |
| 4 medium carrots, quartered | 2 tbsp. butter |
| | ½ tsp. salt |

Heat oven to 450° (hot). Tear off 2½-ft. length of 18″-wide aluminum foil. Place meat in center; sprinkle with soup mix, cover with vegetables. Dot vegetables with butter and sprinkle with salt. Fold foil over and seal securely to hold juices in. Place on baking sheet. Bake 1 to 1½ hr. *4 servings.*

## PEPPER STEAK

| | |
|---|---|
| 1 lb. beef chuck, cut in 3x1″ pieces (about 1″ thick) | 1 cup green pepper, cut in 1″ pieces |
| ¼ cup vegetable oil | 1 cup chopped onions |
| 1 clove garlic, minced | ½ cup chopped celery |
| 1 tbsp. soy sauce | 1 tbsp. cornstarch |
| 1 tsp. salt | 1 cup water |
| ¼ cup water | 2 tomatoes, cut in eighths |
| | 3 to 4 cups cooked rice (1 cup uncooked) |

Brown beef in hot oil; add garlic and cook until yellow. Add soy sauce, salt, and ¼ cup water; cover and cook 45 min. Add all vegetables except tomatoes; cook 10 min. Stir in cornstarch blended with 1 cup water; add tomatoes and cook, without stirring, another 5 min. Serve over hot fluffy rice. *4 servings.*

## CREAMED GROUND BEEF ON BAKED POTATOES

| | |
|---|---|
| ½ cup sliced onions | 1 tsp. salt |
| 1 lb. ground beef | ¼ tsp. pepper |
| 2 tbsp. hot fat | 2 cups milk |
| 3 tbsp. butter | 6 baked potatoes (p. 92) |
| 3 tbsp. flour | |

Brown onions and beef in fat. Season with salt and pepper to taste. Take from skillet. Melt butter in same pan. Add flour, salt, and pepper. Cook over low heat, stirring until smooth and bubbly. Take from heat. Add milk; bring to boil, stirring constantly. Boil 1 min. Add meat. Serve over baked potatoes. *6 servings.*

*Perfect for a Cold Night*

**Creamed Ground Beef
on Baked Potatoes
Buttered Peas and Carrots
Beet Salad (p. 96)
Peach Pie (p. 144)**

## HAMBURGER PIE

| | |
|---|---|
| 1 small onion, chopped | 1 can (1 lb. 4 oz.) green beans |
| 1 lb. ground beef | 1 can (10½ oz.) tomato soup |
| ½ tsp. salt | 2 cups mashed potatoes |
| ¼ tsp. pepper | |
| ½ tsp. monosodium glutamate | |

Heat oven to 350° (mod.). Cook onion in hot fat until yellow; add meat and cook until brown. Add seasonings, drained beans, and soup; pour into 2-qt. baking dish. Spoon mashed potatoes over mixture. Bake 30 min. *6 servings.*

## PORK AND FRUIT SKILLET

| | |
|---|---|
| 6 lean pork chops | 12 cooked prunes, pitted |
| 1 can (13½ oz.) pineapple chunks | 2 tbsp. soy sauce |
| 1 large onion, chopped | ½ tsp. marjoram |
| ¼ cup minced celery leaves | 1 cup diced celery |
| 1 clove garlic, minced | 3 to 4 cups cooked rice (1 cup uncooked) |

Brown chops. Season lightly with salt and pepper. Drain off excess fat. Drain pineapple well; reserve juice. Add all ingredients except diced celery. Cover and simmer over medium heat 20 to 30 min. Add celery and cook 10 min. more, until celery and pork are well done. If mixture seems dry, add a small amount of water. Serve over fluffy white rice. (Use reserved pineapple juice as part of liquid for cooking rice.) *6 servings.*

## VEAL CASSEROLE

| | |
|---|---|
| 1 lb. cubed veal | 1 can (10½ oz.) cream of mushroom soup |
| 1½ cups sliced celery | 1 soup can water |
| 2 small onions, chopped | 2 to 3 tbsp. soy sauce |
| 1 can (10½ oz.) cream of chicken soup | ½ cup uncooked rice |

Heat oven to 325° (slow mod.). Roll meat in flour; brown in hot fat over medium heat; stir in rest of ingredients. Pour into 3-qt. baking dish. Bake, covered, 1½ hr. *6 servings.*

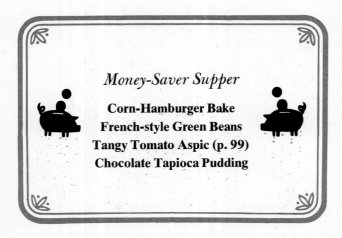

*Money-Saver Supper*

**Corn-Hamburger Bake**
**French-style Green Beans**
**Tangy Tomato Aspic (p. 99)**
**Chocolate Tapioca Pudding**

## CORN-HAMBURGER BAKE

| | |
|---|---|
| 1 large onion, sliced (1 cup) | ¾ cup water or milk |
| 1 lb. ground beef | 1 tsp. salt |
| ¼ cup cut-up celery | ¼ tsp. pepper |
| 2 cans (1 lb. each) cream-style corn (save ½ cup for biscuits) | 1 bouillon cube, if desired |
| | Corn Biscuits (below) |

Heat oven to 425° (hot). Brown onion and ground beef in hot fat. Add rest of ingredients except Biscuits. Bring to boil. Pour boiling meat mixture into 2½-qt. baking dish. Drop Corn Biscuits by tablespoonfuls on top of hot mixture. Bake 25 to 30 min. *8 servings.*

**Corn Biscuits:** Measure 1 cup Gold Medal Flour by dip-level-pour method. Add 1½ tsp. baking powder and 1 tsp. salt. Beat in 1 egg, 2 to 3 tsp. chopped parsley, ½ cup cream-style corn, and 3 tbsp. vegetable oil. Drop into hot mixture.

## BEEF BALL STEW

| | |
|---|---|
| 12 small beef balls (use meat loaf mixture, p. 70) | 6 small potatoes |
| | 1 can (1 lb.) tomatoes (2 cups) |
| 6 small onions | 1 tbsp. salt |
| 4 carrots, sliced | |

Heat oven to 350° (mod.). Shape beef balls; brown in hot fat. Arrange with vegetables and salt in 2-qt. baking dish. Cover and bake 1½ hr. *6 servings.*

## BEEF CRUMBLE ON MUFFIN SQUARES

| | |
|---|---|
| 2 tbsp. chopped onion | 2 cups mixed vegetables |
| 2 tbsp. fat | liquid from vegetables plus water to make 1½ cups |
| 1 lb. ground beef | |
| 1½ tsp. salt | 2 bouillon cubes |
| few grains pepper | 2 tbsp. flour |
| 2 tbsp. chopped green pepper | ¼ cup water |
| | Muffin Squares (p. 119) |

Sauté onion in hot fat over medium heat; add meat and brown. Add seasonings, vegetables, liquid, and bouillon cubes; simmer 15 min. Mix flour and water; slowly blend into mixture, stirring constantly. Cook until thick. Serve over hot split Muffin Squares. *6 to 8 servings.*

## LIMA-CORN BARBECUE

| | |
|---|---|
| 1½ lb. ground beef | 1 tbsp. chili powder |
| 3 tbsp. fat | 1 tbsp. prepared mustard |
| 1 medium onion, chopped | 1 tbsp. Worcestershire sauce |
| 1 medium green pepper, chopped | 1½ tsp. salt |
| 1 can (10½ oz.) tomato soup | 1 can (1 lb.) whole-kernel corn, drained |
| 1 can (1 lb.) baby Lima beans, drained | 1 can (5 oz.) water chestnuts, thinly sliced, if desired |

Brown meat in fat in skillet. Add onion and pepper; cook until just tender. Mix soup, juice from beans, and seasonings. Stir into meat mixture. Cover; cook over slow heat 20 min. Add Lima beans, corn, and water chestnuts. Cook 10 min. more. *6 servings.*

## VEAL SCALLOPINI

| | |
|---|---|
| 1 clove garlic | 2 tbsp. flour |
| 1½ lb. veal, cut thin and in serving pieces | 1½ tsp. salt |
| | ⅛ tsp. pepper |
| ¼ cup vegetable oil | ½ cup water |
| ¾ cup thinly sliced onion | 1 cup tomato sauce (8-oz. can) |
| ¼ lb. mushrooms, sliced, or 1 can (4 oz.) | |

Cook garlic and meat in hot oil until meat is brown. Remove meat and discard garlic. Cook onions and mushrooms in oil until tender. Blend in flour, salt, and pepper; let bubble. Gradually stir in water and tomato sauce; cook until thickened, stirring constantly. Add browned meat and cook 10 min. *4 to 6 servings.*

**For Oven Cookery:** Brown garlic and meat in hot oil; place meat in 1½-qt. baking dish. Make the tomato sauce and pour over. Bake in mod. hot oven (400°) for 15 min.

## EASY LASAGNE

| | |
|---|---|
| 1 lb. ground beef | ¾ tsp. pepper |
| 2 cloves garlic, minced | ½ tsp. oregano |
| 1 can (6 oz.) tomato paste | 1 pkg. (8 oz.) lasagne noodles |
| 1 can (1 lb. 4 oz.) tomatoes (2½ cups) | 1½ cups cut-up Swiss cheese (8 oz.) |
| 1 tsp. salt | 1 carton (12 oz.) cottage cheese |

Brown ground beef and garlic in small amount of fat. Add tomato paste, tomatoes, salt, pepper, and oregano. Cover and simmer 20 min. Cook noodles as directed on pkg. Heat oven to 350° (mod.). Alternate layers of meat sauce, noodles, and cheeses in baking dish, 11½ x 7½ x 1½″, beginning and ending with meat sauce. Bake 20 to 30 min. Sprinkle with grated Parmesan cheese. *6 to 8 servings.*

## FEAST-A PIE

| | |
|---|---|
| Pastry for 8″ One-crust Pie (p. 141) | ½ lb. Mozzarella cheese, grated |
| 4 eggs | ¼ tsp. pepper |
| ¼ cup milk | 1½ tsp. salt |
| ½ cup diced moist salami | ½ tsp. each basil and oregano |
| ½ cup diced pepperoni | |

Heat oven to 425° (hot). Beat eggs and milk together; add meats, cheese, and seasonings; beat well. Pour into pastry-lined pie pan. Bake 35 to 40 min. Serve with Tomato Sauce (p. 103). *6 servings.*

## SPAGHETTI WITH MEAT BALLS

| | |
|---|---|
| Tomato Sauce (below) | 1 clove garlic, cut fine |
| ¾ lb. ground beef | ½ cup milk |
| ¼ lb. ground pork | 2 eggs, beaten |
| 1 cup fine dry bread crumbs | 1½ tsp. salt |
| | ⅛ tsp. pepper |
| ½ cup grated Parmesan cheese | 1 pkg. (8 oz.) spaghetti (cooked) |
| 1 tbsp. minced parsley | |

Prepare Tomato Sauce. Mix rest of ingredients (except spaghetti) lightly and shape into 1″ balls. Brown meat balls on all sides in hot fat. Pour off fat as it collects. Add to sauce 20 min. before sauce is done. Place hot, drained cooked spaghetti on warm platter. Top with Tomato Sauce, surround with meat balls. Serve with grated Parmesan cheese. *4 to 6 servings.*

## TOMATO SAUCE

| | |
|---|---|
| ½ cup chopped onion | 1 can (6 oz.) tomato paste |
| 1 clove garlic, minced | 1 tsp. basil |
| 3 tbsp. olive oil | 2 tbsp. minced parsley |
| 2 cans (1 lb. 4 oz. each) tomatoes, sieved | 2 tsp. salt |
| | ¼ tsp. pepper |
| 1 can (8 oz.) tomato sauce | 1 cup water |

Sauté onion and garlic in olive oil. Add rest of ingredients. Simmer over low heat 1 hr.

## EASY OATMEAL BREAD

*Never baked bread before? Follow this streamlined recipe for sure success. Because it is not kneaded, texture is somewhat coarse but moist and delicious.*

| | |
|---|---|
| ¾ cup boiling water | 1 pkg. active dry yeast |
| ½ cup rolled oats | ¼ cup warm water (not hot—110 to 115°) |
| 3 tbsp. soft shortening | |
| ¼ cup light molasses | 1 egg |
| 2 tsp. salt | 2¾ cups Gold Medal Flour |

Stir together in large mixer bowl boiling water, rolled oats, shortening, molasses, and salt. Cool to lukewarm. Dissolve yeast in warm water. Measure flour by dip-level-pour method. Add yeast, egg, and half the flour to lukewarm mixture. Beat 2 min., medium speed on mixer or 300 vigorous strokes by hand. Scrape sides and bottom of bowl frequently. Add remaining flour and blend in with spoon until smooth. Spread batter evenly in greased loaf pan, 8½x4½x2¾" or 9x5x3". Batter will be sticky. Smooth out top of loaf by flouring hand and patting into shape.

Let rise in warm place (85°) until batter reaches top of 8½" pan or 1" from top of 9" pan, about 1½ hr. (If kitchen is cool, place dough on a rack over a bowl of hot water and cover completely with a towel.)

Heat oven to 375° (quick mod.). Bake 50 to 55 min. To test loaf, tap the top crust; it should sound hollow. Crust will be dark brown. Immediately remove from pan. Place on cooling rack or across bread pans. Brush top with melted butter or shortening. Do not place in direct draft. Cool before cutting. *Makes 1 loaf.*

**Anadama Bread:** Make Easy Oatmeal Bread (above)—except use yellow corn meal in place of rolled oats. Sprinkle dough in pan with a little corn meal and salt before baking.

**Note:** *To use compressed yeast in these recipes and other yeast bread recipes in this book, crumble it into total amount of liquid called for in recipe; liquid should be at 80 to 85°.*

## NO-KNEAD REFRIGERATOR ROLLS

*So handy. Have fresh-baked yeast rolls often. Cut off dough for today's rolls; return rest to refrigerator—it will keep 5 days.*

| | |
|---|---|
| 2 pkg. active dry yeast | 6½ to 7 cups Gold Medal Flour |
| 2 cups warm water (not hot—110 to 115°) | |
| ½ cup sugar | 1 egg |
| 2 tsp. salt | ¼ cup soft shortening |

In mixing bowl, dissolve yeast in warm water. Measure flour by dip-level-pour method. Add sugar, salt, and half the flour to yeast. Beat thoroughly 2 min. Add egg and shortening. Gradually beat in remaining flour until smooth. Cover with damp cloth; place in refrigerator. Punch down occasionally as dough rises in refrigerator. About 2 hr. before baking, cut off amount needed and return remaining dough to refrigerator. Shape (see below) into rolls and place on greased baking sheet. Brush tops with melted butter. Let rise until light (1½ to 2 hr.). If kitchen is cool, place dough on a rack over a bowl of hot water and cover completely with a towel. Heat oven to 400° (mod. hot). Bake 12 to 15 min. *Makes 4 doz. medium rolls.*

**Old-fashioned Biscuits:** Form dough into balls ⅓ size desired. Place close together in a greased round pan.

**Cloverleaf:** Form bits of dough into balls about 1" in diameter. Place 3 balls in each greased muffin cup.

**Picnic Buns:** Use ½ of dough. Divide into 2 parts. Roll each into a 7½" square (½" thick). Cut into 2½" squares. *Makes 18 buns.*

**Crescents:** Roll dough scarcely ¼" thick into a 12" circle. Spread with soft butter. Cut into 16 pie-shaped wedges. Beginning at rounded edge, roll up. Place on pan, point underneath.

## DOUBLE-QUICK DINNER ROLLS

*See picture, pp. 146-147.*

**1 pkg. active dry yeast**
**1 cup warm water (not hot —110 to 115°)**
**2 tbsp. sugar**

**2¼ cups Gold Medal Flour**
**1 tsp. salt**
**1 egg**
**2 tbsp. soft shortening**

In mixing bowl, dissolve yeast in water. Measure flour by dip-level-pour method. Stir sugar, half of flour, and salt into yeast. Beat with a spoon until smooth. Add egg and shortening. Beat in rest of flour until smooth. Scrape down sides of bowl and cover with cloth. Let rise in warm place (85°) until double, about 30 min. If kitchen is cool, place dough on a rack over a bowl of hot water and cover completely with a towel.

Grease 12 large muffin cups. Stir down raised dough. Spoon into muffin cups, filling them ½ full. Again let rise in a warm place until dough reaches top of muffin cups, 20 to 30 min. Heat oven to 400° (mod. hot). Bake 15 to 20 min. *Makes 12 rolls.*

**Seeded Dinner Rolls:** Sprinkle ¼ tsp. poppy or sesame seeds over each Double-quick Dinner Roll (above) after filling muffin cups.

### GARLIC BREAD

*Also delicious with rye or Vienna bread.*

Slice French bread diagonally, not quite through bottom crust. Spread with Garlic Butter (below). Heat loaf at 400° (mod. hot) about 15 min., or until piping hot and crusty. Transfer in loaf shape to basket or bread tray.

**Garlic Butter:** Cream ½ cup (¼ lb.) soft butter with ½ tsp. garlic salt or a few drops garlic juice.

**Onion Bread:** Make Garlic Bread (above)—except spread bread with Onion Butter: cream ½ cup butter with 2 tbsp. minced or grated onion or a few drops onion juice.

### BROWN 'N SERVE ROLLS

Brown 'n serve rolls are available at your neighborhood grocer's. Already raised and partially baked, they need only a few moments' baking to be golden brown and piping hot. Choose cloverleaf rolls, poppy seed rolls, cinnamon rolls, or individual French loaves, to name a few.

### HERB-TOPPED ROLLS

Heat oven to 400° (mod. hot). Brush tops of brown 'n serve rolls with melted butter. Sprinkle lightly with herbs and seasonings of your choice: dried parsley flakes or chives; dill weed; a mixture of 1 tsp. each dried tarragon, sweet basil, and thyme leaves, and ½ tsp. ground sage; onion or garlic salt. Brown in oven 10 to 12 min. Serve immediately.

### RUM-FROSTED ROLLS

Heat oven to 400° (mod. hot). Brush tops of brown 'n serve rolls with melted butter. Brown in oven 10 to 12 min. Brush hot rolls with Rum-flavored Frosting: blend 1½ cups sifted confectioners' sugar, 2 to 3 tbsp. cream, and 1 tsp. rum extract; use just enough cream to make spreading consistency.

## RICH DINNER BISCUITS

| | |
|---|---|
| ¼ cup soft butter or shortening | 2 cups Bisquick |
| | ⅔ cup milk |

Heat oven to 450° (hot). Blend butter into Bisquick. Add milk. Stir with fork into a soft dough. Beat dough vigorously 15 strokes, until stiff and slightly sticky. Roll dough around on cloth-covered board lightly dusted with Bisquick to prevent sticking. Knead gently 8 to 10 times to smooth up dough. Roll out to ½" thick. Biscuits double in size in baking. Dip cutter in Bisquick. Cut close together to save rerolling. Bake on ungreased shiny baking sheet 10 to 15 min.; close together for soft sides, 1" apart for crusty sides. *Makes twelve 2" biscuits.*

## BUTTER DIPS

| | |
|---|---|
| ¼ cup butter | 2 tsp. baking powder |
| 1½ cups Gold Medal Flour | 1 tsp. salt |
| 2 tsp. sugar | ⅔ cup milk |

Heat oven to 450° (hot). Melt butter in 9" sq. pan in oven. Remove pan as soon as butter is melted. Measure flour by dip-level-pour method. Stir dry ingredients together into bowl. Add milk. Stir slowly with fork until dough clings together (about 30 strokes). Turn out on well-floured board. Roll over to coat with flour. Knead lightly about 10 times. Roll out ½" thick into an 8" square. With floured knife, cut dough in half lengthwise, then crosswise to make 18 sticks.

Dip each stick in butter on both sides and lay close together in two rows in pan. Bake 15 to 20 min., until golden brown. Serve hot. *Makes 18 sticks.*

**Garlic Butter Dips:** Just before baking, sprinkle buttered sticks with garlic salt.

**Cheese Butter Dips:** Add ¼ cup grated sharp Cheddar cheese to dry ingredients.

### FOR VARIETY

Your baker can supply you with delicious breads and rolls in fascinating variety. For informal dinners, arrange a plate of assorted rolls. For a more formal dinner, the plainer the rolls, the more style they have.

*DOUBLE-QUICK MUFFINS — When dinner needs an extra something, or when there's an unexpected guest, add a festive touch with piping-hot muffins. In the oven in a minute with our packaged muffin mixes. Pick the family's favorite flavor and try your own variations. Or try one of the special breads below.*

## NUT CRUNCH MUFFINS

Prepare batter for our raisin bran or date muffin mix as directed. Before baking, sprinkle over tops a mixture of ⅓ cup brown sugar, ⅓ cup broken nuts, and ½ tsp. cinnamon. *Makes 12 muffins.*

## SESAME CHEESE CORN BREAD

Heat oven to 400° (mod. hot). Blend 1 egg and 1 cup milk in bowl. Add 1 cup grated sharp Cheddar cheese, ½ tsp. salt, and 1 pkg. (14 oz.) of our corn muffin mix. Stir with fork until blended; batter will be slightly lumpy. Pour into 8 or 9" sq. pan. Sprinkle with 3 tbsp. sesame seeds. Bake 20 to 25 min. *9 to 12 servings.*

## UPSIDE-DOWN ORANGE PUFFS

Heat oven to 400° (mod. hot). Follow directions on our orange muffin mix pkg. for 12 muffins. Place 1 tsp. orange marmalade in bottom of 12 greased muffin cups. Fill cups ½ full of batter. Bake 15 to 20 min. Cool slightly before serving. Serve upside-down. *Makes 12 muffins.*

## QUICK BLUEBERRY NUT LOAF

Heat oven to 375° (quick mod.). Grease a loaf pan, 8½ x 4½ x 2¾". Follow pkg. directions for our wild blueberry muffin mix—except use ⅔ cup milk and add 1 cup chopped nuts. Pour batter into a prepared pan. Bake 45 to 50 min. Store a day before slicing.

## POPOVERS

*See picture, p.98.*

| 1 cup Gold Medal Flour | 1 cup milk |
| ½ tsp. salt | 2 eggs |

Heat oven to 425° (hot). Measure flour by dip-level-pour method. Beat ingredients together with rotary beater just until smooth. Overbeating will reduce volume. Pour into well-greased deep muffin cups (¾ full) or oven-glass cups (½ full). Bake 40 to 45 min., until golden brown. If not baked long enough, they will collapse. Serve at once. *Makes 5 to 9 popovers.*

## BOSTON BROWN BREAD

Rich and tasty with baked beans. Save time by buying it in cans at your grocer's or baker's.

Remove one end of can and loosen the loaf around top of can with a spatula; loaf will then slip out easily.

To heat, cut loaf in even slices with thin, sharp knife; then pile slices back into can. Heat in the uncovered can in same oven in which beans are baking.

Slices of Boston Brown Bread may also be heated in top of double boiler, covered, over hot water. Or they may be toasted lightly, just to warm them through.

## CORN BREAD

| 1 egg | 2 tbsp. sugar |
| 1 cup plus 2 tbsp. milk | 3 tsp. baking powder |
| ½ cup Gold Medal Flour | 1 tsp. salt |
| 1 cup yellow corn meal | 3 tbsp. soft shortening (bacon fat adds flavor) |

Heat oven to 450° (hot). Grease generously 12 muffin cups or corn stick pans or a sq. pan, 9x9x1¾". Heat in oven while mixing batter. Beat egg. Measure flour by dip-level-pour method. Beat all ingredients with rotary beater just until smooth. Pour batter into hot pans until almost full. Bake 10 to 15 min. for corn sticks or muffins, 20 to 25 min. for corn bread. Serve piping hot. *12 servings.*

**Cheese Corn Bread:** Make Corn Bread (above)—except use 2 eggs, decrease milk to ¾ cup, decrease sugar to 1 tsp., and add ⅔ cup grated sharp Cheddar cheese.

## OATMEAL MUFFINS

| 2 tbsp. sugar | 2 cups Bisquick |
| 1 egg | ¾ cup rolled oats |
| ¾ cup milk | |

Heat oven to 400° (mod. hot). Mix all ingredients until blended. Beat vigorously 30 seconds. Fill well-greased muffin cups ⅔ full. Bake 15 min. *Makes 12 muffins.*

**Note:** *For richer muffins, add 2 tbsp. melted shortening or vegetable oil and another 2 tbsp. sugar.*

## CHEESE BREAD

| 1 egg | ¾ cup grated natural |
| 1½ cups milk | sharp cheese, such as |
| 3¾ cups Bisquick | Cheddar |

Heat oven to 350° (mod.). Beat egg and add milk. Stir in Bisquick and cheese. Beat 30 seconds, until well blended. Pour into well-greased waxed-paper-lined loaf pan, 9x5x3". Bake 1 hr. Let cool a few min. Slice ½" thick and serve hot. Wrap remaining bread and refrigerate.

**Garlic Cheese Bread:** Use Cheese Bread (above) to make Garlic Bread (p. 117).

## MUFFIN SQUARES

| 2 cups Bisquick | 1 egg |
| ¼ tsp. dry mustard | 2 tbsp. sugar |
| ⅛ tsp. poultry seasoning | ¾ cup milk |

Heat oven to 400° (mod. hot). Blend all ingredients just until dry ingredients are moistened (batter will be lumpy). Bake in greased 8" sq. pan 20 min. Cut into squares.

## CHOCOLATE CHIP COOKIES

*See picture, pp. 50-51.*

| | |
|---|---|
| ⅔ cup soft shortening (part butter) | 1½ cups Gold Medal Flour |
| ½ cup granulated sugar | ½ tsp. soda |
| ½ cup brown sugar (packed) | ½ tsp. salt |
| | ½ cup chopped nuts |
| 1 egg | 1 pkg. (6 oz.) semi-sweet chocolate pieces |
| 1 tsp. vanilla | |

Heat oven to 375° (quick mod.). Mix shortening, sugars, egg, and vanilla thoroughly. Measure flour by dip-level-pour method. Mix flour, soda, and salt; blend in thoroughly. Add nuts and chocolate pieces. With teaspoon, drop 2" apart on ungreased baking sheet. Bake 8 to 10 min., or until delicately browned. Cool slightly before removing from baking sheet. *Makes 5 doz. cookies.*

**Chocolate Chip Bars:** Spread dough for Chocolate Chip Cookies (above) evenly in oblong pan, 13x9½x2". Bake 20 to 25 min. *Makes 48 bars.*

## CHOCOLATE-COCONUT FILLED COOKIES

| | |
|---|---|
| 1 cup soft shortening | 2¼ cups Gold Medal Flour |
| 1 cup sugar | 1 tsp. salt |
| 2 eggs | ½ tsp. soda |
| 1 tsp. vanilla | 2 large chocolate-coated coconut candy bars (4 pieces) |

Heat oven to 375° (quick mod.). Mix shortening, sugar, eggs, and vanilla. Measure flour by dip-level-pour method. Mix flour, salt, and soda; blend in thoroughly. Cut each small half of candy bar into 12 pieces. Drop teaspoonfuls of dough onto ungreased baking sheet. Place piece of candy on dough. Drop half teaspoon dough on candy. Bake 10 to 12 min., or until lightly browned. *Makes 4 doz. cookies.*

## BANANA SPICE COOKIES

| | |
|---|---|
| ½ cup soft shortening | 2 tsp. baking powder |
| 1 cup brown sugar (packed) | ¼ tsp. soda |
| | ¼ tsp. salt |
| 2 eggs | ½ tsp. cinnamon |
| 1 cup mashed bananas (about 2) | ¼ tsp. cloves |
| | ½ cup chopped nuts |
| 2 cups Gold Medal Flour | |

Mix well shortening, sugar, and eggs. Stir in bananas. Measure flour by dip-level-pour method. Mix dry ingredients and stir in. Blend in nuts. Chill about 1 hr. Heat oven to 375° (quick mod.). Drop rounded tablespoonfuls 2" apart on lightly greased baking sheet. Bake 8 to 10 min. Frost with thin confectioners' sugar icing. *Makes 3 to 4 doz. cookies.*

## APPLESAUCE COOKIES

| | |
|---|---|
| 1 cup soft shortening | 1 tsp. soda |
| 2 cups brown sugar (packed) | 1 tsp. salt |
| | 1 tsp. nutmeg |
| 2 eggs | 1 tsp. cinnamon |
| ½ cup cold coffee | 1 tsp. cloves |
| 2 cups well-drained thick applesauce | 1 cup cut-up raisins |
| | ½ cup coarsely chopped nuts |
| 3½ cups Gold Medal Flour | |

Mix shortening, sugar, and eggs thoroughly. Stir in coffee and applesauce. Measure flour by dip-level-pour method. Mix dry ingredients and stir in. Blend in raisins and nuts. Chill at least 2 hr. Heat oven to 400° (mod. hot). Drop rounded tablespoonfuls about 2" apart on lightly greased baking sheet. Bake 9 to 12 min., until set, and when touched lightly with finger almost no imprint remains. When cool, frost with Lemon Butter Icing (p. 133), if desired. *Makes 7 to 8 doz. cookies.*

## STIR-N-DROP SUGAR COOKIES

2 eggs

⅔ cup vegetable
  oil

2 tsp. vanilla

1 tsp. grated lemon
  rind

¾ cup sugar

2 cups Gold Medal Flour

2 tsp. baking powder

½ tsp. salt

Heat oven to 400° (mod. hot). Beat eggs with fork until well blended. Stir in oil, vanilla, and lemon rind. Blend in sugar until mixture thickens. Measure flour by dip-level-pour method. Mix flour, baking powder, and salt; blend into oil mixture. Drop by teaspoonfuls about 2″ apart onto ungreased baking sheet. Gently press each cooky flat with the bottom of a glass that has been moistened and dipped in sugar. (Continue dipping in sugar before flattening each cooky.) Bake 8 to 10 min., or until a delicate brown. Remove immediately from baking sheet. *Makes 4 doz. 2½″ cookies.*

## BROWN SUGAR DROPS

1 cup soft shortening

2 cups brown sugar
  (packed)

2 eggs

½ cup soured milk,
  buttermilk, or water

3½ cups Gold Medal
  Flour

1 tsp. soda

1 tsp. salt

Mix shortening, sugar, and eggs thoroughly. Stir in liquid. Measure flour by dip-level-pour method. Mix dry ingredients and blend in. Chill at least 1 hr. Heat oven to 400° (mod. hot). Drop rounded teaspoonfuls about 2″ apart on lightly greased baking sheet. Bake 8 to 10 min., or until almost no imprint remains when touched lightly with finger. *Makes about 6 doz. 2½″ cookies.*

## CHOCOLATE DROP COOKIES

½ cup soft shortening
  (part butter)

1 cup sugar

1 egg

2 sq. unsweetened
  chocolate (2 oz.),
  melted and cooled

¾ cup buttermilk or
  soured milk

1 tsp. vanilla

1¾ cups Gold Medal
  Flour

½ tsp. soda

½ tsp. salt

1 cup cut-up pecans or
  other nuts, if desired

Mix shortening, sugar, egg, and melted chocolate thoroughly. Stir in buttermilk and vanilla. Measure flour by dip-level-pour method. Stir dry ingredients together and blend into chocolate mixture. Mix in nuts and chill dough at least 1 hr. Heat oven to 400° (mod. hot). Drop rounded teaspoonfuls about 2″ apart on lightly greased baking sheet. Bake 8 to 10 min., or just until no imprint remains when lightly touched. If desired, frost with Chocolate Butter Icing or Browned Butter Icing (p. 133). *Makes about 3½ doz. 2½″ cookies.*

**Cocoa Drop Cookies:** Make Chocolate Drop Cookies (above)—except omit chocolate and add ½ cup cocoa to dry ingredients.

## OATMEAL DROP COOKIES

½ cup soft shortening

1¼ cups sugar

2 eggs

⅓ cup molasses

1¾ cups Gold Medal
  Flour

1 tsp. soda

1 tsp. salt

1 tsp. cinnamon

2 cups rolled oats

½ cup chopped nuts

1 cup raisins

Heat oven to 400° (mod. hot). Mix shortening, sugar, eggs, and molasses thoroughly. Measure flour by dip-level-pour method. Stir dry ingredients together and blend in. Stir in rolled oats, nuts, and raisins. Drop by rounded teaspoonfuls about 2″ apart onto lightly greased baking sheet. Bake 8 to 10 min., or until lightly browned. *Makes about 6 doz. 2½″ cookies.*

## PLANTATION FRUIT BARS

| | |
|---|---|
| ¼ cup soft shortening | ½ tsp. salt |
| ½ cup sugar | ¼ tsp. soda |
| 1 egg | 1½ tsp. baking powder |
| ½ cup molasses | 1½ cups raisins or cut-up dates |
| ½ cup milk | 1 cup chopped nuts |
| 2 cups Gold Medal Flour | |

Heat oven to 350° (mod. hot). Mix shortening, sugar, egg, molasses, and milk thoroughly. Measure flour by dip-level-pour method. Mix dry ingredients and stir in. Spread evenly in lightly greased oblong pan, 13x9½x 2". Bake about 25 min. While slightly warm, frost with Easy Creamy Icing (p. 133). Cut into bars. *Makes about 4 doz. bars.*

## CANDY-TOPPED OATMEAL BARS

| | |
|---|---|
| 1 cup butter | 1 cup Gold Medal Flour |
| ½ cup brown sugar (packed) | 1 cup rolled oats |
| ½ cup granulated sugar | 6 chocolate bars (1 oz. each) |
| 2 egg yolks | 2 tbsp. butter |
| | ½ cup chopped nuts |

Heat oven to 350° (mod.). Mix butter, sugars, and egg yolks thoroughly. Measure flour by dip-level-pour method. Stir in flour and oats. Spread in greased and floured oblong pan, 13x9½x2". Bake 20 to 25 min. Cool 10 min. Melt chocolate and butter over hot water; spread over cooled cooky layer. Sprinkle with nuts; cut into bars. *Makes 4 doz. bars.*

## BROWNIES

| | |
|---|---|
| 2 sq. unsweetened chocolate (2 oz.) | 2 eggs |
| | ¾ cup Gold Medal Flour |
| ⅓ cup soft shortening or vegetable oil | ½ tsp. baking powder |
| | ½ tsp. salt |
| 1 cup sugar | ½ cup broken nuts |

Heat oven to 350° (mod.). Melt chocolate and shortening together over hot water. Beat in sugar and eggs. Measure flour by dip-level-pour method. Mix dry ingredients and stir in. Mix in nuts. Spread in well-greased square pan, 8x8x2". Bake 30 to 35 min., or until top has dull crust. Cool slightly, then cut into 2" squares. *Makes 16 brownies.*

**Chocolate-frosted Brownies:** Spread Brownies (above), with ½ recipe Chocolate Butter Icing (p. 133).

## PEPPERMINT TEA BROWNIES

*See picture, pp. 50-51.*

Make batter for Brownies (above). Spread in greased and floured oblong pan, 13x9½x2". Bake 20 min. at 350°. Immediately remove from pan. When cool, cut the brownies in half crosswise, making 2 layers about 9½x6½". Spread Peppermint Icing (below) over one oblong layer. Top with other layer. Cut into 2x1" bars. *Makes 2½ doz. brownies.*

**Peppermint Icing:** Mix 1 cup sifted confectioners' sugar, 1 tsp. soft butter, 1⅓ tbsp. milk, and ⅛ tsp. peppermint extract. If desired, tint a delicate green.

## BUTTERSCOTCH BROWNIES

| | |
|---|---|
| ¼ cup butter, soft shortening, or vegetable oil | ¾ cup Gold Medal Flour |
| | 1 tsp. baking powder |
| | ½ tsp. salt |
| 1 cup light brown sugar (packed) | ½ tsp. vanilla |
| | ½ cup coarsely chopped walnuts |
| 1 egg | |

Heat oven to 350° (mod.). Grease an 8" sq. pan. Melt butter over low heat. Remove from heat. Mix in brown sugar until blended; cool. Stir in egg. Measure flour by dip-level-pour method. Mix flour, baking powder, and salt; stir in. Blend in vanilla and walnuts. Spread in prepared pan. Bake 25 min. Do not overbake. Cut into bars while warm. *Makes 18 bars about 2½x1".*

## CRUNCHY NUT COOKIES

| | |
|---|---|
| 1 cup granulated sugar | 3 cups Gold Medal Flour |
| 1 cup brown sugar | |
| ½ cup soft shortening | 1 tsp. soda |
| 2 eggs | ½ tsp. salt |
| 1 tsp. vanilla | 1 cup chopped nuts |

Heat oven to 375° (quick mod.). Mix thoroughly sugars, shortening, eggs, and vanilla. Measure flour by dip-level-pour method. Mix flour, soda, and salt; stir in. Add nuts. Form into balls the size of small walnuts (1 level tbsp.). Place on ungreased baking sheet. Flatten with bottom of greased glass dipped in sugar. Bake 8 to 10 min. *Makes about 5 doz. cookies.*

## SNICKERDOODLES

| | |
|---|---|
| 1 cup soft shortening (part butter) | 2 tsp. cream of tartar |
| 1½ cups sugar | 1 tsp. soda |
| 2 eggs | ¼ tsp. salt |
| 2¾ cups Gold Medal Flour | 2 tbsp. sugar |
| | 2 tsp. cinnamon |

Heat oven to 400° (mod. hot). Mix shortening, sugar, and eggs thoroughly. Measure flour by dip-level-pour method. Mix flour, cream of tartar, soda, and salt; stir in. Form into balls the size of small walnuts. Roll balls in mixture of the 2 tbsp. sugar and cinnamon. Place about 2″ apart on ungreased baking sheet. Bake 8 to 10 min. *Makes about 6 doz. cookies.*

## CHOCOLATE OATMEAL BONBONS

| | |
|---|---|
| ½ cup soft shortening (half butter) | 1½ tsp. vanilla |
| 1 cup sugar | ¾ cup Gold Medal Flour |
| 1 egg | 1 tsp. baking powder |
| 2 sq. unsweetened chocolate (2 oz.), melted | ½ tsp. salt |
| | 1¼ cups rolled oats |

Mix shortening, sugar, and egg thoroughly. Stir in chocolate and vanilla. Measure flour by dip-level-pour method. Mix dry ingredients and stir in. Add oats. Chill dough. Heat oven to 350°. Roll dough into walnut-size balls. Place 2″ apart on greased baking sheet. Bake 10 to 12 min. *Makes 4½ doz. bonbons.*

## PEANUT BUTTER COOKIES

*See picture, pp. 50-51.*

| | |
|---|---|
| ½ cup soft shortening (half butter) | 1 egg |
| ½ cup peanut butter | 1¼ cups Gold Medal Flour |
| ½ cup granulated sugar | ½ tsp. baking powder |
| ½ cup brown sugar (packed) | ¾ tsp. soda |
| | ¼ tsp. salt |

Mix shortening, peanut butter, sugars, and egg thoroughly. Measure flour by dip-level-pour method. Mix rest of ingredients and stir in. Chill dough. Heat oven to 375° (quick mod.). Roll dough into balls the size of large walnuts. Place 3″ apart on lightly greased baking sheet. Flatten, crisscross fashion, with a fork dipped in flour. Bake 10 to 12 min., or until set but not hard. *Makes about 3 doz. 2½″ cookies.*

## CHOCOLATE CRINKLES

*See picture, pp. 50-51.*

| | |
|---|---|
| ½ cup vegetable oil | 2 cups Gold Medal Flour |
| 4 sq. unsweetened chocolate (4 oz.), melted | ½ tsp. salt |
| 2 cups sugar | 2 tsp. baking powder |
| 4 eggs | 1 cup confectioners' sugar |
| 2 tsp. vanilla | |

Mix oil, chocolate, and sugar. Blend in one egg at a time until well mixed. Add vanilla. Measure flour by dip-level-pour method. Stir in salt, flour, and baking powder. Chill several hours or overnight. Heat oven to 350° (mod.). Drop teaspoonfuls of dough into confectioners' sugar. Roll around and shape into a ball. Place about 2″ apart on greased baking sheet. Bake 10 to 12 min. *Makes about 6 doz. cookies.*

## CARAMEL NUT SLICES

½ cup soft shortening
(part butter)

1 cup brown sugar
(packed)

1 egg

½ tsp. vanilla

1¾ cups Gold Medal
Flour

¼ tsp. salt

½ tsp. soda

1 cup finely chopped
nuts

Mix shortening, sugar, egg, and vanilla thoroughly. Measure flour by dip-level-pour method. Mix flour, salt, and soda; stir in. Blend in nuts. Form into two rolls, 2″ in diameter. Wrap in waxed paper and chill overnight. Heat oven to 400° (mod. hot). Cut slices ⅛″ thick; place a little apart on ungreased baking sheet. Bake 8 to 10 min., until set but not hard. *Makes 6½ doz. cookies.*

**Chocolate Slices:** Make Caramel Nut Slices (above)—except add 1½ sq. unsweetened chocolate (1½ oz.), melted, with the shortening. Put cooled baked slices together with icing. *Makes 3 doz. filled cookies.*

## OLD-FASHIONED
## SOUR CREAM COOKIES

½ cup shortening
(part butter)

1 cup sugar

1 egg

1 tsp. vanilla

2⅔ cups Gold Medal
Flour

1 tsp. baking powder

½ tsp. soda

½ tsp. salt

¼ tsp. nutmeg

½ cup commercial
sour cream

Heat oven to 425° (hot). Mix thoroughly shortening, sugar, egg, and vanilla. Measure flour by dip-level-pour method. Mix dry ingredients and add to creamed mixture alternately with sour cream. Divide dough and roll out to ¼″ thick on well-floured pastry cloth. Cut with 2″ cutter; place on greased baking sheet. Sprinkle with sugar. Bake 8 to 10 min., or until delicately golden. *Makes 4 to 5 doz. 2″ cookies.*

## SUMMER PASTELS

*See picture, pp. 50-51.*

2 cups soft butter

2 cups sifted con-
fectioners' sugar

4½ cups Gold Medal
Flour

½ tsp. salt

Mix butter, sugar, and salt thoroughly. Measure flour by dip-level-pour method. Add flour and blend with hands. If dough is dry, add 1 to 2 tbsp. cream. Divide dough into thirds. Add a different food coloring and flavoring from the variations listed below to each third. Mold into 3 long, smooth rolls, about 2″ in diameter. Place on waxed paper and roll in trim. Wrap tightly and chill until stiff (several hours or overnight). Heat oven to 375° (quick mod.). Slice cookies ⅛″ thick. Place on ungreased baking sheet. Bake 7 to 9 min. Do not brown. *Makes about 10 doz. cookies.*

**Green Cookies:** Add 2 tbsp. grated lemon rind, few drops green food coloring. Roll in nonpareils.

**Yellow Cookies:** Add 2 tbsp. grated orange rind, few drops yellow food coloring. Roll in finely chopped nuts.

**Pink Cookies:** Add ½ to 1 tsp. peppermint flavoring, few drops red food coloring. Roll in red crystal sugars.

**Chocolate on Chocolate:** Add 2 sq. semi-sweet chocolate (2 oz.), melted. Roll in chocolate shot.

## DATE COCONUT BALLS

2 cups walnuts

1 cup pitted dates

1 cup brown sugar

2½ cups coconut

2 eggs, slightly
beaten

Heat oven to 350° (mod.). Grind walnuts and dates in food chopper or chop very fine by hand. Add sugar, 1 cup coconut, and eggs; mix well. Drop by teaspoonfuls into remaining coconut. Shape into balls. Bake on lightly greased baking sheet 15 min. *Makes 4 to 5 doz.*

## LOVELIGHT YELLOW CHIFFON CAKE

| | |
|---|---|
| 2 eggs, separated | 1/3 cup vegetable oil |
| 1½ cups sugar | 1 cup milk |
| 2¼ cups Softasilk Cake Flour | 1½ tsp. flavoring |
| 3 tsp. baking powder | Clear Orange Filling (below) |
| 1 tsp. salt | |

Heat oven to 350° (mod.). Grease generously and dust with flour two round layer pans, 8 or 9x1½".

Beat egg whites until frothy. Gradually beat in ½ cup of the sugar. Continue beating until very stiff and glossy. Set this meringue aside. Measure flour by spoon-level-pour method. Stir rest of sugar, flour, baking powder, and salt together in another bowl. Add oil, half of milk, and flavoring. Beat 1 min. medium speed on mixer or 150 strokes by hand. Scrape sides and bottom of bowl constantly. Add rest of milk and egg yolks. Beat 1 more min., scraping bowl constantly. Fold in meringue. Pour into prepared pans. Bake layers 30 to 35 min., until top springs back when lightly touched. Remove from pans. Cool. Spread Clear Orange Filling between layers. Frost sides and top with our fluffy white frosting mix.

## CLEAR ORANGE FILLING

| | |
|---|---|
| 1 cup sugar | 2 tbsp. butter |
| ¼ cup cornstarch | 2 tbsp. grated orange rind |
| ½ tsp. salt | 2 tbsp. lemon juice |
| 1 cup orange juice | |

Mix sugar, cornstarch, and salt in saucepan. Gradually stir in orange juice. Bring to boil over direct heat, stirring constantly. Boil 1 min. Remove from heat; stir in butter and rind. Gradually add lemon juice. Cool thoroughly.

## DATE CAKE

| | |
|---|---|
| 1¼ cups cut-up dates | 1 tsp. vanilla |
| 1 cup boiling water | 1½ cups Gold Medal Flour |
| 1 tbsp. butter | 1 tsp. soda |
| 1 cup sugar | ½ cup chopped nuts |
| 1 egg | Date Topping (below) |

Heat oven to 350° (mod.). Grease and flour a 9" sq. pan. Combine dates, boiling water, and butter in mixer bowl. Measure flour by dip-level-pour method. Add sugar, egg, vanilla, flour, and soda. Beat 2 min., low speed on mixer or 300 vigorous strokes by hand. Blend in nuts. Pour into prepared pan. Bake about 30 min. Cool slightly. Spread with cooled Date Topping.

**Date Topping:** Mix ½ cup sugar, ¼ cup water, and ½ cup dates, cut up. Boil 2 min. Add ½ cup nuts.

## DATE CRUMB CAKE

*Delightful as a dessert or as a coffee cake.*

Make Date Cake (above)—except just beat with spoon until ingredients are thoroughly blended. Sprinkle Crumb Topping (below) over batter. Bake about 40 min. Cool slightly. Omit Date Topping.

**Crumb Topping:** Mix with fingers 2 tbsp. butter, ¼ cup Gold Medal Flour, ¼ cup sugar, and ½ cup chopped nuts until mixture resembles coarse meal.

## EGG YOLK SPONGE CAKE

| | |
|---|---|
| ¾ cup Softasilk Flour | ½ cup sugar |
| 1 tsp. baking powder | ¼ cup boiling water |
| ¼ tsp. salt | 1 tsp. vanilla |
| 3 egg yolks (¼ cup) | ½ tsp. lemon flavoring |

Heat oven to 350° (mod.). Grease and flour one layer pan, 8 or 9x1½", or an 8" sq. pan, or one loaf pan, 8½x4½x2¾". Measure flour by spoon-level-pour method. Mix flour, baking powder, and salt; set aside. Beat egg yolks in small mixer bowl until very thick and lemon colored. Beat in sugar. Blend in water and flavorings, then dry ingredients. Pour into pans. Bake layer or square cake about 25 min., loaf about 30 min., or until top springs back when touched lightly. Let cool upright in pans 8 to 10 min., then remove.

## NEW FUDGE CAKE

| | |
|---|---|
| 1¾ cups Gold Medal Flour | 1½ cups milk |
| 2 cups sugar | 1 tsp. vanilla |
| 2 tsp. baking powder | 2 eggs (⅓ to ½ cup) |
| ¼ tsp. soda | 4 sq. unsweetened chocolate (4 oz.), melted |
| 1 tsp. salt | 1 cup chopped nuts |
| ¼ cup soft shortening | |

Heat oven to 350° (mod.). Grease and flour two layer pans, 8 or 9x1½″, or an oblong pan, 13x9½x2″. Measure flour by dip-level-pour method. Stir together flour, sugar, baking powder, soda, and salt. Add shortening, milk, and vanilla. Beat 2 min., medium speed on mixer or 300 vigorous strokes by hand. Scrape sides and bottom of bowl constantly. Add eggs and chocolate. Beat 2 more min., scraping bowl frequently. Stir in nuts. Pour into prepared pans. Bake layers 35 to 40 min., oblong 40 to 45 min., or until cake tests done. Cool. Ice with a fudge frosting.

## YELLOW CAKE

| | |
|---|---|
| 2 cups Softasilk Flour | ⅓ cup soft shortening |
| 1¼ cups sugar | 1 cup milk |
| 2½ tsp. baking powder | 1 tsp. vanilla |
| 1 tsp. salt | 1 egg (¼ cup) |

Heat oven to 350° (mod.). Grease and flour two layer pans, 8x1½″, or one 9″ sq. pan. Measure flour by spoon-level-pour method. Mix flour, sugar, baking powder, and salt. Add shortening, ⅔ of milk, and vanilla. Beat 2 min., medium speed on mixer or 300 vigorous strokes by hand. Scrape sides and bottom of bowl constantly. Add rest of milk and the egg. Beat 2 more min., scraping bowl frequently. Pour into prepared pans. Bake layers about 30 min., square 30 to 35 min., or until cake tests done. Cool. Frost the layers with White Butter Icing (p. 133) and sprinkle with toasted flaked coconut. Finish the square cake with an easy broiled topping.

## GOLDEN SPICE LOAF

| | |
|---|---|
| 2 cups Gold Medal Flour | ⅔ cup soft shortening (half butter) |
| 1⅓ cups sugar | 1 cup milk |
| 2½ tsp. baking powder | 6 egg yolks |
| ¾ tsp. salt | 1 tsp. vanilla |
| ¾ tsp. mace or nutmeg | |

Heat oven to 350° (mod.). Grease well and lightly flour a loaf pan, 9x5x3″. Measure flour by dip-level-pour method. In a large bowl combine flour, sugar, baking powder, salt, and mace. Add shortening, milk, egg yolks, and vanilla. Beat 3 min., medium speed on electric mixer or 450 vigorous strokes by hand. Pour batter into prepared pan. Bake 65 to 70 min., or until cake tests done. Cool in pan 10 min., then turn out onto rack to finish cooling.

> *USE RIPE BANANAS—Bananas should be medium yellow with brown flecks on the skins, but firm inside. Green-tipped bananas aren't ripe. Never put bananas in the refrigerator.*

## BANANA-NUT CAKE

| | |
|---|---|
| 2½ cups Softasilk Flour | ⅔ cup buttermilk |
| 1⅔ cups sugar | 1¼ cups mashed ripe bananas (about 3) |
| 1¼ tsp. baking powder | 3 eggs (½ to ⅔ cup) |
| 1¼ tsp. soda | ⅔ cup finely chopped nuts |
| 1 tsp. salt | |
| ⅔ cup soft shortening | |

Heat oven to 350° (mod.). Grease and flour two layer pans, 9x1½″, or an oblong pan, 13x9½x2″. Measure flour by spoon-level-pour method. Mix flour, sugar, baking powder, soda, and salt. Add shortening, half of buttermilk, and mashed bananas. Beat 2 min., medium speed on mixer or 300 vigorous strokes by hand. Scrape sides and bottom of bowl constantly. Add eggs and rest of buttermilk. Beat 2 more min., scraping bowl frequently. Fold in nuts. Pour into prepared pans. Bake layers about 35 min., oblong 45 to 50 min., or until cake tests done. Cool. Finish with Butter Icing (p. 133) or "frost" with whipped cream and decorate with banana slices.

# Angel Food Cake

*Fluffy, high, and deliciously tender. Many prefer this cake uniced. Just follow the easy directions on packages of our angel food cake mixes. Whipped cream toppings (p. 135) and butter icings (p. 133) make a beautiful finish.*

### ALMOND ANGEL REFRIGERATOR DESSERT

Bake Angel Food Cake as directed. Cook 1 pkg. (3½ oz.) vanilla pudding and pie filling as directed on package. Add 1 tsp. almond flavoring; cool. Fold in 1 cup whipping cream, whipped, and 1 can (13½ oz.) pineapple tidbits, drained. Reserve half of cooled cake for later use. Tear remainder into small pieces; arrange in baking dish, 11½x7½x1½". Pour whipped cream mixture over pieces. Garnish with toasted slivered almonds and chopped drained maraschino cherries. Cover and chill several hours or overnight. *8 to 10 servings.*

**Note:** *Lemon Chiffon Cake may be substituted for the Angel Food Cake—it makes an equally delicious dessert.*

### CRANBERRY ANGEL CAKE

Bake Angel Food Cake as directed. Split cooled cake, making 3 layers. Spread half of 1 jar (14 oz.) cranberry-orange relish between each layer. Whip 1½ cups whipping cream with ⅓ cup sifted confectioners' sugar; tint with red food coloring, if desired. Frost sides and top of cake. Chill several hours before serving.

### RED, WHITE, AND BLUE CAKE

Bake Angel Food Cake as directed. Cool. Remove from pan and dust top of cake with sifted confectioners' sugar. Serve wedges of cake with fresh raspberries (or strawberries) and blueberries; top with sweetened whipped cream.

### ICE CREAM SANDWICHES

Bake Angel Loaves (below). Cool. Cut cake crosswise into ½" slices. Cut each slice in half and put together with matching slice of cherry-nut or vanilla ice cream. If desired, top with chocolate sauce. *Makes 12 to 14 sandwiches.* Use remaining loaf for another dessert.

**Angel Loaves:** Prepare batter as directed on Angel Food Cake Mix pkg. Pour batter into 2 shiny ungreased loaf pans, 9x5x3". Bake 30 to 35 min. Invert to cool, resting the corners on other pans. When cool, loosen from sides of pan with knife; invert pan and hit sharply on table to remove cake.

### COCONUT CUSTARD ANGEL FOOD CAKE

Bake Lemon Custard Angel Food Cake as directed. Frost top and sides with cooled vanilla pudding (cooked type). Sprinkle toasted coconut over top and sides. Chill before serving.

### NUTMEG LEMON CUSTARD ANGEL FOOD CAKE

Make batter for Lemon Custard Angel Food Cake as directed—except add ½ tsp. nutmeg. Bake as directed. Cool. Frost with lemon fluffy-type frosting mix to which ½ tsp. nutmeg has been added.

# Yellow Cake

*Fluffy, fine-textured, and full-flavored. Follow easy directions on package of our yellow cake mix. It makes a bright sunny cake whether you serve it warm from the oven uniced, with a favorite topping or icing (pp. 133-135), or use it for a special variation (below).*

### BANANA YELLOW CAKE

Make batter as directed—except stir ⅛ tsp. soda into mix before adding liquid. Use ¼ cup less water and add 1 cup mashed bananas (2 to 3 medium). If desired, fold ⅓ cup finely chopped nuts into batter. Pour into prepared oblong or layer pans. Bake. If desired, fill and frost with sweetened whipped cream and sliced bananas.

### BANANA BUTTER-MALLOW CAKE

Bake Banana Yellow Cake (above) in oblong pan. Cool. Prepare butterscotch pudding mix (not instant) as directed on pkg. Spread on top of cake to within ½″ of edge. Frost with Mallow-Nut Frosting (p. 134).

### BUSY DAY CUPCAKES

Make Cupcakes as directed on package. Cool. Spread top of each cupcake with sweet orange marmalade and top with about 10 miniature marshmallows. Broil until marshmallows melt slightly and are golden brown.

### VICTORIA SANDWICH

Bake cake in layers as directed. Split one layer in half to make 2 layers. Fill with ½ cup jelly or preserves. Top with remaining half layer and sift confectioners' sugar over top. Serve in wedges. Use other layer for another dessert.

> *MARBLE CAKE—Rich chocolate and sunny yellow . . . in intriguing marbled effect. Quick and easy to make with our marble cake mix. Frost it with Chocolate Butter Icing (p. 133).*

### PINEAPPLE UPSIDE-DOWN CAKE

Heat oven to 350° (mod.). Melt ½ cup butter in oblong pan, 13x9½x2″. Sprinkle 1 cup brown sugar (packed) evenly over butter. Arrange 8 drained pineapple rings (1-lb. 14-oz. can) over sugar. Decorate with walnut halves and maraschino cherries. Make cake batter as directed. Pour over fruit in pan. Bake 45 to 55 min. Invert at once onto serving plate.

### ORANGE CAKE

Make batter as directed—except fold in 2 tbsp. grated orange rind before baking. Bake as directed. Frost with Orange Butter Icing (p. 133) or serve with Quick Orange Sauce (p. 161).

### PINEAPPLE GLAZED CAKE

Bake cake in oblong pan as directed. Combine 1 can (13½ oz.) crushed pineapple with ½ cup brown sugar (packed). Bring to boil. With point of sharp knife, mark cake into 1″ squares, cutting ½″ deep. Spoon hot pineapple mixture over hot cake. Allow to cool. Serve with whipped cream.

### LEMON MACAROON TORTE

Heat oven to 350° (mod.). Grease an oblong pan, 13x9½x2″, or two 9″ sq. pans. Mix with hand 1 pkg. yellow cake mix, ¼ cup soft shortening, 1 egg, 2 tbsp. water, and 1 cup flaked coconut. Squeeze with fingers until dough is moist enough to hold together. With hand, pat out in pan. Bake 15 to 20 min., until a light golden color. Crust will still be soft when removed from oven. Cool. Prepare lemon pudding mix (not instant) as directed on package. Pour immediately over baked crust. Serve warm or cool. Top with whipped cream. Cut into squares. *18 to 24 servings.*

# White Cake

*You'll serve this snow-white, cloud-light, delicately flavored cake with pride. Just follow simple directions on our white cake mix package. White cake is the perfect partner for rich caramel or chocolate icings or fluffy fruit-flavored toppings.*

### CHOCOLATE CURL CAKE

Bake cake in layer pans as directed—except fold 2 sq. unsweetened chocolate (2 oz.), coarsely shaved, into batter. Spread Dark Chocolate Filling (below) between cooled layers. Frost top and sides with our fluffy white frosting mix. Sprinkle top of cake with additional shaved chocolate.

**Dark Chocolate Filling:** Mix in saucepan 2 large egg yolks, 1 cup sugar, ⅓ cup cream (20% butterfat), 2 tbsp. butter, and 2 sq. unsweetened chocolate (2 oz.), cut up. Cook over medium heat, stirring constantly, only until bubbles appear around edge. Remove from heat. Beat until thick. Cool.

### WHITE NUT CAKE

Bake cake as directed—except fold ⅓ cup finely chopped nuts into batter just before pouring into pan. Finish cake with Fudge-Nut Frosting: add ¾ cup chopped nuts to our chocolate fudge flavor frosting mix.

### POPPY SEED CAKE

Soak ½ cup poppy seeds for 1 hr. in water called for on cake mix pkg. Bake cake in layers as directed—except use poppy seed-water mixture in place of water. Prepare ½ recipe Custard Sauce (p. 135) or ½ of prepared vanilla pudding mix. Spread between cooled layers. Frost top and sides with White Mountain Frosting (p. 134).

### CRANBERRY STACK CAKE

Bake cake in layers as directed. Cool. Split each layer in half, making four layers. For filling, use sweetened whipped cream (1½ cups whipping cream and ⅓ cup sifted confectioners' sugar) and 1 can (1 lb.) whole cranberry sauce. Spread each layer and top of cake with sweetened whipped cream. Spoon ¼ of cranberry sauce over each layer and top of cake, swirling it into the whipped cream. Stack layers together. Chill 1 to 2 hr. before serving.

### MOCHA WHITE CAKE

Make cake as directed—except stir 2 tbsp. powdered instant coffee into mix before adding water. Ice with Mocha Butter Icing (below).

**Mocha Butter Icing:** Make Butter Icing (p. 133)—except omit cream and vanilla and blend in 2 tsp. powdered instant coffee dissolved in 2 tbsp. hot water. If too thick, stir in a few drops of water.

### BROILED PINEAPPLE-COCONUT TOPPING

Mix ½ cup brown sugar (packed), ½ cup well-drained crushed pineapple, and 2 tbsp. softened butter. Spread on one baked layer of cake. Sprinkle ¼ cup chopped nuts and ¼ cup flaked coconut over top; broil until golden brown. Double recipe for oblong cake.

# 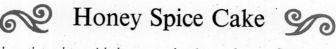 Honey Spice Cake

*Rich and tender, with honey and spice and everything nice. Just follow clear directions on our honey spice cake mix package. Such a wonderful fragrance. Delicious served uniced, warm from the oven, or try one of the easy variations suggested below.*

### APPLESAUCE CAKE

Make batter as directed—except stir ¼ tsp. soda into mix before adding water and eggs. Use ¼ cup less water. Beat 4 min., medium speed on mixer. Fold ¾ cup applesauce into batter. If desired, add ⅓ cup chopped nuts. Bake in oblong or layer pans as directed. Frost with Butter Icing (p. 133).

### HONEY SPICE BANANA CAKE

Make batter as directed—except stir ⅛ tsp. soda into mix before adding liquid and eggs, use ¼ cup less water, and add 1 cup mashed bananas (2 to 3 medium). If desired, fold ⅓ cup nuts into batter. Pour into prepared oblong or layer pans. Bake as directed. Frost with Banana-Nut Frosting (p. 133).

### LEMON SPICE SURPRISE

Heat oven to 350° (mod.). Prepare 1 pkg. lemon pudding mix (not instant) as directed on pkg. Spread in ungreased oblong pan, 13x9½x2″. Arrange 1 can (1 lb.) sliced peaches, drained, over pudding. Make batter as directed. Pour over peaches. Bake about 50 min. Cut into squares and turn upside-down in dessert dishes. Serve warm.

### HONEY COCONUT SQUARES

Bake oblong cake as directed. As soon as cake is removed from oven, drizzle ½ cup honey over top, sprinkle with 1 cup coconut, and slip under broiler a few minutes to toast coconut. Best when served warm.

### ORANGE SPICE CAKE

Make batter as directed—except fold in grated rind of two oranges (about 2 tbsp.). Frost with Orange Butter Icing (p. 133).

### SUGAR 'N SPICE CUPCAKES

Make Cupcakes as directed on pkg. Just before baking, sprinkle batter lightly with confectioners' sugar, a little cinnamon (so some white sugar is still visible), and chopped nuts (1 tsp. for each cupcake). Bake.

### MOCHA-FROSTED SPICE CAKE

Bake cake in layers as directed. Prepare our creamy white frosting mix as directed—except dissolve 2 tsp. powdered instant coffee in the hot water before adding to the dry mix. To 1 cup of the mocha frosting, add ¼ cup each chopped raisins and nuts. Use this to fill and frost top of cake. Frost sides of cake with remaining mocha frosting.

### CIDER 'N SPICE CAKE

Bake cake in layers as directed. Spread Cider Filling (below) between cooled layers. Frost top and sides with White Butter Icing (p. 133).

**Cider Filling:** Mix ½ cup sugar, ¼ tsp. salt, and 3 tbsp. cornstarch in saucepan. Slowly stir in 1 cup apple cider or juice. Bring to boil, stirring constantly. Boil 1 min. Remove from heat. Add 1 tbsp. lemon juice and 2 tbsp. butter. Cool.

*CUPCAKES are so handy for lunch boxes, children's parties, and snacks. Bake them as directed on our layer cake mixes.*

# Chocolate Cake

*Rich, chocolaty, smooth as velvet . . . the flavor the whole family loves. Easy to mix and bake as directed on packages of our chocolate flavored cake mixes. Use your favorite icing or topping (pp. 133-135) or try one of the delectable variations given below.*

### CHERRY-CHOCOLATE CAKE

Drain juice from 1 bottle (4 oz.) maraschino cherries. Add water to make amount called for on cake mix pkg. and add ¼ tsp. almond flavoring. Chop cherries fine and drain. Make batter for Devils Food Cake using cherry juice-water mixture as liquid. Fold in ½ cup finely chopped nuts and chopped cherries. Bake. Frost with our chocolate fudge flavor frosting mix.

### PEANUT BUTTER-CHOCOLATE CAKE

Bake Devils Food Cake in oblong pan as directed. Finish with Peanut Butter Broiled Icing (p. 134).

### FUDGE-NUT CAKE

Make batter for Devils Food Cake as directed—except fold in ½ cup chopped nuts. Bake as directed. Cool. Frost with Chocolate Butter Icing (p. 133).

### MOCHA DEVILS FOOD CAKE

Stir 3 tbsp. powdered instant coffee into Devils Food Cake (dry mix) or use strong cold coffee in place of water. Mix and bake as directed. Cool. Frost with Mocha Butter Icing (p. 129).

### PEP-O-MINT CAKE

Bake Devils Food Cake as directed—except fold in ¼ tsp. peppermint extract or 2 drops oil of peppermint before baking. Cool. Frost with our chocolate fudge flavor frosting mix. Sprinkle ½ cup crushed peppermint candy on top.

### CHOCOLATE WASHINGTON PIE

Bake Devils Food Cake in layers as directed. Cool. Split one layer in half to make two thin layers. Spread Custard Sauce (p. 135) between thin layers. Cover top with whipped cream and decorate with shaved chocolate. Serve in wedges. Serve remaining layer later.

### MILK CHOCOLATE CANDY BAR CAKE

Bake Milk Chocolate Cake in layers as directed. Cut one cake layer in wedges and top with Milk Chocolate Candy Bar Topping: whip 1 cup whipping cream (35% butterfat) with 1 tbsp. confectioners' sugar; fold in 2 milk chocolate nut candy bars (⅞ oz. each), cut in slivers. Frost uncut layer for another dessert.

### MALLOW MILK CHOCOLATE SQUARES

Bake Milk Chocolate Cake in oblong pan as directed. Top warm squares of cake with Marshmallow Sauce (p. 181).

### TRIPLE FUDGE CAKE

*See picture, p. 153.*

Prepare 1 pkg. chocolate pudding mix (cooked type). Blend dry Devils Food Cake Mix into hot pudding. Pour into greased and floured oblong pan, 13x9½x2". Sprinkle with ½ cup chocolate pieces and ½ cup chopped nuts. Bake in 350° (mod.) oven 30 to 35 min.

### "LAZY LADY'S" SPICE CAKE

Make batter for Chocolate Malt Cake as directed—except add 1 tsp. cinnamon, ¼ tsp. cloves, and ¼ tsp. ginger to mix. Add ¾ tsp. lemon extract and ¾ tsp. orange extract. Pour into prepared layer pans. Bake as directed. Frost with Chocolate Butter Icing (p. 133).

# More Easy Cakes

### ALMOND-GLAZED ORANGE CHIFFON CAKE

Bake our orange chiffon cake mix as directed. Cool. Combine ⅓ cup heated milk, 1 tbsp. corn syrup, ¾ tsp. almond extract, and 1 pkg. of our creamy white frosting mix. Beat until smooth. If too thick, add 1 to 2 tbsp. more milk. Pour slowly over cake. Sprinkle top with chopped toasted almonds. Glaze will set within ½ hr. Store any leftover glaze in refrigerator.

### CHIP CHOCOLATE ORANGE CHIFFON CAKE

Make batter for our orange chiffon cake mix as directed—except sprinkle 3 sq. sweet or unsweetened chocolate (3 oz.), shaved, or ½ cup miniature chocolate pieces over top of batter, gently folding in with a few strokes. Bake as directed. Frost with our chocolate fudge flavor frosting mix.

### CHERRY-PINEAPPLE ANGEL CAKE

Bake our angel food cake mix as directed. Blend 1 cup sugar, ½ cup water, 9-oz. can crushed pineapple and 3-oz. pkg. cherry-flavored gelatin in saucepan. Bring to boil; simmer 10 min., stirring occasionally. Chill until partially set, about 2 hr. Whip 2 cups whipping cream; fold into gelatin mixture. Spread generously on top and sides of angel cake; fill center of cake, too. Chill 4 hr. or overnight. *12 to 16 servings.*

**Orange-Pineapple Angel Cake:** Substitute orange-flavored gelatin for cherry in recipe above.

### CHOCOLATE-COCONUT CAKE

Bake our toasted coconut cake mix in oblong pan as directed. Cool. Cut in half. Fill and frost with our chocolate fudge flavor frosting mix. Sprinkle cut almond slices over top.

### LEMON LEI CHIFFON CAKE

Bake our lemon chiffon cake mix in tube pan as directed. Cool. Cut cake in half horizontally. Fill cake with Pineapple Filling (below). Frost with our lemon fluff frosting mix. Make a wreath on top of cake with fresh mint leaves or green leaf gumdrops.

**Pineapple Filling:** Mix ½ cup sugar, 3 tbsp. cornstarch, and ½ tsp. salt in saucepan. Gradually stir in ¾ cup pineapple juice and 1 cup crushed pineapple, well drained. Bring to boil over direct heat, stirring constantly. Boil 1 min. Remove from heat. Stir in 1 tbsp. butter and 1 tsp. lemon juice. Cool thoroughly.

### PRALINE COCONUT CAKE

Bake our toasted coconut cake mix in oblong pan as directed. Finish with Praline Topping (below). *16 servings.*

**Praline Topping:** Mix 3 tbsp. soft butter, 3 tbsp. hot water, and 1 tbsp. light corn syrup thoroughly into 1 pkg. of our caramel fudge frosting mix. Stir in 1 cup flaked coconut and ½ cup chopped nuts. While cake is still warm, spread on topping. Broil 3″ from heat 2 to 3 min., until bubbly. Serve warm.

### STRAWBERRY-LEMON CAKE

Bake our lemon velvet cake mix in layers as directed. Cool. Blend 1 pkg. of our creamy white frosting mix with 3 tbsp. soft butter and ¼ cup mashed fresh strawberries (or ¼ cup thawed frozen strawberries). Beat until smooth, creamy, and fluffy. Use to fill and frost cake. Decorate top of cake with 6 to 8 fresh whole strawberries.

## WHITE BUTTER ICING

⅓ cup soft butter

about 3 tbsp. cream

3 cups sifted confectioners' sugar

1½ tsp. vanilla

Blend butter and sugar thoroughly. Stir in cream and vanilla until smooth. *Makes icing for 2 round layers or 13x9″ oblong.*

**Chocolate Butter Icing:** Add 2 or 3 sq. unsweetened chocolate (2 or 3 oz.), melted.

**Orange or Lemon Butter Icing:** Use 1½ tbsp. grated orange or lemon rind and 3 tbsp. orange or lemon juice in place of vanilla and cream.

**Browned Butter Icing:** Brown butter in pan over medium heat until a delicate brown before blending with confectioners' sugar.

## EASY CREAMY ICING

Blend 1 cup sifted confectioners' sugar, ¼ tsp. salt, ½ tsp. vanilla or other flavoring (lemon, almond, or peppermint), and liquid to make easy to spread (about 1 tbsp. water or 1½ tbsp. cream). If desired, tint with food coloring. Spread on cookies.

## QUICK-AS-A-WINK CHOCOLATE FROSTING

1 pkg. (6 oz.) semi-sweet chocolate pieces

3 tbsp. milk

1 cup sifted confectioners' sugar

2 tbsp. butter

Combine chocolate, butter, and milk in saucepan. Stir over low heat until chocolate is just melted. Remove from heat. Stir in sugar. Beat until smooth, glossy, and easy to spread. If not glossy, stir in a few drops of hot water. *Makes frosting for 8 or 9″ sq. cake.*

## THIN CHOCOLATE ICING

1 sq. unsweetened chocolate (1 oz.)

1 cup sifted confectioners' sugar

1 tsp. butter

2 tbsp. boiling water

Melt chocolate and butter together over hot water. Remove from heat. Blend in sugar and water. Beat only until smooth but not stiff.

---

*FOR PERFECT FROSTED LAYERS—*
*Place one layer upside down on plate; spread on ⅓ of frosting. Place other layer right side up atop filling. Frost sides first, bringing icing up high. Frost the top of the cake last, swirling frosting just to the edge.*

## CHOCOLATE FUDGE FROSTINGS

*Add extra interest to our chocolate fudge flavor frosting mix with one of these suggestions.*

**Rocky Road:** Add 12 marshmallows, finely chopped, or 1 cup miniature marshmallows. For oblong cake.

**Peppermint Fudge:** Add ½ tsp. peppermint flavoring. Or frost cake and sprinkle with ½ cup crushed peppermint candy.

**Mocha:** Add 1 tbsp. powdered instant coffee to dry mix before adding liquid.

**Hobnail:** Frost cake thickly. Press down with bowl of teaspoon, swirl slightly, draw up sharply. Repeat over entire surface of cake.

**Brown Satin:** Sift dry frosting mix. Fold in 1½ cups commercial sour cream. Use to fill and frost cake. Sprinkle with chopped nuts. Refrigerate.

## CREAMY WHITE FROSTINGS

*Start with a package of our creamy white frosting mix.*

**Honey Butter:** Blend ½ cup honey, ½ cup soft butter, and 1 unbeaten egg white with frosting mix. Beat on high speed 1 min. Refrigerate.

**Banana-Nut:** Add 3 tbsp. butter, ⅓ cup mashed banana, and ½ tsp. lemon juice to frosting mix. Blend thoroughly with fork. Frost cake. Sprinkle with ¾ to 1 cup chopped nuts.

## WHITE MOUNTAIN FROSTING

½ cup sugar     2 egg whites (¼ cup)

2 tbsp. water     1 tsp. vanilla

¼ cup light corn syrup

Mix sugar, water, and corn syrup in saucepan. Cover saucepan, bring to rolling boil. Remove cover and cook to 242° or until syrup spins a 6 to 8″ thread. Just before syrup is ready, beat egg whites until stiff enough to hold a point. Pour hot syrup very slowly in a thin stream into the beaten egg whites. Continue beating until frosting holds peaks. Blend in vanilla. When spreading on cake, make pretty swirls with spatula. *Makes frosting for two 8 or 9″ layers or a 13 x 9″ oblong.*

**Satiny Beige Frosting:** Make White Mountain Frosting (above)—except use brown sugar in place of granulated. Use only ½ tsp. vanilla.

## ALLEGRETTI FROSTING

Melt over hot water 1 sq. unsweetened chocolate (1 oz.) with ¼ tsp. shortening. Using a teaspoon, drip chocolate around top edge of cake iced with a fluffy white frosting, letting chocolate run down sides.

## BROILED COCONUT ICING

3 tbsp. soft butter     2 tbsp. cream

  or other shortening     ½ cup shredded

⅓ cup brown sugar       coconut

  (packed)     ¼ cup chopped nuts

Mix all ingredients. Spread over warm 8″ sq. cake in pan. Place 3″ under broiler (low heat) until mixture bubbles, 3 to 5 min. Be careful not to burn icing.

## BROILED PEANUT BUTTER ICING

¼ cup soft butter or     ¼ cup cream (20%

  other shortening       butterfat)

⅔ cup brown sugar     ¼ cup peanut butter

  (packed)     1 cup peanuts, chopped

Mix first four ingredients. Stir in peanuts. Spread on warm 13x9″ oblong cake in pan. Place low under broiler until mixture bubbles and browns, 3 to 5 min. Be careful not to burn.

*TO STORE FROSTED CAKES—Keep frosted cakes fresh and attractive in a cake safe or under an inverted bowl. Fluffy-type frostings are best served the same day. If frosting swirls are mussed in carrying, dip knife in hot water and re-swirl.*

## EASY FROSTING VARIATIONS

*These special frostings all begin with a package of our fluffy white frosting mix.*

**Orange Coconut:** Add 1 tbsp. grated orange rind and ½ cup flaked coconut.

**Chocolate Chip:** Add ½ cup semi-sweet chocolate pieces.

**Spice:** Add ½ tsp. cinnamon, ¼ tsp. nutmeg, and ¼ tsp. cloves.

**Cherry:** Add ⅓ cup chopped, well-drained maraschino cherries and ½ cup chopped nuts.

**Maple:** Add ½ tsp. maple flavoring and ½ cup chopped pecans.

**Peppermint:** Add ¼ tsp. peppermint flavoring and red or green food coloring, if desired.

**Mallow-Nut:** Add 12 marshmallows, cut up. Sprinkle frosted cake with ½ cup chopped nuts.

*TO QUICK-FROST CUPCAKES—Pick up cupcake by the base and dip top into bowl of fluffy frosting, turning as you dip for a pretty effect.*

## FLUFFY WHITE DECORATOR ICING

Make our fluffy white frosting mix as directed on package, beating very stiff. Reserve 1 cup frosting, using remaining frosting to frost an 8″ layer cake or a 13x9″ oblong cake. Blend 1 to 1½ cups sifted confectioners' sugar, 1 tbsp. soft butter, and dash of salt into reserved cup of frosting (frosting should be stiff enough to hold shape). If desired, tint with food coloring. Decorate cake with writing or flowers using decorator tube.

## PINEAPPLE CREAM TOPPING

Combine 1 pkg. instant vanilla pudding mix and 1 can (9 oz.) crushed pineapple, including juice. Fold into 1 cup whipping cream (35% butterfat), whipped; chill. Serve over spice or devils food cake. *Makes 3 cups.*

## SWEETENED WHIPPED CREAM

Place 1 cup chilled whipping cream (35% butterfat) and ¼ cup sifted confectioners' sugar in chilled deep bowl. Using rotary or electric beater, beat until stiff.
**Peanut Crunch Topping:** Fold ½ cup finely crushed peanut brittle into Whipped Cream (above).
**Berry Cream:** Fold 1 pt. crushed and sweetened strawberries or raspberries into Whipped Cream (above).

## COCOA FLUFF TOPPING

In chilled bowl mix 1 cup chilled whipping cream (35% butterfat), ½ cup sifted confectioners' sugar, ¼ cup cocoa, and dash of salt. Beat until stiff.

## CUSTARD SAUCE

| | |
|---|---|
| 1½ cups milk | ¼ cup sugar |
| 4 egg yolks | ¼ tsp. salt |
| (or 2 whole eggs) | 1 tsp. vanilla |

Scald milk in top of double boiler over direct heat. Beat egg yolks in small bowl. Blend in sugar and salt. Gradually stir in scalded milk. Return to double boiler. Cook over simmering (not boiling) water, stirring constantly. When custard coats silver spoon (thin coating), remove from heat. Cool quickly. Blend in vanilla.

## QUICK CUSTARD SAUCE

Prepare vanilla pudding mix as directed on package except use 3 cups milk.

## MAPLE CREAM SAUCE

Mix 1 cup maple syrup and 2 tbsp. butter in saucepan. Boil 3 min. Cool. Stir in ¼ cup undiluted evaporated milk. Add ¼ cup coarsely chopped pecans. Serve over ice cream or warm cake. *Makes 1¼ cups.*

## VANILLA, LEMON, OR NUTMEG SAUCE

| | |
|---|---|
| 1 cup sugar | 2 tsp. vanilla or 2 tbsp. lemon juice with 2 tbsp. grated lemon rind or 2 tsp. nutmeg |
| 2 tbsp. cornstarch | |
| 2 cups boiling water | |
| ¼ cup butter | |

Mix sugar and cornstarch in saucepan. Gradually stir in water. Boil 1 min., stirring constantly. Stir in butter and flavoring. Serve hot over warm white or yellow cake. *Makes 2 cups.*

## CARAMEL SAUCE

| | |
|---|---|
| ½ lb. vanilla caramels (about 36) | ¼ cup water |

Melt caramels in water over hot (not boiling) water. Stir to blend well. Serve hot or cold. *Makes 1 cup.*

## HARD SAUCE

| | |
|---|---|
| ½ cup soft butter | ½ tsp. vanilla or rum flavoring |
| 1 cup sifted confectioners' sugar | |

Cream butter; add sugar gradually and cream until fluffy. Blend in vanilla. Chill about 1 hr. *Makes ¾ cup.*

## RASPBERRY-CURRANT SAUCE

| | |
|---|---|
| 1 pkg. (10 oz.) frozen raspberries, thawed, or 1 cup fresh raspberries | ½ cup currant jelly |
| | 1 tbsp. cold water |
| | 1½ tsp. cornstarch |

Blend berries and jelly; bring to boil. Stir in mixture of water and cornstarch. Boil 1 min., stirring constantly. Cool and strain. Serve with fruit or ice cream. *Makes 1⅓ cups. (Fresh raspberries, ¾ cup.)*

## GLOSSY CHOCOLATE SAUCE

| | |
|---|---|
| 2 sq. unsweetened chocolate (2 oz.) | ½ tsp. vanilla |
| 1 cup light corn syrup | 1 tbsp. butter |

Melt chocolate in corn syrup over low heat. Remove from heat, stir in vanilla and butter. *Makes 1 cup.*

## BAKED CUSTARD

2 eggs or 4
   egg yolks
⅓ cup sugar
¼ tsp. salt

2 cups milk, scalded
½ tsp. vanilla, if desired
nutmeg, for flavoring

Heat oven to 350° (mod.). Beat eggs, sugar, and salt together slightly to mix. Stir in scalded milk and vanilla. Pour into 6 custard cups or a 1½-qt. baking dish and set in pan of hot water (1" up on cups or baking dish). Sprinkle on nutmeg. Bake 45 to 50 min., or until knife inserted 1" from edge comes out clean. *6 servings.*

**Molded Maple Custard:** Add 1 more egg or 2 more egg yolks to Baked Custard (above). Butter custard cups or individual molds; pour 1 to 1½ tbsp. maple syrup into each cup. Pour custard mixture into cups carefully so syrup is not disturbed. Bake. Cool thoroughly before unmolding.

## TAPIOCA CREAM

2 egg yolks,
   slightly beaten
2 cups milk
2 tbsp. sugar
2 tbsp. quick-cooking
   tapioca

¼ tsp. salt
1 tsp. vanilla
2 egg whites
¼ cup sugar

Mix egg yolks, milk, 2 tbsp. sugar, tapioca, and salt in saucepan. Cook over low heat, stirring constantly, until mixture boils. Remove from heat. Cool. Stir in vanilla. Beat egg whites until frothy. Gradually beat in the ¼ cup sugar. Continue beating until stiff and glossy. Fold into mixture in saucepan. Spoon into dessert dishes. Serve with cream or fruit juice. *6 servings.*

**Chocolate Tapioca Cream:** Make Tapioca Cream (above)—except, at the last, fold in ½ cup semi-sweet chocolate pieces.

**Fruit Tapioca Cream:** Make Tapioca Cream (above) —except, at the last, fold in 1 to 1½ cups fresh, frozen, or canned fruits (blueberries, sweet cherries, pineapple, raspberries, or strawberries). Canned and frozen fruits must be thoroughly drained.

**Scotch Tapioca Cream:** Make Tapioca Cream (above) —except use dark brown sugar in place of granulated sugar and add 2 tbsp. butter to cooked mixture.

## RICE AND RAISIN DESSERT

1 cup instant rice
1½ cups milk
3 to 4 tbsp. sugar
½ tsp. salt

¼ tsp. cinnamon
   or nutmeg
¼ cup seedless raisins

Combine all ingredients in saucepan. Bring to full rolling boil, stirring constantly. Remove from heat. Cover and let stand 12 to 15 min., stirring occasionally. Serve warm with cream. *4 servings.*

## RICE CUSTARD CREAM

¼ cup uncooked rice
   (not instant)
2 cups milk
2 egg yolks, well
   beaten

3 tbsp. sugar
¼ tsp. salt
1 tsp. vanilla
2 egg whites
3 more tbsp. sugar

Cook rice and milk over boiling water until tender (about 1 hr.). Into beaten egg yolks stir 3 tbsp. sugar and salt; then stir in some of the hot rice mixture. Return to double boiler and cook 2 min. more, stirring constantly. Cool partially. Stir in vanilla. Beat egg whites until frothy; then beat in 3 tbsp. sugar, a little at a time, continuing until stiff and glossy. Fold into rice-custard mixture. Chill. Serve with or without cream. *6 servings.*

## BUTTERSCOTCH RICE

⅔ cup instant rice
2 cups milk
¼ tsp. salt
3 tbsp. butter

⅓ cup brown sugar
   (packed)
1 tsp. vanilla
½ cup dates, chopped

Mix rice, milk, and salt in large saucepan; cover loosely. Bring to boil and boil gently 15 min., fluffing rice occasionally with fork. Meanwhile, melt butter; add sugar and cook until sugar is dissolved. Add sugar mixture, vanilla, and dates to the cooked rice. Serve warm or chill 1 hr. *4 to 6 servings.*

## FRUIT-FLAVORED DESSERT MIXES

Colorful, light, and delicious desserts can be quickly made with fruit-flavored gelatin or Danish dessert mix. Only liquid need be added, following directions on pkg. When dessert thickens, add cut-up drained fruit, marshmallows, or nuts as you wish.

## LIME-GINGER JELLY

Dissolve 1 pkg. (3 oz.) lime-flavored gelatin in 1 cup hot water. Chill. As mixture thickens, beat with rotary beater until frothy and stir in 1 cup ginger ale. Turn into mold. When set, unmold. Surround with apricot halves on pineapple slices. Serve with Custard Sauce (p. 135) or whipped-cream-in-a-can.

## COOKED PUDDING MIXES

Add milk to these mixes, cook a few minutes, and you have desserts that taste much like old-time cream puddings. Available in a variety of flavors, including vanilla, chocolate, lemon, butterscotch, and caramel. Quickly cooked tapioca pudding mixes are at your market, too.

**For Extra Richness:** After cooking pudding mix as directed on package, stir in 2 tbsp. butter and, if desired, extra flavoring to taste. Then beat with rotary beater and cool.

**Chocolate Swirl Vanilla Pudding:** Stir 5 or 6 cut-up chocolate-covered cream-center mints into hot vanilla pudding; stir just enough to swirl chocolate through pudding.

**Maple-Butterscotch Pudding:** Add ¼ tsp. maple flavoring and 2 drops brandy flavoring to butterscotch pudding.

## INSTANT PUDDING MIXES

A few seconds of beating plus a few minutes for setting are all that are required for these puddings—wonderful for spur-of-the-moment desserts.

**Fruited Vanilla Pudding:** Add fresh berries, sliced bananas, or drained crushed pineapple to vanilla instant pudding. Top with whipped cream and coconut.

## HOT FUDGE PUDDING

*During baking the white pudding cake will rise to the top and a rich chocolate sauce will form at the bottom.*

| | |
|---|---|
| 1½ cups Bisquick | ½ cup brown sugar (packed) |
| ½ cup sugar | 1½ cups boiling water |
| ½ to 1 cup chopped nuts | 1 pkg. (6 oz.) semi-sweet chocolate pieces |
| ½ cup milk | |

Heat oven to 350° (mod.). Mix Bisquick, sugar, nuts, and milk. Turn batter into greased 2-qt. baking dish. Sprinkle brown sugar over batter. Pour boiling water over chocolate pieces and let stand 1 to 2 min., until chocolate melts; then stir until blended. Pour over batter. Bake 40 to 45 min. Let stand 5 min. to cool slightly. Invert servings on plates, dip sauce from baking dish over each. Serve with cream. *6 to 8 servings.*

## SCANDINAVIAN LEMON PUDDING

| | |
|---|---|
| 1 envelope unflavored gelatin (1 tbsp.) | ¼ cup lemon juice |
| ½ cup cold water | 2 tsp. grated lemon rind |
| 5 egg yolks | ⅛ tsp. salt |
| ¾ cup sugar | 5 egg whites |

Soften gelatin in cold water; dissolve over hot water. Beat egg yolks in a large mixer bowl until very thick and lemon colored, about 5 min. Gradually beat in sugar. Blend in lemon juice, rind, and cooled gelatin mixture. Add salt to egg whites and beat until stiff, but not dry. Fold egg whites into egg yolk mixture. Pour into 1½-qt. dish. Chill until firm. Serve in sherbet glasses. Garnish with whipped cream sprinkled with finely ground toasted almonds and a maraschino cherry. *6 to 8 servings.*

## PEARS WITH LEMON VELVET SAUCE

Serve chilled pear halves (fresh or drained canned) in individual dessert dishes. Top with Lemon Velvet Sauce (below). Garnish with curls of unsweetened chocolate.

**Lemon Velvet Sauce:** Prepare 1 pkg. lemon instant pudding as directed. Fold in 1 cup whipping cream, whipped, and 1 tbsp. grated lemon rind.

### GINGERBREAD

Tender, fragrant, hot gingerbread is made in a jiffy from our gingerbread mix. Serve warm squares with Sweetened Whipped Cream (p. 135) or any of the ways suggested below.

**Applesauce Gingerbread:** Heat 1 can (1 lb. 1 oz.) applesauce in saucepan with 1 tsp. cinnamon. Cover top of warm gingerbread with warm applesauce and sprinkle with more cinnamon, if desired. Serve warm. *9 servings. (See picture, p. 108.)*

**Banana Ginger Shortcake:** Split warm squares of gingerbread. Put together with sweetened whipped cream and banana slices. Top with more whipped cream and banana slices. Serve immediately.

**Chocolate Gingerbread:** Add 1 sq. unsweetened chocolate (1 oz.); melted, to batter before pouring into pan.

**Mincemeat Gingerbread:** Spread 1 jar (1 lb. 12 oz.) mincemeat in well-greased 9″ sq. pan. Make gingerbread batter as directed. Pour over mincemeat. Bake about 50 min. at 350°, or until top of cake is firm to touch. Run knife around edge of cake to loosen from pan. Immediately invert onto serving plate. Leave pan over cake for 5 min. Remove pan and serve warm with hard sauce or whipped cream. *12 to 16 servings.*

**Cream Cheese Topping for Gingerbread:** Soften 2 pkg. (3 oz. each) cream cheese in bowl at room temperature. Blend with 2 tbsp. orange juice and ½ cup sifted confectioners' sugar. Spoon on squares of warm gingerbread. Sprinkle with grated orange rind.

**Marshmallow Topping:** Spread ½ cup orange marmalade on hot gingerbread. Place 18 marshmallow halves on top, arranging 2 on each serving. Place about 3″ under broiler until delicately browned, about 1 min. Serve immediately.

### APPLE DATE DOWDY

Heat oven to 375° (quick mod.). Arrange 4 cups sliced, peeled tart apples in greased 9″ sq. pan. Mix ⅔ cup brown sugar (packed), ½ tsp. cinnamon, ½ tsp. nutmeg, and ½ to 1 tsp. orange rind. Sprinkle over apples. Pour on 2 tbsp. orange juice. Dot with 2 tbsp. soft butter.

Mix date filling from 1 pkg. of our date bar mix with ¼ cup hot water. Add crumbly mix and 1 egg. Mix thoroughly. Drop mixture by spoonfuls evenly over fruit. Bake 35 to 40 min. *8 servings.*

### PUDDING CAKES

Hot and homey, sweet and satisfying—so simple to make with our pudding cake mixes. Just mix the cake batter, sprinkle on the sauce mixture, and pour on water. While baking, the cake and pudding magically change places.

**Lemon-Fruit Pudding Cake:** Follow directions on lemon pudding cake mix pkg.—except stir ½ cup currants or finely cut uncooked prunes into cake batter.

**Chocolate Marshmallow Pudding Cake:** Follow directions on chocolate pudding cake mix pkg.—except sprinkle ½ cup miniature marshmallows over batter in baking dish.

**Caramel Raisin Pudding Cake:** Follow directions on caramel pudding cake mix pkg.—except sprinkle ½ tsp. nutmeg and ½ cup raisins over batter in baking dish.

## PEARADISE SNOWCAP DESSERT

1 cup miniature marsh-
mallows

1 cup commercial sour
cream

1 can (1 lb.) pear halves
(reserve liquid)

1 pkg. (3 oz.) raspberry-
flavored gelatin

1 pkg. (10 oz.) frozen
raspberries, thawed
and drained

Melt marshmallows over hot water, stirring constantly. Fold sour cream into melted marshmallows. Pour into well-oiled 1-qt. mold. Chill until firm. Combine pear liquid with water to make 1¼ cups; heat. Dissolve gelatin in hot liquid. Chill until slightly thickened; whip until fluffy. Fold in raspberries. Fill mold with whipped gelatin; chill several hours or overnight. Unmold and garnish with sliced pears. *8 servings.*

## CRANBERRY-APPLE CRUMB DESSERT

3 tbsp. butter, melted

½ lb. vanilla wafers,
finely crushed

½ cup butter

1 cup sifted con-
fectioners' sugar

1 egg

2 cups cranberries,
chopped

3 medium apples,
peeled and chopped

1 cup (8-oz. can)
crushed pineapple,
drained

1 cup granulated
sugar

1 cup miniature
marshmallows

1 cup whipping cream,
whipped and sweetened

Combine melted butter and crumbs. Press half of crumbs into oblong pan, 13x9½x2". Beat butter, confectioners' sugar, and egg 7 to 8 min. Spread evenly over crumbs in pan. Mix fruits, sugar, and marshmallows, draining off any juice. Spread over butter mixture in pan. Top with whipped cream. Sprinkle on remaining crumbs. Refrigerate overnight. *15 servings.*

## BOSTON CREAM PIE

This early American dessert, said to have been originated by Martha Washington, is now "easy as pie" when cake, filling, and chocolate glaze come from packets in our Boston cream pie package. *8 servings.*

**Cocoa Cream Delight:** Follow directions on Boston cream pie pkg. for filling and cake. Complete except for icing. Mix 1 cup whipping cream, chocolate icing mix (from packet), and 1 tsp. vanilla in chilled bowl; beat until stiff. Frost sides and top of filled cake with chocolate whipped cream. Chill until served.

**Coconut Boston Cream Pie:** Sprinkle ⅓ cup flaked coconut on filling before putting top layer in place and sprinkle another ⅓ cup flaked coconut atop chocolate glaze.

## BROWNIE RIBBON DESSERT

Heat oven to 350° (mod.). With aluminum foil, line a jelly roll pan, 15½x10½x1". Grease. Follow directions for Fudgy Brownies on our fudge brownie mix pkg.—except omit nuts. Spread in pan. Bake 15 to 20 min. Cool in pan 15 min. Lift foil and brownies out of pan in one piece. Cut 5 strips, each about 3" wide. Whip 2 cups whipping cream with ¼ cup sifted confectioners' sugar. Spread ½ cup on one strip. Stack with ½ cup whipped cream between each strip. Turn stack on its side on serving plate. Cover with remaining whipped cream. Chill 6 hr. or overnight. Garnish with finely chopped nuts. Slice and serve with chocolate sauce. *12 servings.*

## EASY TIPSY TRIFLE

Line 1½-qt. baking dish or 9" sq. glass baking dish with sponge cake from the bakery or leftover yellow cake. Mix ⅓ cup orange juice and 2 tbsp. sherry flavoring; pour over cake. Spread with strawberry or raspberry jam. Cook 1 pkg. vanilla pudding mix according to pkg. directions. Spread over jam. Chill until set. Whip ½ cup whipping cream with 2 tbsp. confectioners' sugar and spread over trifle. Decorate with toasted slivered almonds. *9 servings.*

## SURPRISE CHEESECAKE

| | |
|---|---|
| Graham Cracker Crust (below) | 1 pkg. lemon fluffy-type frosting mix |
| 1 pkg. (8 oz.) cream cheese | 1 cup commercial sour cream |
| ½ tsp. salt | 1 pkg. frozen sliced strawberries |
| 1½ cups dry curd cottage cheese | |

Heat oven to 350° (mod.). Press graham cracker mixture evenly over bottom and sides of 8″ sq. pan. Soften cream cheese to room temperature. Mix salt into cottage cheese. Press cottage cheese through sieve into large mixer bowl with cream cheese; set aside. Beat frosting mix as directed on pkg. Mix cheeses and gradually beat in prepared frosting. Pour into prepared pan. Bake 35 min. Carefully spread with sour cream. Cool at room temperature. Chill. Serve with strawberries. *9 to 10 servings.*

**Graham Cracker Crust:** Blend 1½ cups fine graham cracker crumbs (18 to 20 crackers), ⅓ cup brown sugar (packed), and ½ tsp. cinnamon. Add ⅓ cup butter, melted, and mix well.

## APPLE ASKA

Heat oven to 400° (mod. hot). Mix 2 sticks of our pie crust mix and ⅓ cup sugar together until crumbly. Press firmly into bottom of square pan, 9x9x1¾″. Bake 15 min. (crust will not be brown). Cool. Mix 1 can (1 lb.) applesauce and ½ tsp. cinnamon; spread over crust. Prepare Meringue for 9″ pie (p. 146) and spread over applesauce. Bake 15 to 20 min., until golden. Cool. *9 servings.*

## PARTY PEACH MELBA

Stud 6 canned peach halves with toasted almonds; put one in each individual dessert dish. Using 1 pkg. (10 oz.) thawed frozen raspberries, 1 can (8 oz.) red raspberries, or 1 cup sweetened fresh raspberries, spoon berries over peaches. Chill. Whip 1 pt. vanilla ice cream to pouring consistency; blend in rum flavoring to taste; pour over peaches. *6 servings.*

## POT DE CRÈME AU CHOCOLAT

| | |
|---|---|
| 4 oz. German sweet chocolate | 2 egg yolks, slightly beaten |
| 1 tbsp. sugar | ½ tsp. vanilla |
| ½ cup cream | |

Combine chocolate, sugar, and cream in saucepan. Heat over medium heat, stirring constantly, until chocolate melts and mixture becomes smooth and blended. Remove from heat; slowly pour into egg yolks, stirring constantly. Blend in vanilla. Pour into small serving dishes such as demitasse cups; chill. Serve with whipped cream. *4 to 6 servings.*

## CHEESE-STUFFED PEACHES WITH CARAMEL SAUCE

Chill 1 can (1 lb. 13 oz.) Cling peach halves; drain. Mix 1 pkg. (3 oz.) cream cheese with cream or milk until soft; add ¼ cup chopped pecans. Make balls of cheese-nut mixture and place in peach halves. Cover with Caramel Sauce (p. 135). *About 10 servings.*

## STRAWBERRY BLINTZES

| | |
|---|---|
| Pancakes (below) | 3 tbsp. lemon juice |
| 1 cup cottage cheese (small curd) | ¼ cup sugar |
| 1 pkg. (3 oz.) cream cheese | 1 pkg. (10 oz.) frozen strawberries, thawed |
| 1½ tbsp. lemon rind | 1 tbsp. lemon juice |
| | ¼ tsp. almond extract |

Heat oven to 400° (mod. hot). Combine cheeses, rind, 3 tbsp. lemon juice, and sugar; whip until creamy. Place ¼ cup filling on each pancake and roll up. Place rolled-side-down in 11x7″ baking dish. Heat in oven for 10 min. just before serving. Heat the strawberries, 1 tbsp. lemon juice, and almond. Spoon over pancakes. Serve immediately. *6 servings.*

**Pancakes:** Add 1 egg and 1 cup milk to 1 cup Bisquick. Beat until smooth. Bake six 5″ pancakes. Keep pancakes warm between towels until ready.

## 🙢 Standard Pastries 🙠

### FOR 8 OR 9″ TWO-CRUST PIE

*(Baked with filling.)*

**2 cups Gold Medal
Flour**
**1 tsp. salt**

**⅔ cup lard\***
**¼ cup water**

Measure flour by dip-level-pour method. Mix flour and salt. Cut in shortening. Sprinkle with water; mix with fork. Round into ball. Roll a little more than half of dough 1″ larger than inverted pie pan. Ease into pan, fill, and trim edge. Roll out the other half in the same way. Cut slits near center. Fit over filling, seal, and flute. Bake as directed for special pie being made.

\***Note:** *Or use ⅔ cup plus 2 tbsp. hydrogenated shortening.*

### FOR 8 OR 9″ BAKED PIE SHELL

*(Baked, then filled.)*

**1 cup Gold Medal
Flour**
**½ tsp. salt**

**⅓ cup lard\***
**2 tbsp. water**

Heat oven to 475° (very hot). Measure flour by dip-level-pour method. Mix flour and salt. Cut in shortening. Sprinkle with water; mix with fork. Round into ball. Roll out 1″ larger than inverted pie pan. Ease into pan, flute, and prick pastry. Bake 8 to 10 min. Finish according to recipe.

\***Note:** *Or use ⅓ cup plus 1 tbsp. hydrogenated shortening.*

### FOR 8 OR 9″ ONE-CRUST PIE

*(Baked with filling.)*

Follow recipe for Baked Pie Shell (above)—except do not prick and do not bake until filling is added. Then bake as directed for special pie being made.

> *PASTRY MADE WITH A MIX—Just follow directions on package of our pie crust mix.*
>
>

## 🙢 1-2-3 Pastries 🙠

### FOR 8 OR 9″ TWO-CRUST PIE

**1¾ cups Gold Medal
Flour**
**1 tsp. salt**

**½ cup vegetable oil**
**3 tbsp. cold water**

Heat oven to 425° (hot). Measure flour by dip-level-pour method. Mix flour and salt. Blend oil in thoroughly with fork. Sprinkle all of water over mixture; mix well. Press dough firmly into ball with hands. If too dry, add 1 to 2 tbsp. more oil.

Divide dough about in half. Use the larger part for bottom pastry. Flatten slightly and immediately roll out between 2 pieces of waxed paper. Wipe table with damp cloth to prevent paper from slipping. Peel off top paper, place pastry in pan, paper-side-up. Peel off paper and fit pastry loosely into pan. Fill as desired, Roll remaining dough in similar manner for top crust. Cut slits and place over filling. Trim ½″ beyond rim of pan; fold under. Seal and flute edges. Bake 35 to 40 min., or until juice begins to bubble through slits in top crust, except fresh apple 50 to 60 min. To prevent overbrowning of edges, cover with a 1½″ strip of aluminum foil; remove 15 min. before end of baking time.

### FOR 8 OR 9″ ONE-CRUST PIE OR PIE SHELL

**1 cup plus 2 tbsp.
Gold Medal Flour**
**½ tsp. salt**

**⅓ cup vegetable oil**
**2 tbsp. water**

Heat oven to 450° (hot). Measure flour by dip-level-pour method. Mix flour and salt. Blend oil in thoroughly with fork. Sprinkle all of water over mixture; mix well. Press dough firmly into ball with hands. If too dry, add 1 to 2 tbsp. more oil.

Flatten dough slightly; immediately roll into 12″ circle between 2 pieces of waxed paper. Wipe table with damp cloth to keep paper from slipping. Peel off top paper; place pastry in pan, paper-side-up. Peel off paper; fit pastry loosely into pan. Trim ½″ beyond pan edge. Fold extra pastry back and under and build up fluted edge. Prick thoroughly. Bake shell 12 to 15 min. Do not prick if crust and filling are to be baked together. Bake as recipes directs.

## EASY-PERFECT
## PATTY OR TART SHELLS

*For creamed chicken or sea foods, for ice cream or fruit, or for cream pie fillings.*

**In Advance:** Roll Pastry for Two-crust Pie (p. 141) to thickness of pie crust. Cut into eight 5″ rounds. Prick with fork. Stack, using waxed paper between rounds. Place in plastic bag or in aluminum foil and freeze.

**When Ready to Use:** Heat oven to 475° (very hot). Place frozen circles on inverted custard cups on baking sheet, or on backs of muffin cups. Bake 8 to 10 min. During baking, pastry takes shape of cups. *Makes 8 patty shells.*

## SIMPLIFIED TARTS

*Crispy pastry rounds or squares make a delicious dessert when topped with a favorite filling.*

Heat oven to 475° (very hot). Roll Pastry (p. 141) ⅛″ thick. Cut into 3″ rounds or squares. Place on ungreased baking sheet. Prick with fork. Bake until delicately browned, 8 to 10 min.

**Top Tarts**—with softened cream cheese and sweetened or glazed fruit, or with chocolate or other cream pie filling and whipped cream.

**Put together, shortcake fashion**—with sweetened fresh or frozen fruit and Custard Sauce (p. 135); top with more fruit and Custard Sauce or whipped cream.

## EASY FOIL TARTS

| | |
|---|---|
| 1½ cups Gold Medal Flour | ½ cup hydrogenated shortening |
| ¾ tsp. salt | 3 tbsp. water |

Heat oven to 475° (very hot). Measure flour by dip-level-pour method. Mix flour and salt. Cut in shortening. Sprinkle with water; mix with fork. Round into ball. Divide pastry into 8 equal parts. Place each part on square of heavy-duty aluminum foil. Roll dough into 5″ circle. Trim edges of dough and foil to make neat 5″ circle. Shape into tart by turning up edges 1″; flute. Prick bottoms of tarts with fork. Bake 8 to 10 min. on baking sheet. Cool and fill with your favorite cream filling. *Makes 8 tarts.*

## GRAHAM CRACKER CRUST

Heat oven to 350° (mod.). Mix 1½ cups graham cracker crumbs (18 crackers) and 3 tbsp. sugar in bowl. Add ⅓ cup butter, melted; mix thoroughly. Press mixture firmly and evenly against bottom and sides of 9″ pie pan. Bake 10 min. Cool; fill with chiffon or cream filling.

## VANILLA FRUIT TARTS

Bake Easy-Perfect Patty Shells (left)—except make ten 4″ squares or rounds. Cook vanilla pudding mix according to pkg. directions—except use only 1½ cups milk; add ⅓ cup sugar and 2 egg yolks with milk. Cool. Beat 2 egg whites until foamy. Gradually add ¼ cup sugar, beating until stiff but not dry. Fold this meringue into cooled pudding until well blended. Prepare 1 cup fresh strawberries or orange sections, cubed (2 or 3 oranges). Place 3 or 4 pieces of fruit in shell. Add filling and garnish with more fruit. Refrigerate several hours, until set. *Makes 10 tarts.*

## FRUIT TARTS À LA MODE

Fill baked tart shells with fruit (sweetened whole or sliced strawberries, blueberries, green or Tokay grapes, or raspberries; peaches; crushed pineapple; or applesauce). Top with ice cream, whipped cream, or Custard Sauce (p. 135).

## FROZEN FUDGE TARTS

Divide contents of our chocolate fudge flavor frosting mix in half. Blend 1½ cups chilled whipping cream into half the dry frosting mix and chill; beat until stiff. Pour into Easy Foil Tarts (left). Garnish with toasted almonds. Freeze until firm. *8 servings.*

# PEACH PIE

| Pastry for 9″ Two-crust Pie (p. 141) | ½ tsp. cinnamon |
| --- | --- |
| 1 cup sugar | 4 cups sliced firm peaches |
| ¼ cup Gold Medal Flour | 1½ tsp. butter |

Heat oven to 425° (hot). Mix sugar, flour, and cinnamon. Mix lightly through peaches. Pour into pastry-lined pie pan. Dot with butter. Cover with top crust which has slits cut in it. Seal and flute. Cover edge with 1½″ strip of aluminum foil to prevent excessive browning. Bake 35 to 45 min., or until crust is nicely browned and juice begins to bubble through slits in crust. Serve slightly warm, not hot.

# APPLE PIE

| FOR 9″ PIE | FOR 8″ PIE |
| --- | --- |
| Pastry for 9″ Two-crust Pie (p. 141) | Pastry for 8″ Two-crust Pie (p. 141) |
| ¾ to 1 cup sugar | ½ to ¾ cup sugar |
| 1 tsp. cinnamon or nutmeg | ¾ tsp. cinnamon or nutmeg |
| 6 to 7 cups sliced pared apples | 4 to 5 cups sliced pared apples |
| 1½ tbsp. butter | 1 tbsp. butter |

Heat oven to 425° (hot). Mix sugar and cinnamon. Mix lightly through apples. Heap up in pastry-lined pie pan. Dot with butter. Cover with top crust which has slits cut in it. Seal and flute. Cover edge with 1½″ strip of aluminum foil to prevent excessive browning. Bake 50 to 60 min., or until crust is nicely browned and apples are cooked through (test with fork).

**Raspberry-Apple Pie:** For filling, combine 1 pkg. (10 oz.) frozen raspberries, thawed and well drained, 4 cups sliced pared apples, 1 cup sugar, 2 tbsp. flour, ½ tsp. salt, and ¼ tsp. nutmeg. *Makes 9″ pie.*

**Cranberry-Apple Pie:** For filling, combine 3 cups sliced pared apples, 2 cups whole fresh or thawed frozen cranberries, 1¾ cups sugar, and ¼ cup Gold Medal Flour. Bake 40 to 50 min. *Makes 9″ pie.*

**Brown Sugar Apple Pie:** Use brown sugar in place of granulated sugar.

**Dutch Apple Pie:** Five min. before pie is done, remove from oven and pour ½ cup whipping cream through slits in top crust. Return to oven and bake 5 min. more.

# RHUBARB PIE

| Pastry for 9″ Two-crust Pie (p. 141) | ⅓ cup Gold Medal Flour |
| --- | --- |
| 1⅓ to 2 cups sugar | 4 cups cut-up rhubarb |
| | 1½ tbsp. butter |

Heat oven to 425° (hot). Mix sugar and flour. Mix lightly through rhubarb. Pour into pastry-lined pie pan. Dot with butter. Cover with top crust which has slits cut in it. Sprinkle with sugar. Seal and flute. Cover edge with 1½″ strip of aluminum foil to prevent excessive browning. Bake 40 to 50 min., or until crust is nicely browned and juice begins to bubble through slits. Serve slightly warm.

# MINCEMEAT PIE

Heat oven to 425° (hot). Make Pastry for 8″ Two-crust Pie (p. 141). Fill pastry-lined pie pan with 2½ cups mincemeat (add some chopped apples, if you wish). Seal and flute. Bake 40 to 45 min.

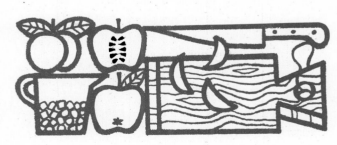

## FRESH BERRY PIE

Pastry for 9" Two-crust Pie (p. 141)

1 to 1½ cups sugar

⅓ cup Gold Medal Flour

½ tsp. cinnamon

4 cups fresh berries (blueberries, black-berries, raspberries, strawberries, loganber-ries, or boysenberries)

1½ tbsp. butter

Heat oven to 425° (hot). Mix sugar, flour, and cinnamon. Mix lightly through berries. Pour into pastry-lined pie pan. Dot with butter. Cover with top crust which has slits cut in it. Seal and flute. Cover edge with 1½" strip of aluminum foil to prevent excessive browning. Bake 35 to 45 min., or until crust is nicely browned and juice begins to bubble through slits in crust. Serve slightly warm, not hot.

**Note:** *If time is short, use prepared pie filling available in many delicious fruit and berry flavors. Just pour the filling into the crust!*

## STRAWBERRY-PINEAPPLE PIE

Pastry for 9" Two-crust Pie (p. 141)

1 pkg. (10 oz.) frozen strawberries

1 can (13½ oz.) pine-apple tidbits

1 tbsp. fresh lemon juice

½ cup sugar

¼ cup quick-cooking tapioca

¼ tsp. salt

2 tbsp. butter

Heat oven to 425° (hot). Thaw berries just enough to separate. Combine berries, pineapple (and juice), and lemon juice. Combine sugar, tapioca, and salt; stir into fruit; pour into pastry-lined pie pan. Dot with butter. Cover with top crust which has slits cut in it. Seal and flute. Cover edge with 1½" strip of aluminum foil. Bake 40 to 50 min., removing foil strip 15 min. before end of baking. Serve at room temperature.

**Raspberry-Pineapple Pie:** Substitute frozen raspberries for strawberries.

## CANNED CHERRY PIE

Pastry for 9" Two-crust Pie (p. 141)

¾ to 1 cup sugar

¼ cup Gold Medal Flour

½ tsp. cinnamon

½ cup fruit juice

3½ cups drained, pitted cherries

1 tbsp. butter

Heat oven to 425° (hot). Mix in saucepan sugar, flour, cinnamon, and fruit juice. Cook over medium heat, stirring constantly, until mixture thickens and boils. If desired, brighten color with red food coloring. Pour hot thickened juice over cherries. Mix lightly. Pour into pastry-lined pie pan. Dot with butter. Cover with top crust which has slits cut in it. Seal and flute. Cover edge with 1½" strip of aluminum foil to prevent excessive browning. Bake 35 to 45 min., or until nicely browned and juice begins to bubble through slits in crust. Serve warm.

**Canned Blueberry or Boysenberry Pie:** Make Canned Cherry Pie (above)—except use drained canned blue-berries or boysenberries in place of cherries. Add 2 tbsp. lemon juice before pouring mixture into pastry-lined pie pan.

**Canned Apple, Peach, or Apricot Pie:** Make Canned Cherry Pie (above)—except use canned sliced apples, peaches, or apricot halves and juice in place of cherries and juice.

**Note:** *Frozen fruit which retains its shape when thawed (such as cherries, blueberries, peaches, and apricots) may be sub-stituted for canned fruit—except reduce sugar about ½ cup.*

## ICE CREAM DATE PIE

Heat oven to 400° (mod. hot). Mix ¼ cup softened butter and crumbly mix from our date bar mix pkg. with fork. Spread in oblong pan, 13x9½x2". Bake 10 min. Do not overbake. Take from oven; stir with spoon. Press hot crumbly mixture against bottom and sides of 9" pie pan, reserving ½ cup for topping. Cool. Add ½ cup hot water to date filling mix. Cool. Spoon 1 pt. vanilla ice cream into pie shell and spread date filling over ice cream. Sprinkle remaining crumbly mixture over pie. Serve at once or freeze until firm.

## VANILLA CREAM PIE

8″ Baked Pie Shell
(p. 141)
½ cup sugar
2 tbsp. cornstarch
½ tsp. salt

2 cups milk
2 egg yolks, slightly
beaten
2 tsp. butter
1 tsp. vanilla

Mix sugar, cornstarch, and salt in saucepan. Slowly stir in milk. Boil 1 min. over medium heat, stirring constantly. Remove from heat. Stir half of mixture into egg yolks, then blend into hot mixture in pan. Boil 1 more min., stirring constantly. Remove from heat. Blend in butter and vanilla. Pour into baked pie shell and chill about 2 hr. Just before serving, top with whipped cream.

## QUICK VANILLA CREAM PIE

Prepare 1 pkg. vanilla pudding or pie filling mix as directed on pkg. Pour into 8″ Baked Pie Shell (p. 141). Chill about 2 hr. Just before serving, top with whipped cream.

**Berry Cream Pie:** Cover cooled filling with raspberries, blueberries, sliced strawberries, or sweetened blackberries. Top with whipped cream.

**Mocha Cream Pie:** Add 1½ tsp. powdered instant coffee to filling mix before cooking.

**Coconut Cream Pie:** Fold ¾ cup moist shredded coconut into cooled filling just before pouring into pie shell. Sprinkle ¼ cup coconut over whipped cream topping.

**Date Cream Pie:** Add ¾ cup chopped pitted dates to cooled filling.

## CHOCOLATE CREAM PIE

Make Quick Cream Pie (above) using 1 pkg. chocolate pudding or pie filling mix.

**Peppermint Cream Pie:** Decorate Chocolate Cream Pie with Peppermint Cream Topping (whip ½ cup whipping cream; fold in 2 tbsp. confectioners' sugar, ¼ tsp. peppermint flavoring, and a few drops red food coloring). Trim with chocolate candy wafers, whole or broken, or with chocolate shavings. Chill until ready to serve.

## DOUBLE-QUICK BANANA CREAM PIE

9″ Baked Pie Shell
(p. 141)
3 medium bananas
1 cup (8 oz.) commercial
sour cream

1 cup milk
1 pkg. (3½ oz.)
instant vanilla
pudding

Slice 2 bananas into cooled baked pie shell. Combine cream and milk. Stir in instant pudding; blend well until mixture is smooth and slightly thick, then pour over bananas. Garnish with additional banana slices; chill. Top with whipped cream.

**Chocolate Banana Cream Pie:** Use chocolate instant pudding instead of instant vanilla pudding.

**Toasted Coconut Cream Pie:** Omit bananas. Add 1 cup toasted coconut to vanilla filling to make 8″ pie.

## CHERRY CREAM PIE

Prepare 1 pkg. (3½ oz.) vanilla pudding and pie filling mix (not instant) as directed on pkg. Pour into 9″ Baked Pie Shell (p. 141). Chill at least ½ hr. Spread 1 can (1 lb.) cherry pie filling over vanilla filling. Chill at least 3 to 4 hr.

## CREAM PARTY PIE

Graham Cracker Crust
(p. 142)
1 pkg. vanilla pudding
or pie filling mix
1 tsp. unflavored
gelatin

2 cups milk
1 cup whipping cream,
whipped stiff

Mix mix, gelatin, and milk. Cook according to directions on pudding mix pkg. Cool, covered, until it begins to set. Fold in half of whipped cream. Pour into Graham Cracker Crust. Spoon rest of whipped cream on top. Chill. Garnish gaily with fresh berries.

**Flavored Cream Party Pie:** Flavor the cream filling as desired with rum, brandy, or sherry flavoring.

## LEMON MERINGUE PIE

| | |
|---|---|
| 9" Baked Pie Shell (p. 141) | 3 egg yolks, slightly beaten |
| 1½ cups sugar | 3 tbsp. butter |
| ⅓ cup cornstarch | ¼ cup lemon juice |
| 1½ cups water | 1 tbsp. grated lemon rind |

Mix sugar and cornstarch in saucepan. Gradually stir in water. Cook over medium heat, stirring constantly, until mixture thickens and boils. Boil 1 min. Slowly stir at least half the hot mixture into egg yolks. Then blend into hot mixture in saucepan. Boil 1 min. longer, stirring until smooth. Blend in butter, lemon juice, and rind. Pour into baked pie shell. Finish with Pie Meringue (right). Serve as soon as cool.

## PIE MERINGUE

| FOR 8" PIE | FOR 9" PIE |
|---|---|
| 2 egg whites | 3 egg whites |
| ¼ tsp. cream of tartar | ¼ tsp. cream of tartar |
| ¼ cup sugar | 6 tbsp. sugar |
| ¼ tsp. flavoring | ½ tsp. flavoring |

Heat oven to 400° (mod. hot). Beat egg whites with cream of tartar until frothy. Gradually beat in sugar, a little at a time. Continue beating until stiff and glossy. Beat in flavoring. Pile onto hot pie filling, being careful to seal the meringue onto edge of crust. Bake 8 to 10 min., or until delicately browned. Cool away from drafts.

## AMBROSIA PIE

**8″ Baked Pie Shell (p. 141)**
**¾ cup flaked coconut**
**3 to 4 bananas, sliced**
**1 tbsp. lemon juice**

**1 can (11 oz.) mandarin oranges, drained and chilled**
**1 cup Sweetened Whipped Cream (p. 135)**

Sprinkle ½ cup coconut evenly in baked pie shell. Add layers of bananas sprinkled with lemon juice; top with orange sections. (Reserve 6 to 8 orange sections for garnish.) Spoon on whipped cream and sprinkle with a little nutmeg, if desired. Garnish pie with remaining coconut and oranges. Serve immediately.

## LEMON SWIRL PIE

Bake and cool 9″ Baked Pie Shell (p. 141). Prepare lemon chiffon pie filling, using your favorite recipe or pkg. mix. Melt 3 sq. semi-sweet chocolate (3 oz.) over hot water. Brush inside of cooled baked pie shell with thin coating of melted chocolate. Pile half the filling into shell. With spoon, dribble 2 tbsp. melted chocolate over top of filling. Add remaining filling and dribble remaining chocolate in thin line swirl over top of filling. Refrigerate several hours until set.

*Friday Favorite*
**Broiled Halibut Steak with Tartar Sauce**
**Hurry-up Potatoes (p. 92)     Buttered Peas**
**Best Tossed Salad (p. 94)**
**Double-quick Dinner Rolls (p. 117)**
**Lemon Swirl Pie**

## CHOCOLATE BROWNIE PIE

| | |
|---|---|
| Pastry for 9" One-crust Pie (p. 141) | 3 eggs |
| | ½ cup sugar |
| 2 sq. unsweetened chocolate (2 oz.) | ¾ cup dark corn syrup |
| 2 tbsp. butter | ¾ cup pecan halves |

Heat oven to 375° (quick mod.). Melt chocolate and butter together over hot water. Beat eggs, sugar, chocolate mixture, and syrup together with rotary beater. Mix in pecan halves. Pour into pastry-lined pie pan. Bake 40 to 50 min., just until set. Serve slightly warm or cold with ice cream or whipped cream.

**Cocoa Brownie Pie:** Omit chocolate and sift ½ cup cocoa with the sugar. Then add ¼ cup melted butter to the egg and sugar mixture.

## CREAMY MINCE-PECAN PIE

| | |
|---|---|
| Pastry for 9" Two-crust Pie (p. 141) | 3 tbsp. brown sugar (packed) |
| 1 cup whipping cream, whipped | 2 tbsp. flour |
| | ½ cup pecan halves |
| 1 jar (28 oz.) mincemeat | |

Heat oven to 425° (hot). Fold whipped cream into mincemeat and spread in pastry-lined pie pan. Combine brown sugar and flour. Sprinkle over mincemeat. Arrange pecan halves on top of mixture. Cover with top crust which has about ten 1" slits cut in it. Seal well by folding top crust under bottom crust and flute. Bake 40 to 45 min. Cool slightly before serving.

## CREAM PIE WITH CHOCOLATE MERINGUE

| | |
|---|---|
| 9" Baked Pie Shell (p. 141) | 3 egg whites |
| | 6 tbsp. sugar |
| 1 pkg. vanilla pie filling mix | 1 tbsp. cocoa |

Heat oven to 400° (mod. hot). Prepare pie filling as directed on pkg. Pour into pie shell. Beat egg whites until frothy. Gradually beat in 4 tbsp. of sugar. Continue beating until stiff and glossy. Combine cocoa and 2 tbsp. sugar; fold and blend completely into meringue. Pile by spoonfuls on top of hot pie filling, spread to edge to seal. Bake 8 to 10 min. Serve cold.

---

### *Festive Holiday Dinner*

**Roast Turkey (p. 78)**

**Mashed Potatoes     Giblet Gravy**

**Cranberry Sauce**

**Spinach Gourmet (p. 93)**

**Orange-Pineapple Salad (p. 101)**

**Brown 'n Serve Rolls**

**Pumpkin Pie     Creamy Mince-Pecan Pie**

## CREAMY PUMPKIN PIE

| | |
|---|---|
| Pastry for 9" One-crust Pie (p. 141) | 1 large egg |
| | ½ tsp. salt |
| 1¾ cups mashed cooked or canned pumpkin | ½ tsp. cinnamon |
| | ¼ tsp. nutmeg |
| 1⅓ cups sweetened condensed milk (15-oz. can) | ¼ tsp. ginger |
| | 1 cup hot water |

Heat oven to 375° (quick mod.). Beat all ingredients together with rotary beater. Pour into pastry-lined pie pan. Bake 50 to 55 min. Garnish with whipped cream.

## EASY CUSTARD PIE

| | |
|---|---|
| Pastry for 9" One-crust Pie (p. 141) | ¼ tsp. salt |
| | 1 tsp. vanilla |
| 4 eggs, slightly beaten | 2½ cups scalded milk |
| ½ cup sugar | |

Heat oven to 450° (hot). Cover edge of pastry with 1½"-wide strip of aluminum foil. Thoroughly mix eggs, sugar, salt, and vanilla. Slowly stir in hot milk; pour immediately into unbaked pie shell. (To avoid spills, fill at oven.) Sprinkle top with nutmeg. Bake about 20 min., or until silver knife inserted 1" from side of filling comes out clean. The center may still look a bit soft, but will set later. Serve slightly warm or chilled.

## BERRY MINUTE CREAM PIE

**Graham Cracker Crust (p. 142)**

**1 pkg. (10 or 16 oz.) frozen strawberries or raspberries**

**1 pkg. (3 oz.) strawberry- or raspberry- flavored gelatin**

**1 pt. vanilla ice cream**

Place strawberries in large saucepan. Break up with fork and bring to boil. Add gelatin and stir until gelatin is dissolved. Add ice cream to mixture and stir until melted. Place in refrigerator to partially set. (Mixture mounds slightly when dropped from spoon.) Pour into cooled baked crust. Chill until completely set. If desired, garnish with whipped cream.

**Ambrosia Minute Cream Pie:** Make Berry Minute Cream Pie (above)—except use 1 can (1 lb.) fruit cocktail and 1 pkg. (3 oz.) orange-flavored gelatin in place of berries and berry-flavored gelatin.

**Pineapple Minute Cream Pie:** Make Berry Minute Cream Pie (above)—except use 1 can (1 lb. 4½ oz.) crushed pineapple and 1 pkg. (3 oz.) lemon-flavored gelatin in place of berries and berry-flavored gelatin.

## STRAWBERRY MINUTE PIE

**8″ Baked Pie Shell (p. 141)**

**1 pkg. (3 oz.) strawberry- flavored gelatin**

**1 cup boiling water**

**1 pkg. (16 oz.) unthawed frozen sweetened sliced strawberries**

Dissolve gelatin in water. Add unthawed frozen berries. Break up berries with a fork. As berries thaw, gelatin thickens. When partially set, pour into cooled pie shell. Chill until completely set. Just before serving, garnish with Sweetened Whipped Cream (p. 135).

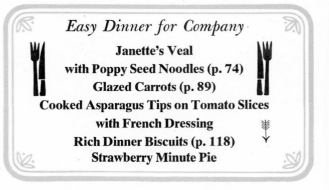

*Easy Dinner for Company*

**Janette's Veal with Poppy Seed Noodles (p. 74)**
**Glazed Carrots (p. 89)**
**Cooked Asparagus Tips on Tomato Slices with French Dressing**
**Rich Dinner Biscuits (p. 118)**
**Strawberry Minute Pie**

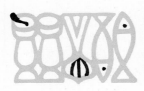

*Everyone loves to eat outdoors. And every year more and more families discover the fun of cooking and eating in the backyard, on the porch or patio, and at the park or seashore. Equipment need not be elaborate: a folding grill that can be packed in the car or a brazier with removable legs for easy transportation will do the job.*

## FIRE TIPS

Light charcoal 45 min. to 1 hr. before time to start grilling food.

Use gloves and tongs to protect hands from heat of fire.

Knock gray ash from charcoal from time to time for greatest heat.

Be sure fire is out before leaving picnic site: douse charcoal in bucket of water or smother wood embers with sand.

## FOOD TIPS

Meat and poultry should be at room or outdoor temperature before barbecuing for best flavor.

Start chicken with cut-side-down as bones hold heat in.

Keep barbecue sauce warm or hot while basting meat, fish, or poultry.

Do not overcrowd grill as it will be difficult to turn foods and intensity of heat will be lessened.

## POTATOES ROASTED IN FOIL

Rub skins of medium baking potatoes with oil or butter. Wrap each potato securely in heavy-duty aluminum foil. Roast directly on coals or on grill over coals, depending on how meat is being prepared; turn often. Roast potatoes on coals 35 to 45 min., on grill about 1 hr., or until potatoes are soft when gently pressed with asbestos-gloved thumb. Make crosswise slits through foil and potato. Fold foil back and squeeze until potato pops up through opening. Dot with butter; season with salt and pepper.

*Steak—Everybody's Favorite*

**Charcoal Broiled Steak**
**Potatoes Roasted in Foil**
**Sliced Tomatoes and Cucumbers**
**Garlic Bread (p. 117)**
**Almond Angel**
**Refrigerator Dessert (p. 127)**

## CHARCOAL BROILED STEAK

Choose a sirloin, porterhouse, T-bone, or club steak cut 1 to 2″ thick. Bring to room temperature before grilling. Slash fatty edge at 2″ intervals to keep from curling. For ease in cleaning grill, rub with oil or piece of fat. If desired, rub meat on both sides with cut cloves of garlic.

Lay steak on grill and lower it as close to briquets as possible. Sear steak 2 min. to seal in juices. Raise grill to 3″ above briquets and continue cooking. When juice comes to top and bubbles on uncooked surface, steak is ready to turn. Use tongs or spatula to turn steaks (a fork pierces meat and allows juices to run out). Season with salt and pepper. Lower grill and sear second side 2 min. Raise again and complete cooking. Season second side. If desired, steak may be basted with barbecue sauce last few minutes of cooking. To determine if steak is done as desired, use a small sharp knife and make a slit along bone.

|  | 1″ thick | 2″ thick |
|---|---|---|
| **Rare** | 6 to 8 min. each side | 10 to 15 min. each side |
| **Medium to Well done** | 10 to 15 min. each side | 15 to 20 min. each side |

### ISLAND PINEAPPLE

Select a fully ripe fresh pineapple. Remove top, but do not peel. Cut lengthwise into 8 segments or wedges. Place in oblong pan, 13x9½x2″. Brush 3 tbsp. honey over fruit. Marinate 1 hr., turning occasionally so pineapple is thoroughly coated with honey. Place skin-side-down on grill 3 to 4″ from hot coals. Grill 15 to 20 min., or until pineapple is steaming hot. *8 wedges.*

### HEARTY HAM STEAK

Buy 1½- to 2-lb. precooked ham steak, cut about 1″ thick. Place on slightly greased grill over hot coals. Baste frequently with Chef's Special Sauce (below). Grill 5 to 7 min. per side, until steak is a rich brown color. Serve remaining Sauce with ham. *About 6 servings.*

**Chef's Special Sauce:** Mix ¼ cup prepared mustard, ¼ cup pineapple juice, 2 tbsp. brown sugar, ½ tsp. horse-radish, and dash of salt.

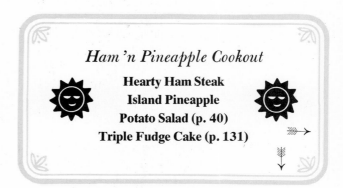

*Ham 'n Pineapple Cookout*

**Hearty Ham Steak**
**Island Pineapple**
**Potato Salad (p. 40)**
**Triple Fudge Cake (p. 131)**

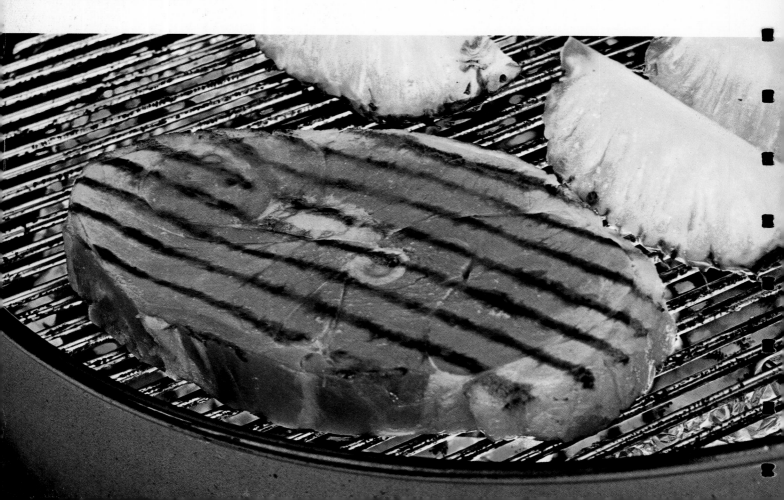

### BEEF TERIYAKI

Marinate ¼ to ½″ slices of beef sirloin in Teriyaki Sauce (below) overnight in refrigerator. Turn occasionally. Place on greased grill 6 to 8″ from hot coals. Turn only once; baste with marinade. Grill 25 min. for well done.

**Teriyaki Sauce:** Mix ½ cup soy sauce, ¼ cup honey, ½ tsp. monosodium glutamate, and 1 clove garlic, minced, or ½ tsp. ginger.

*Oriental-Style Barbecue*

**Beef Teriyaki**
**Cooked Rice Heated in Foil**
**Green Salad with Sliced Mushrooms**
**Fruit Kabobs (p. 61)**

*Gone Fishin'*

**Barbecued Trout**
**Potato Chips**
**Tomatoes Vinaigrette**
**Quick Date-Pineapple Cake (p. 181)**

### BARBECUED TROUT

Brush trout inside and out with lemon or lime juice before refrigerating—this keeps fish fresh in appearance and aroma. Place fish in shallow pan; pour on Marinade (below) and let stand an hour. Use drained Marinade for basting during barbecuing. Tuck a sprig or two of fresh herbs in cavity. Place on grill over bed of coals and barbecue until done, 10 to 15 min.

**Marinade:** Measure ½ cup soy sauce, ½ cup cooking sherry, 1 tbsp. lime or lemon juice, ¼ cup vegetable oil, and 1 clove garlic, crushed, into large jar. Shake well to blend.

## BARBECUED SPARERIBS

| | |
|---|---|
| 4½ lb. loin back ribs | 1½ tbsp. cornstarch |
| ½ cup soy sauce | Texas Barbecue Sauce (below) |

Place ribs in a large kettle with a cover and add 3 cups of water. Bring to a boil and cook 5 min. Remove ribs from water and drain well. Brush ribs with a mixture of the soy sauce and cornstarch. Continue to brush both sides of ribs, until all the soy-cornstarch mixture is gone. This should be done periodically over a period of 30 to 45 min. to allow the mixture to penetrate into the meat. Place ribs, bone side down, on grill 3″ from medium coals. Cook 30 min.; turn and cook 30 to 40 min. longer, turning and basting the ribs frequently with Texas Barbecue Sauce. Serve immediately with remaining sauce. *6 servings.*

**Texas Barbecue Sauce:** Mix in saucepan 1 cup tomato juice, ½ cup water, ¼ cup catsup, ¼ cup vinegar, 2 tbsp. Worcestershire sauce, 2 tbsp. brown sugar, 1 tbsp. paprika, 1 tsp. dry mustard, 1 tsp. salt, ¼ tsp. chili powder, ⅛ tsp. cayenne pepper. Simmer 15 min.

## VAGABOND STRAWBERRY SHORTCAKE

Make Fruit Shortcake Dough (below). Spread dough in greased pie pan. Cover with another pie pan. Bake on charcoal grill about 15 min. Turn pan over and bake on the other side for 15 min., until browned.

Split shortcake, spoon sweetened strawberries (⅔ to 1 cup sugar to 3 cups berries; let stand 1 hr. at room temperature) on lower half; replace top, spoon on more berries. Serve warm, cut into wedges, with plain or whipped cream.

**Fruit Shortcake Dough:** Add ¾ cup cream (or ½ cup milk plus ¼ cup butter, melted) to 2 cups Bisquick. Add 2 tbsp. sugar, if desired. Mix thoroughly with fork.

*PLANNING—This is the key word for a successful barbecue. After lighting the all-important match, while waiting for the coals to become hot gray, assemble everything you need: plates, napkins, glasses, eating utensils, barbecue tools, seasonings—and, of course, the food!*

*Spareribs 'n Shortcake*

**Barbecued Spareribs
with Texas Barbecue Sauce
Mashed Potatoes in Foil
Vegetable Relishes in Variety
Vagabond Strawberry Shortcake**

## CHARCOAL GRILLED BARBECUED CHICKEN

Brush chicken broiler pieces with barbecue sauce or marinate in sauce while getting the fire ready. Drain off excess sauce. Set chicken on grill 6 to 8″ from coals. If distance has to be less, watch carefully to avoid charring. Keep turning chicken every 5 min., basting with sauce. Grill 30 to 60 min., depending on size.

## ROAST CORN

Allow time for gray ash to cover charcoal briquets, about 45 min. Discard outer husks. Strip inner husks to end of cob; do not tear off. Pull out silk. Soak in ice water 20 min. Drain corn on towel; leave husks wet. Spread corn generously with butter. Rewrap in husks; then in double thickness of heavy-duty aluminum foil. Cook on ash-gray coals 10 to 15 min., turning once.

*Chick-N-Que*

**Pink Lemonade
Barbecued Chicken
Roast Corn
Onion-Cucumber Salad (p. 97)
with Sliced Tomatoes
Sliced Peaches          Gingersnaps (p. 52)**

## BEEFBURGERS

2 lb. ground beef
2 tsp. salt
1 tsp. pepper
¼ cup grated onion
1 tsp. monosodium glutamate

herbs, grated cheese, or chopped pickle
¼ cup water, broth, or milk for extra juicy burgers

Mix ingredients lightly. Form lightly into 8 thick patties. Place on grill over bed of coals and barbecue until done, 15 to 20 min. Baste with barbecue sauce while cooking.

## REFRESHING LEMON TEA

6 tea bags
1 qt. boiling water
1 can (6 oz.) lemonade concentrate

2 qt. cold water
¼ cup sugar

Steep tea bags in boiling water 15 min. Add concentrate, stirring until melted. Add cold water and sugar. Chill. Serve over ice in glasses. *Makes 12 glasses (8 oz. each) of tea.*

## LAZY MAN'S CHILI BEANS

4 cloves garlic
2 tsp. salt
¼ cup sugar
1 can (10 oz.) Spanish chili

4 slices bacon, diced
2 large onions, sliced ⅛″ thick
2 cans (1 lb. 4 oz. each) red kidney beans
1 cup water

Mash garlic, salt, and sugar to a paste; blend into chili. Fry bacon until golden; add onions and cook until soft and transparent. Stir in kidney beans, water, and chili mixture; simmer 20 to 30 min. May be made ahead and reheated. *8 servings.*

### *Teen Barbecue*

**Grilled Beefburgers or Franks**
**Buttered Toasted Buns**
**Lazy Man's Chili Beans**
**Cole Slaw**
**Ice Cream Balls    Summer Pastels (p. 124)**
**Refreshing Lemon Tea**

### *Breakfast Picnic*

**Peeled Oranges**
**Fried Eggs (p. 8)**
**Cherry Butterscotch Ring (p. 17)**
**(bake at home, reheat in foil over coals)**

# Good and Easy Suggestions for Leftovers

| FOOD | USE IN |
|---|---|
| **Beef or Lamb** | Beef Spanish Rice, p. 36<br>Sandwich Fillings, p. 26<br>French-toasted Sandwiches, p. 27<br>Monday Macaroni, p. 159<br>Heat sliced meat in gravy, serve with mashed potatoes or bread. |
| **Bread** | Croutons, p. 25<br>Cheeseburger Casserole, p. 37<br>Toast Cups, p. 107<br>Bread Stuffing, p. 82<br>Toasty Applesauce Dessert, p. 161<br>Mock Angel Food, p. 161 |
| **Cake** | Chocolate Refrigerator Dessert, p. 161<br>Singed Angel Wings, p. 161 |
| **Cheese** | Carrots au Gratin, p. 89<br>Cheese Delight, p. 101<br>Cheese Butter Dips, p. 118 |
| **Chicken or Turkey** | Chicken Salad, pp. 38, 43<br>Meat-Macaroni Salad, p. 43<br>Chicken-Tomato-Cole Slaw Sandwich, p. 30<br>Chicken or Turkey Spread for Canapés, p. 62<br>Chicken à la King, p. 80<br>Chicken Dinner Pie, p. 80<br>Easy Turkey Divan, p. 160<br>Chicken-Wild Rice Casserole, p. 109 |
| **Egg Whites** | White Mountain Frosting, p. 134<br>Forgotten Meringues, p. 170<br>Prune or Apricot Whip, p. 46 |
| **Egg Yolks** | Egg Yolk Sponge Cake, p.125<br>Millie's Mustard Sauce, p. 103<br>Add to Scrambled Eggs, p. 9<br>Baked Custard, p. 136 |

| FOOD | USE IN |
|---|---|
| **Fruits** | Ginger-Applesauce Bars, p. 52<br>Fruit-Tapioca Cream, p. 136<br>Fruit Gelatin Mold, p. 101<br>Use in fruit cups for appetizers or desserts. |
| **Ham** | Chef's Salad, p. 43<br>Ham-Potato Salad, p. 40<br>Ham with Potatoes, p. 35<br>Ham-Potato-Cheese Casserole, p. 35<br>Creamed Ham and Eggs, p. 37<br>Scalloped Corn and Ham, p. 90<br>Four-layer Dinner, p. 160<br>Macaroni Cups, p. 160<br>Sandwich Fillings, p. 26 |
| **Pork** | Chinese Pork and Rice, p. 36<br>Subgum, p. 159<br>Heat in barbecue sauce, serve in buns. |
| **Shrimp** | Sea Food Salad, p. 43<br>Sea Food Newburg, p. 85<br>Shrimp Circles, p. 63 |
| **Tuna or Salmon** | Sea Food Salad, p. 43<br>Sandwich Fillings, p. 26<br>Creamed Tuna or Salmon and Eggs, p. 37 |
| **Veal** | Garden Supper Casserole, p. 159<br>Monday Macaroni, p. 159<br>Savory Meat Pie, p. 159 |
| **Vegetables** | Mexican Green Bean Salad, p. 42<br>Quick Cream of Vegetable Soup, p. 24<br>Green and Gold Salad, p. 40<br>Potato-Egg Scramble, p. 37<br>Beef Crumble on Muffin Squares, p. 114<br>Salmon Supper, p. 106<br>Sweet Potato Balls, p. 92<br>Hashed Creamed Potatoes, p. 159 |

*Thanks to modern wrapping materials and freezing and refrigeration methods, leftover foods need never be wasted. You can transform them into tempting and nutritious dishes with a little planning, a bit of imagination, and a few recipe suggestions.*

## GARDEN SUPPER CASSEROLE

2 cups cubed soft bread
  (about 2 slices)

½ cup grated sharp
  cheese

2 tbsp. butter, melted

1 cup cooked peas
  or other vegetable

1½ cups Medium Cream
  Sauce (p. 103)

2 tbsp. chopped onion

1 cup cut-up cooked
  meat, tuna, or 3 hard-
  cooked eggs, sliced

1 large tomato, sliced

Heat oven to 350° (mod.). Mix bread cubes, cheese, and butter; spread half this mixture in greased 1-qt. baking dish. Add peas. Make Cream Sauce, browning onion in the butter. Add meat; pour over peas. Arrange tomato over top and cover with remaining bread mixture. Bake 25 min. *4 servings.*

## SUBGUM

*See picture opposite.*

1 can (4 oz.) sliced
  mushrooms (drained,
  reserving liquid)

2 cups diced cooked pork
  from pork roast

1 tbsp. butter

2 cups sliced celery

1½ cups leftover
  gravy

1 can (1 lb. 4 oz.)
  bean sprouts

Sauté mushrooms and pork in butter. Add celery, mushroom liquid, and gravy; cook over low heat until celery is just tender, about 30 min. Add water if mixture becomes too thick. Add drained bean sprouts; heat through. Serve on hot fluffy rice or crisp Chinese noodles. *4 servings.*

*Simple-to-Make Supper*

**One of the Main Dishes Pictured
Fresh or Canned Fruits in Variety
with Vanilla-Mayonnaise Topping (p. 102)
Ranch Pudding (p. 183)**

## SAVORY MEAT PIE

*See picture opposite.*

¼ cup chopped onion

2 tbsp. chopped green
  pepper

2 cups diced cooked meat
  (beef, lamb, or veal)

2 cups diced cooked vege-
  tables (carrots, celery,
  peas, corn, turnips,
  green beans)

1½ to 2 cups well-
  seasoned gravy,
  thinned with milk
  or stock

Biscuit dough (p. 44)
  or pastry for Baked
  Pie Shell (p. 141)

Heat oven to 425° (hot). Sauté onion and pepper in hot fat. Combine with meat, vegetables, and gravy in 2-qt. baking dish. Top with biscuits or pastry. Cut slits in top for steam to escape. Bake 20 min. *4 servings.*

## MONDAY MACARONI

*See picture opposite.*

2 onions, minced

2 tbsp. butter

1 tbsp. vegetable oil

1 cup finely chopped
  cooked meat

1 can (6 oz.) tomato
  purée

2 tsp. minced parsley

bit of bay leaf

1 cup cooked vegetables

1 cup meat stock

hot boiled macaroni
  (8 oz. uncooked)

Sauté onions in butter and oil. Add meat and cook 5 min. Add tomato purée, parsley, and bay leaf; simmer 15 min. Add vegetables and meat stock. Heat through; pour over macaroni on hot platter. Sprinkle with grated sharp Cheddar or Parmesan cheese. Serve immediately. *4 servings.*

## HASHED CREAMED POTATOES

Chop leftover boiled or baked potatoes finely. Add half as much cream as potatoes; season. Heat in saucepan 10 to 15 min., or until thick. Or pour into baking dish, top with buttered crumbs, and heat in moderate oven until bubbly.

## FOUR-LAYER DINNER

Heat oven to 350° (mod.). Drain 1 can (15½ oz.) green beans; place in bottom of 8" sq. or 1½-qt. baking dish. Top with 8 slices of leftover ham. Combine 1 can (10½ oz.) cream of celery soup, ¼ cup mayonnaise, and 1 tsp. prepared mustard; pour over ham and beans. Top with ¼ cup fine dry bread crumbs and ¼ lb. grated natural Cheddar cheese. Bake 30 min. *6 to 8 servings.*

**Note:** *1 can (12 oz.) luncheon meat, cut in 8 slices, may be substituted for ham.*

## MACARONI CUPS

Heat oven to 400° (mod. hot). Combine 2 cups cooked macaroni (1 cup uncooked), ½ to 1 cup cubed leftover ham, 1 cup cubed cheese, 1 tsp. prepared mustard, 1 tsp. horse-radish, and 1 cup Medium Cream Sauce (p. 103). Place in greased individual casseroles or 1-qt. baking dish. Top with buttered crumbs or crushed Wheaties. Bake 20 to 25 min. *4 servings.*

## EASY TURKEY DIVAN

| | |
|---|---|
| 2 pkg. (10 oz. each) frozen broccoli spears | 1 can (14½ oz.) evaporated milk |
| 6 slices turkey or 2 cups pieces of turkey | 1 can (10½ oz.) mushroom soup |
| 6 slices cheese | 1 can (3½ oz.) French-fried onion rings |

Heat oven to 350° (mod.). Cook broccoli to crisp-tender stage. Put in bottom of oblong baking dish, 11½ x 7½ x 1½". Cover with turkey; top with cheese slices and cover with mixture of milk and soup. Bake 25 min. Cover with onion rings and bake 5 min. more. *4 to 6 servings.*

 *Holiday Week Supper*

**Easy Turkey Divan**
**Pear-Cranberry Salad (p. 96)**
**Herb-topped Rolls (p. 117)**
**Pep-O-Mint Cake (p. 131)**

## CHOCOLATE REFRIGERATOR DESSERT

Prepare 1 pkg. chocolate pudding mix as directed on pkg.; cool. Whip 1 cup whipping cream with ⅓ cup confectioners' sugar and fold into cooled pudding. Cut up 1 layer leftover white, yellow, or chocolate cake and line bottom of 8″ sq. baking dish. Pour pudding over cake. Sprinkle ½ cup chopped nuts over pudding, if desired. Chill several hours. *4 to 6 servings.*

## INDIVIDUAL COOKY TORTES

| | |
|---|---|
| ½ cup whipping cream | 12 leftover sandwich cookies |
| ¼ cup confectioners' sugar | |
| 1 tbsp. cocoa | chopped salted peanuts |

Beat cream, sugar, and cocoa until stiff. For each torte, split 2 sandwich cookies; spread cocoa whipped cream between each layer; frost top and sides. Continue until you have 6 individual cooky tortes. Garnish with peanuts. Chill overnight. *6 servings.*

## TOASTY APPLESAUCE DESSERT

| | |
|---|---|
| 6 slices whole wheat or white bread | ½ tsp. cinnamon |
| soft butter | 1 can (1 lb.) applesauce |
| ½ cup sugar | ⅓ cup raisins |
| | ¼ cup maple-flavored syrup |

Heat oven to 350° (mod.). Trim crusts from bread slices. Cut each trimmed slice into 3 strips; butter both sides of bread strips. Combine sugar and cinnamon. Sprinkle 2 tbsp. sugar mixture in bottom of 8″ baking pan. Place half of bread strips in bottom of pan; sprinkle with 2 more tbsp. sugar mixture. Cover with applesauce; sprinkle with raisins. Top with remaining bread strips. Sprinkle remaining ¼ cup sugar mixture over bread strips. Pour syrup over all. Bake 30 min., or until bread strips are golden brown. Serve warm with cream. *6 servings.*

## COCONUT BALLS

Cut leftover angel food cake into pieces 2″ square. Gently mold into balls. Dip into a fluffy white frosting. Roll in moist shredded coconut.

## MOCK ANGEL FOOD

Dip several-day-old bread slices in sweetened condensed milk, then in flaked coconut. Place on baking sheet and toast in hot oven until bread is hot through and coconut brown.

## FRUIT FRAPPÉ

Save leftover fruit juice, syrup from canned fruit, and fresh canned or frozen fruit in a jar in refrigerator. When you have 3 to 4 cups, freeze solid in refrigerator tray. To serve: break into chunks with spoon, then whip with electric mixer or blender until frozen pieces are fine. Serve with a straw.

## SINGED ANGEL WINGS

Brush cut sides of wedges of angel food or chiffon cake with melted butter. Lightly brown on both sides under broiler, about 1 min. on each side. Serve with Quick Orange Sauce (below).

**Quick Orange Sauce:** Combine 1 cup sugar, 2 tbsp. cornstarch, and 1 tsp. salt in pan. Blend well; gradually stir in 1 cup water. Add 2 tbsp. butter. Cook, stirring constantly, until mixture boils; boil 1 min. Remove from heat; stir in 1 can (6 oz.) undiluted frozen orange juice concentrate. *Makes 2 cups sauce.*

# ❦ Freezing Tips ❧

## WRAPPING SOLID FOODS

For meat, cake, pie, bread, etc., use freezerweight paper such as heavy-duty aluminum foil or transparent plastic. Polyethylene bags may be used for baked goods. Use freezer tape for sealing. It may also be used as a label on hard-to-mark wrapping materials. Label wrapped goods with china marking pencil of felt pen.

## PACKING LIQUID FOODS

Package liquids in heavily waxed cartons, glass freezer jars, or plastic or aluminum containers. Choose a size of container that holds enough for one meal. Use containers with wide openings so food may be removed when only partially thawed. Casserole dishes may be frozen in the baking dish, ready to reheat.

## TIME CHART FOR KEEPING FROZEN BAKED FOODS

| FOOD | STORAGE TIMES | DEFROSTING TIMES | TIPS |
|---|---|---|---|
| **Yeast Breads** (loaves, coffee cake, and rolls) | Baked: 2 to 3 mo. (freezing dough not recommended) | Cakes and rolls: 325° oven, about 20 min. Loaves: room temp. 3 hr. (wrapped) | Cool thoroughly before wrapping. Bake to light golden brown to prevent separation of upper crust from interior of loaf. |
| **Quick Breads** (nut and fruit breads, biscuits, muffins, coffee cakes, waffles, and pancakes) | Baked: 2 to 3 mo. (freezing dough not recommended) | Biscuits, muffins, cakes: 325° oven, 25 min. Nut breads: room temp. 1½ to 2 hr. (wrapper on). | Do not overbake, as this makes breads dry when reheated. Cool thoroughly, then freeze immediately. |
| **Pies** (fruit, pumpkin, and mince) (chiffon) | Baked: 4 to 6 mo. 2 to 3 mo. Unbaked Pies: 2 to 3 mo. | Baked: room temp. 30 min., then reheat in 325° oven 30 min. Chiffon: room temp. 45 min. or in refrigerator 2 to 3 hr. Unbaked: bake frozen pies at given temp. 15 to 20 min. *longer* than time given in recipe. | Unbaked frozen pies may tend to have a soggy bottom crust. Bake or reheat on lower oven shelf. |
| **Cookies** (rolled, bar, drop, and refrigerator) | Baked: 9 to 12 mo. Dough: 9 to 12 mo. | Baked: 10 to 15 min. at room temp. (not in oven). Dough: thaw slightly before rolling, slicing. | Be sure to wrap cookies tightly for freezing or they may dry out. Frost cookies after thawing to prevent sogginess. |
| **Cakes** (butter, angel food, chiffon, double-quick, pound, fruitcakes, and cupcakes) | Unfrosted: 6 mo. Frosted: 2 to 3 mo. (freezing dough not recommended) | Large cake: 2 to 3 hr. at room temp. Layers: 1 hr. (room temp.). Cupcakes: 30 min. (room temp.). | If possible, fill and frost after thawing. However, confectioners' sugar-type freezes best of all frostings. |

# Meals on Time

*Ever have the problem of getting all the food for a meal ready at the same time? A little planning on paper will help you have everything finished at that "magic moment."*

*After a few times, detailed planning as shown below won't be necessary. However, it will still be helpful to list the food for dinner in order of preparation with main starting times jotted down.*

*And when you are preparing dinner for guests, a detailed list helps you organize your work, keeps you from becoming confused, and allows you to enjoy your own dinner party.*

---

### Family Dinner

**Oven-fried Chicken (p. 79)**

**Mashed Potatoes**      **Cream Gravy**

**Buttered French-style Green Beans**

**Old-fashioned Cabbage Slaw (p. 97)**

**Cherry Cobbler (p. 48)**

**Milk or Coffee**

---

### Holiday Dinner

**Roast Chicken, Turkey, Duckling, or Goose (p. 78)**

**with Stuffing (p. 82)**

**Mashed Potatoes**      **Giblet Gravy**

**Savory Green Limas (p. 87)**

**Mashed Squash or Rutabagas**

**Cranberry Sauce**      **Hot Rolls**

**Pickles and Olives**

**Sherbet with Fruitcake**

---

## FOR DINNER AT 6:30 P.M.

### Approximate Preparation Times

| | |
|---|---|
| Oven-fried Chicken | 1 hr. |
| Mashed Potatoes<br>Using our mashed Potato Buds. | 10 min. |
| Green Beans<br>Using frozen beans, ready to cook. | 12 min. |
| Cole Slaw<br>Make ahead and chill in refrigerator. | 15 min. |
| Cherry Cobbler<br>Allow 15 min. for mixing, 25 min. for baking. | 40 min. |

### Preparation Steps

| | |
|---|---|
| 5:00 | Prepare chicken for oven. |
| 5:15 | Have chicken in oven. |
| 5:15–5:45 | Free time.<br>Turn chicken. Prepare cobbler. Mix salad. |
| 6:00 | Set table. |
| 6:15 | Start green beans. Remove chicken from oven. Make coffee. |
| 6:20 | Make gravy. Start mashed potatoes. |
| 6:25 | Serve food. Remove cobbler from oven. |
| 6:30 | *The Magic Moment.* |

## PLAN AHEAD

**Do These Things Two Days Ahead**

1. Do all possible marketing.
2. Plan table arrangement and centerpiece.
3. Check over table linens, china, silverware, and glassware needed. See that linens are fresh and that silverware, glassware, and china are shining and bright.

**Do These Things One Day Ahead**

1. Wash and dry the chicken, turkey, duckling, or goose. Store in refrigerator ready for stuffing.
2. Make stuffing, cool and store it in plastic bag or covered bowl in refrigerator. (Don't stuff bird until just before roasting.)
3. Make cranberry sauce. If sauce is not jellied, place in serving dish and cover.
4. Bake rolls.
5. Simmer giblets, chop and refrigerate ready for gravy.
6. Arrange centerpiece. Fresh flowers will keep well if room is at moderate temperature and if plant food is added to water.

# Herbs

*Remember . . . use a very light touch at first! Then taste before adding more.*

| | APPETIZERS AND SOUPS | MEATS AND POULTRY | CHEESE, EGGS, AND FISH | VEGETABLES AND SALADS |
|---|---|---|---|---|
| **Basil** | Tomato juice or soup. Sea food dips or spreads. Vegetable or pea soup. | Beef, pork, veal, lamb. Fried or broiled chicken or liver. Marinades. Stuffing. | All egg or cheese dishes. On fish prepared any way. Also shellfish. | Tomatoes in any form. Italian vegetables or salads. Squash, beans, carrots, beets, peas. |
| **Dill** | Any cheese dip or spread. Tomato juice or soup, borsch, pea soup. Smoked fish. | Lamb chops or steaks. Corned beef. Italian spaghetti. Creamed chicken. | All egg and cheese dishes. Fish sauces, such as tartar or cream sauce. | In peas, cauliflower, sautéed potatoes. In sour cream salad dressings. |
| **Marjoram** | Avocados, patés, cream cheese. Clam chowder, onion soup. Tomato juice. | Beef, pork, veal. Stews. Chicken or meat pie. Sausages. Stuffings. | Any cheese or egg dish. Sprinkle on fish before baking. Creamed fish. | Tossed green salad. Zucchini, peas, mushrooms, carrots, fried potatoes. |
| **Oregano** | Guacamole. Pizza. All mushroom appetizers, tomato juice. Bean or tomato soup. | Spaghetti sauces. All game. Mushroom sauces. Broiled or fried chicken. | Baked or poached eggs, omelets. Any shellfish dish. Fish stuffings. | Avocado salad. All mushroom dishes. Spanish sauces for vegetables. Onions. |
| **Rosemary** | Jams and jellies. Fruit cups. Chicken, pea, or turtle soup. | Veal or lamb, stews, pot roast. All chicken dishes. Marinades. Stuffings. | Scrambled or shirred eggs, omelets. Baked or fried fish. | Cabbage, broccoli, Brussels sprouts, potatoes, mushrooms. Fruit salads. |
| **Savory** | Patés. Vegetable juice. Consommé, chowders, bean or lentil soup. | Smoked turkey, pork, veal, lamb. Chicken or meat loaf. Stews. Stuffings. | Cream cheese. Baked fish. Scrambled or shirred eggs, omelets. | Green, tomato, vegetable, or potato salad. Artichokes, asparagus. |
| **Tarragon** | Chicken livers. Vegetable juices. Cheese spreads or dips. Any soup or chowder. | Any chops or steaks. Chicken, turkey, or game. Beef or lamb stew. Marinades. | All egg dishes. Baked or broiled fish or lobster. Tartar sauce. | Sea food salad, tomato aspic, salad dressing. Asparagus, beans, beets, chard. |
| **Thyme** | Cheese or sea food dips or spreads. Fish or clam chowders. Oyster stew. | Lamb in any way, veal, pot roast, stew, game, meat loaf, creamed chicken. | Scrambled eggs or omelet. Cheese sandwiches, soufflé, or fondue. Fish. | Sea food or chicken salad, tomato aspic, cabbage slaw, sliced tomatoes. Beets. |

# Table of Food Equivalents

| FOOD | WEIGHT | APPROXIMATE MEASURE |
|---|---|---|
| Apples | 1 lb. | 3 medium (3 cups sliced) |
| Bananas | 1 lb. | 3 medium (2½ cups sliced) |
| Berries | 1 qt. | 3½ cups |
| Bread crumbs, fresh | 1-lb. loaf | 8 cups fresh bread crumbs |
| Butter, margarine, other fats | 1 oz. | 2 tbsp. |
| | 1 stick (¼ lb.) | ½ cup |
| | 1 lb. | 2 cups |
| Candied fruit | ½ lb. | 1½ cups |
| Cheese, Cheddar or American | ¼ lb. | 1 cup grated |
| Cheese, cottage | 12-oz. carton | 1½ cups |
| Cheese, cream | 3-oz. pkg. | 6 tbsp. |
| Coffee, ground | 1 lb. | 80 tbsp. (to make 40 cups) |
| Chocolate, unsweetened | ½-lb. pkg. | 8 1-oz. squares |
| Cocoa | 4 oz. | 1 cup |
| Coconut, shredded | 1 lb. | 5 cups |
| Cream, commercial sour | 12-oz. carton | 1½ cups |
| Cream, whipping | ½ pt. | 1 cup (2 cups whipped) |
| Dates, pitted | 7½-oz. pkg. | 1¼ cups, cut up |
| Egg whites | 4 | ½ cup |
| Egg yolks | 6 | ½ cup |
| Flour | | |
| All-purpose | 1 lb. | 3½ cups unsifted |
| Cake | 1 lb. | 4 cups unsifted |
| Rye | 1 lb. | 4½ to 5 cups unsifted |
| Whole wheat | 1 lb. | 3½ cups unsifted |
| Lemon | 1 medium | 1½ to 3 tsp. grated rind and 2 to 3 tbsp. juice |
| Macaroni | 7- or 8-oz. pkg. | 4 cups cooked |
| Marshmallows | ¼ lb. | 16 |
| Milk | | |
| Evaporated | 6-oz. can | ¾ cup |
| | 14½-oz. can | 1⅔ cups |
| Sweetened condensed | 15½-oz. can | 1½ cups |
| Noodles | 5- or 6-oz. pkg. | 2½ cups cooked |
| Nuts, in shell | | |
| Almonds | 1 lb. | 1 to 1¾ cups nutmeats |
| Peanuts | 1 lb. | 2¼ cups nutmeats |
| Pecans and walnuts | 1 lb. | 1⅔ cups nutmeats |
| Nuts, shelled | | |
| Almonds | 1 lb. | 3½ cups nutmeats |
| Peanuts | 1 lb. | 3 cups nutmeats |
| Pecans and walnuts | 1 lb. | 4 cups nutmeats |
| Oranges | 1 medium | 1 to 2 tbsp. grated rind and ⅓ to ½ cup juice |
| Potatoes, sweet | 1 lb. | 3 medium (3 cups sliced) |
| Potatoes, white | 1 lb. | 3 medium (2⅓ cups sliced) |
| Raisins | 15-oz. pkg. | 3 cups |
| Rice, white | 1 cup | 3 to 4 cups cooked |
| Rice, wild | 1 cup | 3 cups cooked |
| Spaghetti | 7- or 8-oz. pkg. | 4 cups cooked |
| Sugar | | |
| Brown | 1 lb. | 2¼ cups (packed) |
| Confectioners' | 1 lb. | 4½ cups (sifted) |
| Granulated | 1 lb. | 2 cups |

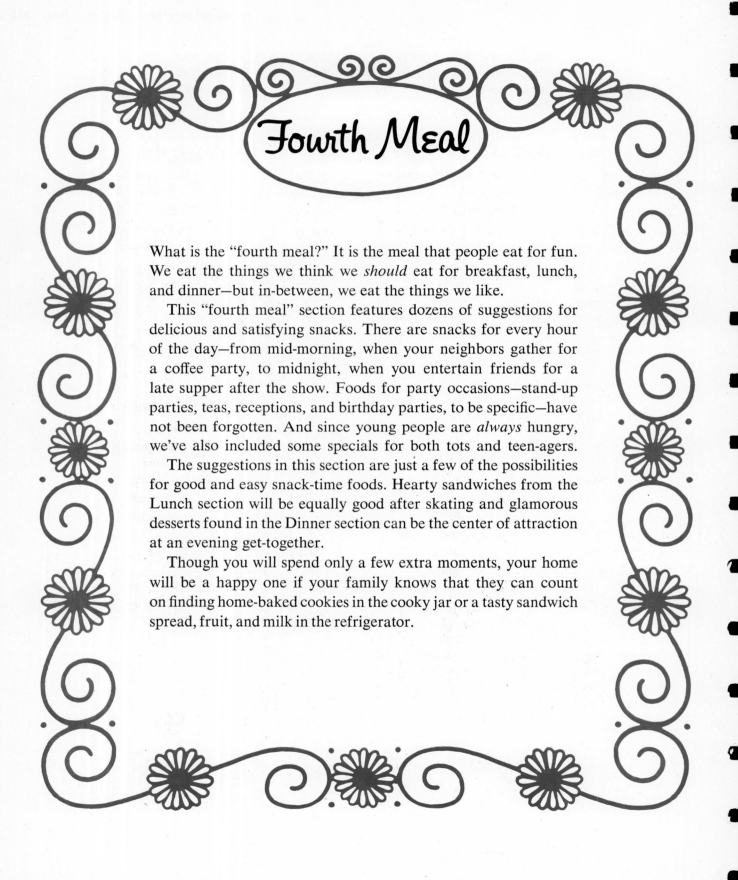

# Fourth Meal

What is the "fourth meal?" It is the meal that people eat for fun. We eat the things we think we *should* eat for breakfast, lunch, and dinner—but in-between, we eat the things we like.

This "fourth meal" section features dozens of suggestions for delicious and satisfying snacks. There are snacks for every hour of the day—from mid-morning, when your neighbors gather for a coffee party, to midnight, when you entertain friends for a late supper after the show. Foods for party occasions—stand-up parties, teas, receptions, and birthday parties, to be specific—have not been forgotten. And since young people are *always* hungry, we've also included some specials for both tots and teen-agers.

The suggestions in this section are just a few of the possibilities for good and easy snack-time foods. Hearty sandwiches from the Lunch section will be equally good after skating and glamorous desserts found in the Dinner section can be the center of attraction at an evening get-together.

Though you will spend only a few extra moments, your home will be a happy one if your family knows that they can count on finding home-baked cookies in the cooky jar or a tasty sandwich spread, fruit, and milk in the refrigerator.

*The old German "Kaffee Klatsch" tradition has been eagerly adopted in America. And well it might, for it affords time to relax and enjoy your neighbors and friends. With little work, you can proudly serve a homemade treat.*

## BLUEBERRY BUCKLE

¾ cup sugar
¼ cup soft shortening
1 egg
½ cup milk
2 cups Gold
   Medal Flour

2 tsp. baking powder
½ tsp. salt
2 cups fresh or drained
   canned blueberries
Crumb Topping (below)

Heat oven to 375° (quick mod.). Mix thoroughly sugar, shortening, and egg. Stir in milk. Measure flour by dip-level-pour method. Mix flour, baking powder, and salt; stir in. Blend in berries. Spread in greased and floured 9″ sq. pan. Sprinkle with Crumb Topping. Bake 45 to 50 min., until toothpick stuck into center comes out clean. Serve warm. *Makes nine 3″ squares.*

**Crumb Topping:** Mix ½ cup sugar, ⅓ cup flour, ½ tsp. cinnamon, and ¼ cup soft butter.

## FRENCH BREAKFAST PUFFS

⅓ cup soft shortening
½ cup sugar
1 egg
1½ cups Gold
   Medal Flour
1½ tsp. baking
   powder

½ tsp. salt
¼ tsp. nutmeg
½ cup milk
⅓ cup butter, melted
½ cup more sugar
1 tsp. cinnamon

Heat oven to 350° (mod.). Mix shortening, ½ cup sugar, and egg. Measure flour by dip-level-pour method. Mix flour, baking powder, salt, and nutmeg; stir in alternately with milk. Fill greased muffin cups ⅔ full. Bake 20 to 25 min., until golden brown. Immediately roll in melted butter, then in mixture of ½ cup sugar and cinnamon. *Makes 12 medium puffs.*

## EASY SUGAR BUNS

2 cups Bisquick
2 tbsp. sugar
1 tsp. nutmeg
⅛ tsp. cinnamon

⅔ cup cream or
   ½ cup milk
1 egg
¼ cup butter, melted
½ cup sugar

Heat oven to 400° (mod. hot). Mix Bisquick, 2 tbsp. sugar, and spices. Add cream and egg. Mix thoroughly. Drop dough into greased muffin cups, filling cups ½ full. Bake about 15 min.

Dip warm buns in melted butter, then into the ½ cup sugar, coating all sides. Serve warm. *Makes 10 to 12 medium buns.*

## DATE-AND-NUT BREAD

1½ cups boiling
   water
1½ cups cut-up dates
½ cup brown sugar
   (packed)
1 tbsp. soft shortening

1 egg
2¼ cups Gold Medal
   Flour
1 tsp. soda
½ tsp. salt
1 cup broken nuts

Heat oven to 350° (mod.). Grease a loaf pan, 9x5x3″. Pour boiling water over dates; let cool. Mix sugar, shortening, and egg thoroughly. Stir in the dates. Measure flour by dip-level-pour method. Mix dry ingredients and stir in. Blend in nuts. Pour into greased pan. Bake 60 to 70 min.

## TEA BREAD TOPPINGS

Toast plain or nut bread slices, split English muffins, biscuits, or other muffins. Butter lightly. Serve with one or more of the following spreads:

Cream cheese mixed with chopped dates or raisins.

Grated orange or lemon rind mixed with sugar.

Maple butter (whip 1 cup maple syrup into ½ cup soft butter until fluffy).

Cinnamon-sugar (keep in shaker for easy serving).

Cream cheese mixed with a little orange juice and grated orange rind.

Orange marmalade or favorite jams or preserves.

Pineapple cheese spread (from a jar).

Brown sugar, butter, and coconut.

Cinnamon-flavored honey (shake cinnamon into honey to taste).

## COFFEE ELEGANT

**Café au Lait:** Pour equal amounts of strong coffee and hot milk into serving cup at the same time.

**South American Coffee:** Mix equal amounts of hot chocolate and coffee.

**Vienna Coffee:** Serve strong black coffee in tiny demitasse cups topped with whipped cream.

**Cocoa-Coffee:** Stir 1 tbsp. cocoa into 6 cups hot black coffee.

**Café Mexican:** Fill demitasse cups with strong black coffee; top with Spiced Whipped Cream: add 1 tbsp. confectioners' sugar, ⅛ tsp. each of cinnamon and nutmeg to ½ cup whipping cream, whipped.

**Double Iced Coffee:** Make coffee ice cubes by freezing coffee in ice cube trays. Put in tall glasses; pour double strength coffee over. Top with Spiced Whipped Cream (see Café Mexican).

## PINEAPPLE-CARAMEL-NUT ROLLS

Heat oven to 375° (quick mod.). Combine ½ cup brown sugar (packed), ¼ cup butter, and 2 tbsp. molasses in small pan. Stir over medium heat until butter is melted and a smooth syrup forms. Put about 1 tbsp. syrup in each of 12 medium muffin cups. Sprinkle 3 or 4 pecan halves over syrup. Drain 1 can (9 oz.) crushed pineapple. Divide pineapple equally between muffin cups. Place unbaked brown 'n serve clover leaf rolls, bottom-side-down, on top of mixture. Bake 15 min. Remove from oven and invert immediately. Let rolls stand a few minutes before removing from pan. Serve pineapple-side-up. *Makes 12 rolls.*

## QUICKIE KOLACHES

In each of 12 brown 'n serve rolls, cut a hole from the top with a melon ball cutter or a teaspoon. Fill hole with cherry jam. Place on ungreased baking sheet. Bake 15 min. in quick mod. oven (375°). Spread a mixture of 1 cup sifted confectioners' sugar and 2 tbsp. milk over hot rolls.

## EASY SNACK COOKIES

*Use cookies purchased at your neighborhood bakery or grocery.*

Serve in two's, with favorite confectioners' sugar frosting, bright jam, or toasted marshmallow between.

Stack together with whipped cream and nuts between. Chill to mellow.

Serve softer cookies, perhaps brownies, as a base for ice cream, top with sauce for luscious, easy dessert.

Frost chocolate drop cookies with peppermint icing, sugar cookies with pastel-tinted icing, peanut butter cookies with chocolate icing.

## VELVET CRUMB CAKE

| | |
|---|---|
| **1⅓ cups Bisquick** | **1 egg** |
| **¾ cup sugar** | **¾ cup milk** |
| **3 tbsp. soft shortening** | **1 tsp. vanilla** |

Heat oven to 350° (mod.). Grease and flour an 8″ sq. pan or a round layer pan, 9x1½″. Mix Bisquick and sugar. Add shortening, egg, and ¼ cup of milk. Beat vigorously 1 min. Gradually stir in remaining milk and vanilla. Beat ½ min. Pour into pan. Bake 35 to 40 min., until top springs back when lightly touched. While warm, cover with Broiled Coconut Icing (p. 134). Serve warm.

## VELVET CRUMB UPSIDE-DOWN CAKE

Melt over low heat 2 tbsp. butter in an 8″ sq. pan. Sprinkle with ¼ cup brown sugar. Arrange fresh or well drained canned fruit over sugar. Make Velvet Crumb Cake batter (above); pour over fruit in pan. Bake 40 to 45 min. Invert pan at once on serving plate.

## VELVET FUDGE CAKE

Make Velvet Crumb Cake (above)—except add ⅓ cup cocoa to Bisquick. Pour half of batter into prepared 8″ sq. pan. Spread with half of Chocolate-Coconut Topping (below). Pour remaining batter into pan. Bake 35 to 40 min. Immediately spread with rest of topping. Serve warm.

**Chocolate-Coconut Topping:** Mix ⅓ cup water, 2 cups finely chopped coconut, and ½ cup semi-sweet chocolate pieces, melted.

## EASY BUTTER MIX COOKIES

*Richly elegant cookies made with cake mix!*
Heat oven to 375° (quick mod.). Mix ⅓ cup butter, ½ cup shortening (do not use all butter or all shortening), 2 egg yolks, and ½ tsp. vanilla. Thoroughly blend in 1 pkg. of our layer cake mix (any flavor but Marble)—⅓ at a time. If dough seems dry, add 1 to 1½ tsp. water. Add ½ cup chopped nuts, if desired. Form scant teaspoonfuls into balls. Bake 8 to 12 min. on ungreased baking sheet. *Makes 6 to 8 doz. cookies.*

**Pressed Cookies:** Omit nuts; press dough through cooky press into favorite shapes. Bake 8 to 10 min.

**Refrigerated Cookies:** Omit nuts; mold dough in long, smooth roll 1½″ in diameter. Roll in finely chopped nuts. Wrap in waxed paper; chill until stiff. With sharp thin knife, slice ⅛″ thick. Bake 6 to 8 min.

## CHOCOLATE CHIP COCONUT CHEWS

Heat oven to 325° (slow mod.). Prepare 1 pkg. of our fluffy white frosting mix as directed on pkg. With a fork, stir frosting into 1 pkg. (8 oz.) shredded coconut (3 cups) and 1 pkg. (6 oz.) chocolate pieces (1 cup). With two forks, drop lightly into little mounds (about tablespoon-size) on lightly greased baking sheet. Bake 17 to 20 min. *Makes about 3½ doz. cookies.*

*COOKIES ABRACADABRA!! — Keep packaged cooky mixes on hand for delicious coffee-time treats.*

*Another easy way for cookies-in-a-hurry... make your favorite refrigerator cookies in long rolls and freeze. When guests come, remove rolls from freezer, thaw about 10 min.—they're ready to be sliced and baked.*

## VELVET CREAM CAKE

*A fluffy whipped cream filling nestled between layers of tender, light cake.*

Bake your favorite flavor of any of our layer cake mixes in 9″ layers as directed on pkg. Split each layer, making 4 layers. Choose a matching flavor of our creamy-type frosting mix (chocolate fudge with devils food or yellow cake mix, creamy white with white or marble cake mix, and caramel fudge with honey spice cake mix).

Add 2 cups dry frosting mix to 1½ cups whipping cream (35% butterfat) and 1 tsp. vanilla for filling. Chill 1 hr.; whip. Put filling between layers. Spread top with Thin Icing (below), letting some dribble down sides. Sprinkle top of cake with chopped nuts, if desired. Chill. *About 12 servings.*

**Thin Icing:** Blend rest of dry frosting mix, 2 to 3 tbsp. hot water, and 1 tbsp. light corn syrup. Beat until smooth. Add 1 to 2 tsp. more water, if necessary.

## FORGOTTEN MERINGUES

*They bake while you sleep.*

6 egg whites (¾ cup)     2 cups sugar
1½ tsp. lemon juice or
   ½ tsp. cream of tartar

Heat oven to 400° (mod. hot). Beat egg whites with lemon juice or cream of tartar until frothy. Gradually beat in sugar a little at a time. Beat until stiff and glossy. Drop by small spoonfuls in circles on baking sheet covered with brown paper, or heap into high mounds and hollow out with back of spoon. Put into oven, close door, turn off oven. (Don't peek!) Let stand overnight in oven. To serve: fill meringues with ice cream; top with fresh fruit or with butterscotch or chocolate sauce and salted pecans or almonds. *Makes 12 meringues.*

## NUT-GLAZED FRUIT PIE

Blend 2 tbsp. soft butter and ¼ cup brown sugar (packed). Stir in 1½ tbsp. cream and ¼ cup pecan halves. Spread over baked fruit pie (frozen or from the bakery, warm or cooled). Place under broiler 3″ from source of heat. Broil 3 to 5 min., or until glaze bubbles and browns. Serve while glaze is still warm.

## FROZEN CHOCOLATE CREAM PIE

9″ Baked Pie Shell (p. 141)     1 cup chocolate-flavored syrup
2 cups whipping cream (35% butterfat)     ¼ to ½ cup chopped nuts
½ tsp. vanilla

Whip cream until stiff. Carefully fold in vanilla and syrup. Pile filling into pie shell. Sprinkle with nuts. Freeze overnight, or until firm. Remove from freezer 10 min. before serving.

## ORANGE REFRIGERATOR DESSERT

½ angel food cake     1 cup orange juice, fresh or diluted concentrated
1 envelope unflavored gelatin (1 tbsp.)     1 cup sugar
¼ cup cold water     2 cups whipping cream, whipped
¼ cup boiling water

Break cake in small pieces. Place in oblong pan, 13x9½x2″. Soften gelatin in cold water; dissolve in boiling water. Mix orange juice, sugar; blend in gelatin. Chill until slightly thickened. Beat. Mix gelatin mixture and whipped cream. Pour over cake. Chill. If desired, sprinkle grated orange rind over top. *12 large servings.*

---

## PERFECT FOR DESSERT PARTIES

Surprise Cheesecake, p. 140.
Pot de Crème au Chocolat, p. 140.
Cranberry Stack Cake, p. 129.
Strawberry-Lemon Cake, p. 132.
Brownie Ribbon Dessert, p. 139.
Pearadise Snowcap Dessert, p. 139.
Ambrosia Pie, p. 147.

*For a formal tea or reception at home, arrange the dining table with simple elegance, the tea service at one end, the coffee at the other. And an open house at holiday time is a wonderful way to entertain family, neighbors, and friends.*

### Easy Tea or Reception

**Tea and Coffee**
**Floating Island Punch**
**Special Party Sandwiches (p. 172)**
**Little Cakes and Fancy Cookies**
**Salted Nuts          Fondant Mints**

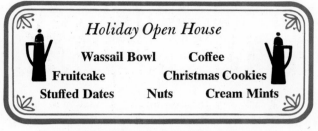

### Holiday Open House

**Wassail Bowl          Coffee**
**Fruitcake          Christmas Cookies**
**Stuffed Dates          Nuts          Cream Mints**

## HOT TEA

Put 1 to 1½ tsp. tea for each cup or person in scalded teapot. Pour over it freshly boiled water. Let stand in warm place 3 to 5 min. Strain. Serve at once. Have pot of hot water to dilute tea as desired. Serve with thin half slices of lemon or milk and sugar.

**Note:** *Tea ball or bag may be placed in cup and boiling water poured over. After 3 min. or less, remove bag or ball.*

**Iced Tea:** Fill glass ⅓ full with cracked ice, strain double-strength fresh tea over. Serve with lemon.

## FLOATING ISLAND PUNCH

½ cup sugar

2 cups water

1 can (6 oz.) frozen concentrated lemon juice

3 cans (6 oz. each) frozen concentrated orange juice

1 qt. ginger ale

1 qt. sparkling water or white grape juice

1 bottle (4 oz.) maraschino cherries and juice

1 orange, sliced thin

ice cubes

1 pt. lemon or orange sherbet

Heat sugar and water until sugar dissolves; cool. Combine fruit juices, ginger ale, sparkling water, and fruit. Add syrup. Pour into punch bowl. Add ice cubes. Drop in sherbet by spoonfuls or in small balls using an ice cream dipper. *25 to 30 servings.*

## COFFEE FOR A CROWD

1 whole egg, washed

1 lb. regular grind coffee

1 cup cold water

7 qt. cold water

Break egg; mix (shell and all) with coffee. Add 1 cup water. Tie coffee in cheesecloth bag large enough to allow room for coffee to swell. Measure 7 qt. water into large coffee pot. Immerse coffee bag in water, bring to boil. Remove pot from heat. Leave bag of coffee in water 3 to 4 min., remove and stir. *Serves 20 (40 6-oz. cups).*

**Note:** *If preferred, use boiling water to start, bring to boil. Stir. Remove from heat, let stand 10 min. Remove bag.*

## WASSAIL BOWL

*Serve it hot and spicy to delight holiday guests.*

3 whole oranges

whole cloves

6 cups apple cider or juice

1 cinnamon stick

¼ tsp. nutmeg

¼ cup honey

3 tbsp. lemon juice

1 tsp. lemon rind

1 can (1 lb. 4 oz.) unsweetened pineapple juice (2½ cups)

Heat oven to 325° (slow mod.). Stud oranges with cloves (about ½" apart). Place in baking pan with a little water (just enough to cover bottom of pan). Bake 30 min. Heat cider and cinnamon stick in large pan. Bring to boil and simmer covered 5 min. Add remaining ingredients and simmer uncovered 5 min. longer. Place in punch bowl and float baked oranges on top.

Serving note: keep hot over low heat or heat in small amounts as guests arrive. *Makes 20 cups.*

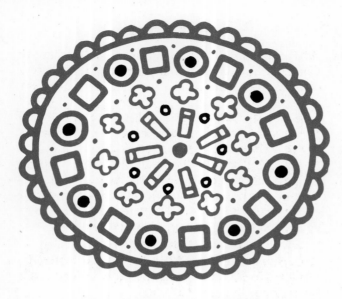

## OPEN-FACED SANDWICHES

Cut thin bread slices with shaped cutters—flowers, diamonds, hearts, rings. Spread with butter and a canapé spread (right). Decorate with water cress, olive slices, minced parsley or pimiento, or capers. Bunches of sweet green grapes, whole strawberries and grapes, or strawberry or mint leaves on plates add a gay touch.

## RIBBON SANDWICHES

Trim crusts from two unsliced loaves of bread, one white and one whole wheat. Cut 6 lengthwise ⅓" slices from each. Put 4 slices (2 light, 2 dark—alternating colors) together with butter or Cheese Butter: cream ¼ lb. grated Cheddar cheese with ½ lb. butter. Make 2 more loaves, using all the bread. Wrap; chill; slice.

## CORNUCOPIAS

Spread trimmed bread squares with filling. Spread soft butter under corner of square; roll into cornucopias. Fasten with toothpicks; chill until butter will hold sandwich in shape.

## FOLD-UPS

Spread trimmed bread squares with filling; fasten opposite corners at center with toothpicks.

# Special Sandwich Spreads

## CHICKEN, CRABMEAT, OR TUNA

| | |
|---|---|
| 1 cup diced cooked chicken or 1 can (6½ oz.) crabmeat or tuna, flaked | salt and pepper to taste |
| ½ cup finely chopped celery | 1 or 2 hard-cooked eggs, chopped |
| 1½ tsp. lemon juice | ¼ cup mayonnaise |

Combine all ingredients lightly. Spread on buttered bread or toast (cut in fancy shapes). Garnish with pimiento or top with another slice of bread or toast for double sandwich.

## HAWAIIAN HAM

Mix thoroughly ¼ cup ground leftover ham, ¼ cup cream cheese, and ¼ cup drained crushed pineapple. Spread on white, rye, or whole wheat bread, hot biscuits, or homemade rolls.

## OLIVE-NUT-CREAM CHEESE

| | |
|---|---|
| 1 pkg. (3 oz.) cream cheese | 3 tbsp. finely chopped stuffed olives |
| 2 tbsp. soft butter | 2 tbsp. finely chopped nuts |
| 2 tbsp. milk | ⅛ tsp. onion juice |

Mix ingredients thoroughly. Spread on bread, toast rounds, or pastry rounds.

## CREAM CHEESE-PINEAPPLE

Mix thoroughly 2 pkg. (3 oz. each) cream cheese, 2 tbsp. drained crushed pineapple, and 1 tbsp. minced chives or young onion tops. Spread on bread or toast rounds or pastry rounds. Garnish with water cress.

## CANDY STRAWBERRIES

**1 pkg. (1 lb.) flaked or shredded coconut**

**1 pkg. (4 or 5 oz.) blanched almonds**

**1 pkg. (3 oz.) strawberry-flavored gelatin**

**2 tbsp. sugar**

**1 can (15½ oz.) sweetened condensed milk**

Put coconut and almonds through food grinder or blender. Combine with gelatin, sugar, and milk. Add food coloring to desired shade. With teaspoonful of dough, roll into ball and shape into strawberry. (Dampen hands frequently for ease in handling dough.) Roll in red sugar, if desired; prick with toothpick to simulate seeds. Cut green spears from cherries or gumdrops and insert as stems. Store in airtight container. Candies freeze well. *Makes about 6 doz.*

## GOLDEN NUGGETS

*See picture, pp. 50-51.*

**1 cup dried apricots, coarsely cut up**

**½ cup water**

**1 cup soft shortening (part butter)**

**½ cup brown sugar (packed)**

**½ cup granulated sugar**

**1 egg**

**1 tsp. vanilla**

**½ tsp. almond flavoring**

**1¾ cups Gold Medal Flour**

**½ tsp. salt**

**2 tsp. baking powder**

**1½ to 2 cups flaked coconut**

**toasted whole almonds**

Cook apricots in water over low heat 5 to 10 min. Do not drain. (Water should be absorbed.) Mix shortening and sugars until fluffy. Add egg, flavorings, and cooled apricots. Measure flour by dip-level-pour method. Mix flour, salt, and baking powder; stir in. Chill dough several hours. Heat oven to 350° (mod.). Drop heaping teaspoonfuls of dough into coconut to coat. Place 2" apart on baking sheet and top with an almond. Bake 12 to 15 min., or until lightly browned. *Makes about 6 doz. cookies.*

## VARIETY TARTS

Heat oven to 450° (hot). Prepare 1-2-3 Pastry for One-crust Pie (p. 141). Roll pastry between 2 pieces of waxed paper into a 12" square. Remove top piece of waxed paper. Using the bottom piece of waxed paper, transfer pastry to baking sheet, placing it dough-side-down. Remove waxed paper. Cut tarts with knife or pastry wheel into 2" squares, 3x1" fingers, 3x2" rectangles, 3" triangles, or 2" rounds. Bake 10 to 12 min., or until golden brown. Cool. Put two together with Creamy Butter Filling (below). Garnish with pistachio nuts, maraschino cherry, chocolate curl, orange curl, or mint leaf, using ¼ tsp. filling to hold garnish in place. *Makes 1 to 2 doz. double tarts.*

**Creamy Butter Filling:** Blend ¼ cup soft butter, ¾ cup sifted confectioners' sugar, 1 egg yolk, and 1 tsp. vanilla (or any desired flavoring).

## HIDDEN TREASURE PASTRIES

Make Pastry for Two-crust Pie (p. 141) or use 2 sticks of our instant mixing pie crust mix. Pat about 1 tsp. into a thin round in hands, then wrap around a maraschino cherry (drained), 6 to 8 mint-flavored chocolate pieces, or a pineapple chunk, drained. Bake at 450° 10 to 15 min., or until light brown. Roll immediately in confectioners' sugar. If desired, roll again in sugar before serving. *Makes 3 doz.*

## TWO-FOR-TEA CAKES

Make batter from either our white or yellow cake mix as directed on pkg. Spread in greased and floured jelly roll pan, 15½x10½x1". Bake 22 to 28 min. at 350°.

Heat oven to 500° (very hot). Prepare 1 pkg. of our cherry fluff or lemon fluff frosting mix as directed on pkg. Spread frosting on cooled cake, forming a slight ridge with knife to mark cake in 2 parts. Sprinkle one part with ⅓ cup chopped nuts, the other with ½ cup flaked coconut. Place in oven 3 to 5 min., until topping is brown. Cut cake into 1½" squares. *Makes 70 squares.*

### Mother's Birthday Dinner

**Hamburger Stroganoff (p. 69)**
**on Buttered Noodles**
**Broccoli with Chopped Almonds**
**Raspberry Gelatin Salad with Peaches**
**Biscuits          Butter**
**Daisy Cake**

### Father's Birthday Buffet

**Ham Loaf (p. 73)**
**Baked Potatoes with Sour Cream**
**Buttered Asparagus          Tossed Salad**
**Birthday Pie**

### Supper Honoring Grandfather

**Oven Barbecued Steaks (p. 67)**
**Parsley Potatoes          Green Peas**
**Lime Gelatin Salad with Blushing Pears**
**Herb-buttered French Bread**
**Happy Birthday Telegram Cake**

### Daughter's Afternoon Party

**Chicken Salad Sandwiches**
**Birthday Bouquets          Ice Cream**

### Supper for Son's Birthday

**Spaghetti and Meat Balls**
**Greens with Oil-and-Vinegar Dressing**
**Crusty Hard Rolls with Garlic Butter**
**Tarts to Suit His Fancy**

### Children's Party Refreshments

**Clown Cupcakes**
**Strawberry Ice Cream**
**Milk or Chocolate Milk**

## DAISY CAKE

Fill and frost a layer cake with yellow frosting. Snip 3 marshmallows into 6 sections, cutting about ¾ of way through marshmallows. Spread sections, gently pinching to resemble petals. Arrange at one side on top of frosted cake. In center of each flower, place small yellow gumdrop. At side of each flower, make leaves with green gumdrops.

## BIRTHDAY PIE

Make father's favorite pie—Lemon Meringue, Blueberry, Pumpkin, Apple, or whatever his choice is (see pp. 143-150). Just before serving, place candles on top and light them.

## HAPPY BIRTHDAY TELEGRAM CAKE

Frost an oblong cake with yellow frosting. Pipe chocolate frosting around edges for border (use decorators' tube or improvise by cutting off corner of envelope and using as tube). In left hand corner, write Western Union return address, then happy birthday message, making it look like a telegram.

## BIRTHDAY BOUQUETS

Frost cupcakes and decorate with icing swirls or flowers. Place each cupcake on a lacy paper doily which has streamers of colored ribbons taped under it.

## TARTS TO SUIT HIS FANCY

Make individual tart shells (p. 142). Fill with the "birthday boy's" favorite ice cream. Stick candles in ice cream and light just before serving. Pass sundae sauce after candles are removed.

## CLOWN CUPCAKES

Frost cupcakes all over with tinted frosting. Pointed ice cream cone makes hat; gumdrops make mouth and eyes. Place on paper doily "ruffles."

*Stand-up parties are an easy, informal way to entertain a maximum number of friends in a minimum of space and with a minimum of effort. Guests all but entertain themselves as they move about helping themselves to canapés and punch. Set the buffet table with tiny napkins, small plates, and canapés and dips arranged in your most attractive accessories.*

**Shrimp Circles (p. 63)**
**Franko Corn Thins**
**Spicy Tomato Soup**

**Ha' Penny Snacks (p. 61)**
**Deviled Eggs**
**Crisp Vegetable Relishes**
**Minted Lemon-ale**

### FRANKO CORN THINS

Heat oven to 400° (mod. hot). Grease well a jelly roll pan, 15½ x 10½ x 1". Blend 2 eggs and ¾ cup milk in bowl. Add 1 pkg. (14 oz.) of our corn muffin mix, ¾ tsp. salt, and ¼ cup grated Parmesan cheese. Stir until blended. Pour into pan. Slice 5 frankfurters like pennies; arrange over batter. Sprinkle with another ¼ cup grated Parmesan cheese, garlic salt, and celery seeds. Bake 15 to 20 min. Serve warm. *Makes 25 3x2" thins.*

### SPICY TOMATO SOUP

Heat 1 can tomato soup with a slice of onion, pinch of cinnamon, clove and bay leaf. Add an equal amount of rich milk. Heat again. *4 servings.*

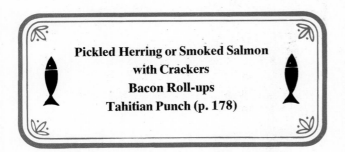

**Pickled Herring or Smoked Salmon**
**with Crackers**
**Bacon Roll-ups**
**Tahitian Punch (p. 178)**

### BACON ROLL-UPS

Roll pineapple wedges, cooked shrimp, cooked chicken livers, dates, or 1" pieces of frankfurter in half-slices of bacon; secure with toothpicks. Broil until bacon is crisp. Serve hot.

### DEVILED EGGS

**6 hard-cooked eggs**      ½ tsp. dry mustard
**½ tsp. salt**                  **about 3 tbsp. salad dress-**
**¼ tsp. pepper**                **ing or vinegar or cream**
                                 **(enough to moisten)**

Cut hard-cooked eggs in halves. Slip out yolks. Mash with fork. Mix in rest of ingredients. Refill whites with egg yolk mixture, heaping it up lightly.

### MINTED LEMON-ALE

Wash and remove leaves from 10 sprigs fresh mint. Pour 1 cup lemon juice (about 5 lemons or use frozen lemon juice reconstituted), ½ cup sugar, and ½ cup water over mint leaves. Let stand 30 min. Add 1 qt. chilled ginger ale, crushed ice. Stir vigorously until pitcher is frosted. *8 to 10 servings.*

### MORE EASY STAND-UP PARTY FOODS

**Peppy Potato Chips:** Spread potato chips on baking sheet. Sprinkle lightly with garlic or onion salt, grated cheese, lemon juice, minced parsley or chives, or any other flavor-adding condiment you wish. Slide into hot oven a few minutes and serve piping hot.

**Nuts and Bolts:** Mix 1½ cups Kix, 1 cup Cheerios, 2 cups tiny cheese crackers, 2 cups pretzel sticks, and ½ lb. mixed nuts in shallow baking pan. Melt ¼ cup butter; add ½ tsp. Worcestershire sauce, ¼ tsp. garlic salt, and ¼ tsp. celery salt; pour over mixture. Stir and salt lightly. Bake at 250° (slow) for 1 hr., stirring every 15 min. *Makes 6 cups.*

*A wonderful way to entertain 10 or more friends is a midnight supper on a Friday or Saturday evening. Guests arrive about 9 p.m.; then after cards, dancing, or a special television program, the hostess serves a festive main dish or dessert or both with tea, coffee, or hot chocolate. Buffet service is easiest for you, the hostess.*

## HAMBURGER PIZZA

1 pkg. active dry yeast
¾ cup warm water (not hot—105 to 115°)
2½ cups Bisquick
¾ cup chopped onion
1 clove garlic, chopped
2 cups tomato sauce
1 lb. ground beef, cooked
½ cup chopped green pepper
salt and pepper to taste
2½ cups grated Mozzarella cheese or 2 pkg. (6 oz. each) sliced Mozzarella cheese (cut into thin strips)
oregano

**To Make Dough:** Dissolve yeast in warm water. Add Bisquick and beat vigorously. Turn dough onto surface well dusted with Bisquick. Knead until smooth, about 20 times. Divide dough into 4 pieces. Roll each piece paper-thin into a circle, about 10″ in diameter. Place on ungreased baking sheets or in shallow pie pans.

**To Make Filling:** Mix onion, garlic, tomato sauce, ground beef, green pepper, salt, and pepper; spread on dough. Sprinkle grated cheese over all or lay cheese strips on top. Sprinkle with oregano to desired taste. Heat oven to 425° (hot). Bake 15 to 20 min., until crust is brown and filling is hot and bubbly. Serve immediately. To eat, cut into pie-shaped wedges. Fold each wedge over and eat with fingers.

**Note:** *Unbaked Pizzas may stand while others are baking.*

## INDIVIDUAL MUFFIN PIZZAS

Brush halves of English muffins with olive oil or butter. Toast under broiler. Cover each with tomato slices, catsup, or tomato paste; onion rings; salami or pepperoni; and a few anchovies. Sprinkle with olive oil, salt, pepper, garlic salt, and oregano. Top with a slice of Mozzarella or Cheddar cheese and a mushroom cap. Return to broiler until cheese melts and bubbles. Serve hot.

**Hamburger Pizza**
**Banana Butter-Mallow Cake (p. 128)**

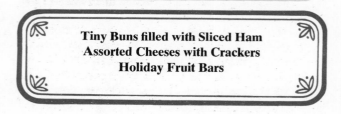

*MAKE YOUR OWN PIZZA*—Everyone has a favorite combination of toppings for pizza. Make pizza and let your family and friends take their choice of meat or sausage, cheese, mushrooms, onions, olives, herbs.

**Tiny Buns filled with Sliced Ham**
**Assorted Cheeses with Crackers**
**Holiday Fruit Bars**

## HOLIDAY FRUIT BARS

⅔ cup soft shortening (part butter)
1 cup sugar
1 egg
1 tbsp. grated orange rind
¼ cup orange juice
2½ cups Gold Medal Flour
1 tsp. soda
½ tsp. salt
½ tsp. cinnamon
½ tsp. nutmeg
1 cup raisins
1 cup mixed candied fruit
½ cup chopped nuts

Heat oven to 400° (mod. hot). Cream shortening, sugar, and egg until fluffy. Stir in rind and juice. Measure flour by dip-level-pour method or by sifting. Blend dry ingredients; stir into creamed mixture. Mix in fruit and nuts; pat dough in greased pan, 15½ x 10½ x 1″. Bake 15 to 18 min. Cut into bars. *Makes about 3 doz.*

## MILLIE'S PEANUT BRITTLE

| | |
|---|---|
| 3 cups sugar | 1 lb. raw Spanish peanuts |
| 1 cup water | (round, with red skins |
| ½ cup light corn | on) |
| syrup | 1 tsp. soda |
| 1 tbsp. butter | 1 tsp. vanilla |

Boil sugar, water, and corn syrup to 242°, or until syrup spins a 6 to 8″ thread. Add butter and peanuts; cook slowly to 300°, stirring occasionally. Meanwhile, heat buttered baking sheet in 200° oven. Add soda and vanilla. (It will foam up.) Turn out onto warmed baking sheet; pull out thin as it cools. When cold, break into pieces with knife handle. *Makes 3 lb.*

## TOFFEE FUDGE

| | |
|---|---|
| 1 cup pecans, chopped | 1 large milk chocolate bar |
| ¾ cup brown sugar | (4½ oz.), broken in |
| (packed) | pieces, or ½ cup semi- |
| ½ cup butter | sweet chocolate pieces |

Grease a 9″ sq. pan. Spread pecans over bottom of pan. In saucepan, slowly boil brown sugar and butter for 7 min., stirring constantly. Remove from heat and spread over nuts immediately. Sprinkle chocolate over hot mixture. Cover pan so heat will melt chocolate. Spread chocolate evenly over candy. Cut into squares while hot. Refrigerate to set the chocolate. *Makes 36 1½″ pieces.*

## CREAM PRALINES

| | |
|---|---|
| 1 pkg. (1 lb.) light brown | 2 tbsp. butter |
| sugar (2¼ cups) | 2 cups pecan halves |
| ⅛ tsp. salt | (½ lb.) |
| ¾ cup evaporated milk | |

Mix sugar, salt, milk, and butter in 2-qt. pan. Cook, stirring constantly, over low heat until sugar is dissolved. Add pecans and cook over medium heat to soft ball stage (234°), stirring constantly. Remove from heat; let cool 5 min. Stir rapidly until mixture thickens and coats pecans. Working quickly, drop teaspoonfuls on waxed paper, forming patties. Let stand until cool and set. *Makes about 4 doz. pralines.*

## THREE-MINUTE FUDGE

| | |
|---|---|
| 1 small can (6 oz.) evaporated milk, undiluted (⅔ cup) | 1½ pkg. (6 oz. each) semi-sweet chocolate pieces (1½ cups) |
| 1⅔ cups sugar | 1 tsp. vanilla |
| ½ tsp. salt | ½ cup chopped nuts |
| 1½ cups diced marshmallows (16 medium) | |

Combine milk, sugar, and salt in saucepan. Cook over low heat until mixture boils. Boil 3 min., or until candy thermometer registers 225°, stirring constantly. Remove from heat. Add marshmallows, chocolate pieces, vanilla, and nuts. Stir until marshmallows and chocolate pieces are melted. Pour into buttered 9″ sq. pan. Refrigerate until firm. *Makes 2 lb.*

## GOOD 'N EASY FUDGE

Melt 2 tbsp. soft butter in 3 tbsp. water in top of double boiler. Add 1 pkg. of our chocolate fudge flavor frosting mix; stir until smooth. Heat over boiling water 5 min., stirring occasionally. Add ½ cup chopped nuts. Pour into buttered 9x5x3″ pan. Let stand until firm. *Makes 1 lb. or 32 squares.*

**Cherry Opera Fudge:** Follow directions above using 1 pkg. of our creamy white frosting mix instead of chocolate fudge. Add ½ cup candied cherry halves.

## TING-A-LINGS

| | |
|---|---|
| 2 pkg. (6 oz. each) semi-sweet chocolate pieces or equal amount milk chocolate | 4 cups Wheaties, Cheerios, or Kix |

Melt chocolate over hot water. Cool at room temperature. Gently stir in cereal until well coated. Drop with tablespoon onto waxed paper. Place in refrigerator until chocolate is set, dry, and hard (2 hr.). *Makes 3 to 3⅓ doz.*

**Noodle Clusters:** Make Ting-A-Lings (above)—except use 1 cup Spanish peanuts and 1 to 2 cups chow mein noodles in place of cereal.

**Haystacks:** Make Noodle Clusters (above)—except use 2 pkg. (6 oz. each) caramel or butterscotch pieces in place of chocolate pieces.

## FLAVORED MILKS

**1 cup milk, thoroughly chilled**          **fruit, chocolate, or other flavoring (below)**

Shake or beat milk with fruit or other flavoring until well blended. Serve cold. If desired, top with whipped cream or sprinkle with nutmeg. *1 serving.*

**Chocolate Milk:** Use 1½ to 2 tbsp. Chocolate Sauce (commercial or recipe at right).

**Banana Milk:** Use ½ banana, mashed.

**Orange Blossom Milk:** Use ¼ to ⅓ cup orange juice, ⅛ tsp. almond flavoring, and 1 tsp. sugar.

**Strawberry Milk:** Use ¼ cup crushed sweetened strawberries or 1 tbsp. strawberry ice cream topping.

**Caramel Milk:** Add 1½ to 2 tbsp. commercial caramel or butterscotch syrup.

## STRAWBERRY ICE CREAM SODA

**¼ cup crushed strawberries**          **carbonated water**

**1 tsp. sugar (omit if using frozen berries)**          **1 scoop strawberry or vanilla ice cream**

Mix strawberries and sugar in tall glass. Fill glass ⅔ full with carbonated water. Add ice cream; stir vigorously. Fill to top with carbonated water. *Makes 1 soda.*

**Chocolate Ice Cream Soda:** Make same as Strawberry —except use 3 tbsp. chocolate syrup in place of strawberries and chocolate ice cream instead of strawberry.

## ROOT BEER FLOAT

Place a scoop of ice cream in the bottom of a tall glass. Fill with ice-cold root beer.

**Other Fancy Floats:** Use other flavors of ice creams with other carbonated beverages. Experiment until you've found your favorite blend.

## MINTY CHOCOLATE FLIP

**¾ cup Chocolate Fudge Sauce (below)**          **1½ tsp. vanilla**

**¼ cup malted milk powder**          **¼ to ½ tsp. peppermint extract**

**2 cups milk**          **2 cups (1 pt.) vanilla ice cream, slightly softened**

Combine Sauce and malted milk powder; stir until smooth. Slowly blend in milk and flavorings. Chill. When ready to serve, add ice cream; mix just enough to blend. Serve immediately. For a thicker shake, use 1½ pt. ice cream. *4 servings.*

**Chocolate Fudge Sauce:** Combine our chocolate fudge flavor frosting mix, 2 tbsp. light corn syrup, and 3 tbsp. soft butter in top of double boiler. Gradually add ⅔ cup milk. Stir occasionally over rapidly boiling water for 5 min. Store in covered container in refrigerator. *Makes 1 pt.*

## TAHITIAN PUNCH

**⅔ cup sugar**          **1 can (46 oz.) canned pineapple-orange juice drink**

**⅔ cup water**

**8 whole cloves**          **⅔ cup lemon juice**

**2 sticks cinnamon (4″ sticks)**          **2 tbsp. rum extract**

          **2 cups ginger ale, chilled**

Combine sugar, water, and spices in saucepan; simmer covered 5 min. Cool; strain. Combine sugar-water mixture, pineapple-orange drink, and lemon juice. Chill. At serving time add rum extract and pour over ice cubes in punch bowl, or pitcher. At the last minute, pour ginger ale carefully down side. Garnish by floating strawberries or well-drained maraschino cherries with fresh mint leaves in punch. *Makes 2 qt. or 10 to 16 servings.*

## BANANA POPS

Make Good 'N Easy Fudge (p. 177). Peel bananas, cut crosswise in 3 or 4 pieces, and place each on a wooden skewer. Dip in fudge mixture or spread with spatula. Roll in chopped nuts, candies, or cut-up coconut (toasted, if desired). Chill until fudge coating is firm.

## ICE CREAM LOLLIPOPS

Write name on handle of each wooden teaspoon. Insert bowl of spoon into square (individual serving) of brick ice cream. Place in freezing compartment until hard. Dip in melted milk chocolate. When chocolate is partially set, dip in chopped nuts or chocolate shot.

## LOLLIPOPCORN BALLS

Empty contents of 1 pkg. of our caramel fudge frosting mix into large saucepan. Add ½ cup soft butter, ½ cup cream (20% butterfat), and ½ cup light corn syrup. Mix thoroughly; cook over medium heat to 250° or hard ball stage.* Pour over 10 cups popped corn and ½ cup peanuts, if desired, in buttered bowl; stir constantly. Butter hands; shape mixture lightly and quickly around 6 or 8 lollipops, depending on size, to make balls about 3″ in diameter. Cool and wrap in waxed paper or cellophane. Tie with colored ribbon. *Makes 6 to 8.*

*Drop a little syrup into a cupful of cold water. When the syrup can be pressed together to hold a firm ball that is still plastic but not rigid, it has reached the hard ball stage, 250°.

## SNACK TIME

**Spread-Your-Own:** Have bread, butter, jelly, and peanut butter on the table. Children love to help themselves to this combination! Salty crackers and peanut butter or graham crackers and jelly or icing are favorites with children, too.

**Sip-Your-Own:** Children can easily make their own flavored milks or milk shakes, using recipes on p. 178. Nutritious, too!

## TO TEASE TOTS' APPETITES

**Pink Applesauce:** Add a drop of red food coloring or cook sauce with tiny red cinnamon candies.

**Custard-N-Candy:** Multi-colored tiny candies in bright designs make custards or puddings a new treat.

**Animal Bread:** When time permits, cut bread slices in shapes of animals with cooky cutters and serve buttered with hot soup.

**Pink Milk or Lemonade:** Add a drop of food coloring or a little strawberry or raspberry juice to tint milk or lemonade pink.

**Mashed Potato Clowns:** Serve hot buttered mashed potatoes in small dishes; add carrot noses and mouths and Lima bean eyes (or use your imagination with available vegetables).

**Colorful Frostings:** Tint frostings for cookies or cupcakes several colors. Let child choose favorite colors.

## TRAFFIC LIGHT COOKIES

*Teach the children the "stop and go" rules with these cookies.*

Make your favorite rolled sugar cooky, such as Sour Cream Cookies (p. 124), or make Ginger Cutouts (p. 52). Cut into rectangles 3x2″ or into 3″ circles. Make 3 indentations in a straight line lengthwise, using end of thimble (not hollow end). Bake. While still soft, make indentations again. Cool. Fill with icing (tinted red, yellow, and green) or with orange marmalade (tint some red and some green, leave some yellow).

## PIXIE PEACH CUPS

Buy your family's favorite doughnuts. Spread the tops with sweetened whipped cream. Drain canned Cling peach halves. Top cream with a peach half, cut-side-up. Place a drained maraschino cherry and a sprig of mint in each peach cavity.

## SHRIMP TOWERS

Split an English muffin and toast bottom side. Butter untoasted side of muffin half; top with tomato slice, cheese slice, 4 shrimp, and 2 pieces (each 2″ long) partially cooked bacon (in this order). Then place under broiler until bacon is crisp and cheese melts, 2 to 3 min. Garnish top with slice of pimiento-stuffed olive. Serve piping hot.

## CHICKEN OR TUNA BURGERS

1 can (6½ or 7 oz.) tuna or 1 cup cut-up cooked chicken

1 cup chopped celery

½ cup diced Cheddar cheese

½ cup chopped ripe olives

¼ cup mayonnaise

1 small onion, minced

6 hamburger buns

Mix all ingredients for filling. Add salt and pepper to taste. Split buns; butter, and sprinkle with paprika. Fill with tuna mixture, replace tops. Put in waxed paper sandwich bags; fold and fasten tops of bags with paper clips. Or wrap in aluminum foil. Just before serving, heat on baking sheet in mod. oven (350°) 15 to 20 min. *6 sandwiches.*

## INDIVIDUAL PO' BOY OR HERO SANDWICHES

Slice and butter frankfurter rolls or small French loaves. Cover bottom of roll or loaf with leaf lettuce, then pile with several kinds of sliced cold meat, sliced cheese, tomato slices, hard-cooked egg slices, and green pepper rings. Spread mustard inside top of roll. To be eaten, whole or sliced, with the fingers.

## DOUBLE DECKERS

For each sandwich, use 3 slices of buttered bread or toast, alternating with fillings. Use suggestions below or make combinations to suit your individual taste.

Sliced chicken or turkey, tomato slices, crisp bacon, and mayonnaise.

Sliced ham, sliced Cheddar cheese, lettuce, sweet pickle, and sauerkraut.

Salami and corned beef, Mozzarella cheese, tomato slices, lettuce, and mayonnaise.

Ham salad, sliced turkey, and sliced olives.

Hamburger patties, Bleu or pimiento cheese spread, mayonnaise, and lettuce.

## CAVATZONE

1 lb. ground lean pork

½ cup chopped onion

¼ cup grated Parmesan cheese

½ cup grated Swiss cheese

1 large egg, beaten

¼ tsp. Tabasco

1½ tsp. salt

2 tbsp. minced parsley

Mayonnaise Biscuit Dough (below)

Heat oven to 400° (mod. hot). Cook pork and onion over low heat until no longer pink. (Do not brown. Stir with fork to break up as it cooks.) Cool.

Mix in rest of ingredients. Make Mayonnaise Biscuit Dough. Spread half of it in well-greased 8″ sq. pan; spread meat mixture over dough. With fingers, spread rest of dough over mixture. (The top will even out during baking.) Brush with beaten egg yolk to give crusty glaze. Bake 25 to 30 min. Cut in slices about ½″ thick and serve hot or cold. *9 servings.*

**Mayonnaise Biscuit Dough:** Add ⅔ cup milk and ¼ cup mayonnaise to 2 cups Bisquick. Mix well.

## QUICK DATE-PINEAPPLE CAKE

*Teens can whip up this yummy cake themselves.*

Heat oven to 375° (quick mod.). Lightly grease a square pan, 8x8x2″. Using 1 pkg. of our date bar mix, mix date filling and ½ cup hot water. Blend in crumb mixture (from pkg.), 2 eggs, 1 tsp. baking powder, ½ cup chopped walnuts, and half the fruit from 1 can (9 oz.) crushed pineapple, drained. Spread in prepared pan. Bake about 35 min., until a deep golden brown. Frost with Pineapple Butter Icing (below). *9 to 16 servings.*

**Pineapple Butter Icing:** Blend 3 tbsp. soft butter and 1½ cups sifted confectioners' sugar. Stir in rest of pineapple (about 3 tbsp.) until spreading consistency.

## SHAGGY DOGS

*Easily made by dipping toasted marshmallows in chocolate syrup, then coconut.*

Melt milk chocolate candy bars, adding milk to make a thin syrup (one 5¢ candy bar plus about 1 tbsp. milk makes enough syrup for about 2 marshmallows). Put shredded or flaked coconut in flat dish. Toast marshmallows on fork or stick over campfire or range surface unit in kitchen; then dip in chocolate and coconut. Eat directly from fork.

## CHERRY CRUNCH

Heat oven to 350° (mod.). Cut ½ cup butter into 1 pkg. of our yellow cake mix (dry mix). Reserve 1 cup mixture. Pat remaining mixture lightly into oblong pan, 13x9½x2″, building up ½″ edge. Spread 2 cans (1 lb. 4 oz. each) cherry pie filling over cake mixture to within ½″ of pan edge. Blend ½ cup chopped walnuts and the 1 cup reserved mixture. Sprinkle over top. Bake 45 to 50 min. Serve warm with cream, whipped cream, or ice cream. *12 to 15 servings.*

**Note:** *For a crisper, thinner dessert, use 1 can cherry pie filling; bake 35 to 40 min.*

## RECORD CAKE

Bake your favorite chocolate cake in two 8 or 9″ layers. Prepare 1 pkg. of our chocolate fudge flavor frosting mix and 1 pkg. of our creamy white frosting mix as directed. Spread white frosting between layers, saving 1 cup. Frost top and sides of cake with fudge frosting, reserving ½ cup for decorating. Frost center of cake with small amount of white frosting to resemble label on record.

To give effect of grooves on record, draw tines of fork round and round through fudge frosting on top of cake. Using cake decorator tube or paper envelope with tiny corner cut off, write Happy Birthday or other greeting with fudge frosting on "label." Decorate sides of cake with musical symbols in white frosting. Finish with 2 small dancing figures fashioned out of pipe cleaners.

## MAKE YOUR OWN SUNDAES

Bring out a large bowl or plate of ice cream balls in many flavors. Offer a choice of Quick Fudge or Marshmallow Sauce (below), or other favorite sauces. (For hurry-up serving, make the ice cream balls ahead of time; place on a baking sheet and freeze in freezer.) Serve with a variety of cookies.

**Quick Fudge Sauce:** Melt 1 pkg. (6 oz.) semi-sweet chocolate pieces over hot water. Beat in 1 can (5½ oz.) evaporated milk and ⅛ tsp. salt. Serve hot or cold. *Makes about 1½ cups.*

**Marshmallow Sauce:** Cook ½ cup sugar and ⅓ cup hot water just until sugar dissolves. Take from heat, stir in 16 finely cut-up marshmallows (¼ lb.) or 2 cups miniature marshmallows until melted. Pour slowly into 1 unbeaten egg white, beating with electric or rotary beater until mixture thickens. *Makes 2 cups.*

## A Quartet of Toasty Treats

### HAM-CHEESE TOASTEES

**8 slices buttered bread**

**4 slices boiled ham
(fat removed)**

**4 slices Swiss cheese**

**about ½ cup softened
butter**

Make 4 sandwiches from buttered bread, ham, and cheese. Spread outsides of sandwiches with butter. Cut in halves. Brown slowly on both sides on electric grill or in skillet. Serve at once. *8 toastees.*

### STRAWBERRY TOASTEES

**12 slices bread**

**¾ cup strawberry
preserves**

**¾ cup butter**

Make 6 sandwiches, filling each with 2 tbsp. preserves. Spread outsides with the butter (about 2 tbsp. per sandwich). Brown on both sides in skillet. Sprinkle with a little confectioners' sugar. Serve immediately. *6 toastees.*

### BEEF TOAST

**10 slices bread**

**prepared mustard**

**catsup**

**1 lb. ground beef**

**½ to ¾ cup finely
chopped onion**

Heat oven to 400° (mod. hot). Toast bread in oven until lightly browned on both sides. Spread with mustard and catsup. Do not butter bread as meat contains enough fat to moisten. Crumble meat evenly over toast. Salt and pepper meat to taste; sprinkle with onion. Turn oven to 500° (very hot). Bake toast 3 to 5 min., or until meat is done. Cut slices in halves or quarters to serve. *10 servings.*

### CHEESE DREAMS

Put a slice of cheese (American or Cheddar) between 2 slices of bread. Butter outside of both bread slices generously. Just before serving, brown lightly in heavy skillet (low heat) or electric grill until cheese melts. *1 serving.*

## Frosty Favorites

### STRAWBERRY ICE

**1 pkg. (3 oz.) strawberry-
flavored gelatin**

**½ cup sugar**

**1½ cups boiling
water**

**1 pkg. (16 oz.) frozen
sliced strawberries,
partially thawed**

**¼ cup orange juice**

**¼ cup lemon juice**

Mix gelatin and sugar. Add water and stir until gelatin is dissolved. Add berries and stir until berries are broken up. Add juices. Divide into 2 freezer trays; freeze until just set (somewhat mushy), about 1 hr. Spoon into bowl and beat with rotary beater until smooth. Return to freezer trays and freeze until firm, about 1 hr. Serve in sherbet cups with brownies or crisp cookies. *8 to 10 servings.*

### ORANGE FREEZE

Combine 1 qt. vanilla ice cream and 1 can (6 oz.) slightly thawed frozen orange juice concentrate; beat on high speed on mixer or in blender until well blended. Spoon into dessert dishes; garnish with mandarin oranges and toasted coconut. Refrigerate until ready to serve. Or use Orange Freeze as a topping for fresh, frozen, or canned fruit. *8 dessert servings; 16 servings when spooned over fruit.*

### BISCUIT TORTONI

Combine ⅓ cup fine coconut macaroon crumbs, 2 tbsp. diced candied cherries, and ¼ cup chopped salted almonds. Slightly soften 1 pt. vanilla ice cream and fold in cherry-almond mixture. Spoon into ice cube tray or little paper cups in ice cube tray. Freeze until firm. *4 servings.*

## PEANUT CLUSTERS

| | |
|---|---|
| 1 cup sugar | ½ tsp. vanilla |
| ¼ cup butter | 1 cup rolled oats, uncooked |
| ⅓ cup evaporated milk | |
| ¼ cup crunchy peanut butter | ½ cup Spanish peanuts |

Mix sugar, butter, and milk in saucepan. Bring to rolling boil; boil 3 min., stirring frequently. Remove from heat. Stir in peanut butter and vanilla. Fold in oats and peanuts. Drop by scant tablespoonfuls onto waxed paper on baking sheet. Let stand until set. *Makes 2½ doz.*

## KIX NOUGAT BARS

| | |
|---|---|
| 3 tbsp. butter | ½ cup moist shredded coconut |
| ½ lb. marshmallows | |
| 4 cups Kix | ½ tsp. salt |
| ¼ cup coarsely chopped nuts | 4 oz. sweet or semi-sweet chocolate, melted |

Melt butter and marshmallows over hot water, stirring constantly. Remove from heat. Fold in Kix, nuts, coconut, and salt. Turn out into buttered 8 or 9″ sq. pan. With hand, protected by a piece of waxed paper, pat out mixture evenly in pan. Pour melted chocolate over top. With rubber scraper or spatula, spread chocolate in a thin layer over the top of Kix mixture. Chill until set, 45 to 60 min. Cut into bars. *Makes 32 bars, each about 2x1″.*

**Wheaties or Trix Nougat Bars:** Make Kix Nougat Bars —except substitute Wheaties or Trix for Kix.

## QUICK SPICE CAKE

| | |
|---|---|
| 2 cups brown sugar (packed) | ½ tsp. cloves |
| | ½ tsp. nutmeg |
| 2½ cups Gold Medal Flour | 1½ tsp. soda |
| | 1 egg |
| ½ cup soft shortening | 1¼ cups soured milk |
| 1 tsp. cinnamon | Custard Sauce (p. 135) |

Heat oven to 350° (mod.). Grease and flour two round layer pans, 9x1½″. Measure flour by dip-level-pour method. Mix sugar, flour, shortening, and spices. Reserve ½ cup for topping. Add soda, egg, and soured milk to mixture in bowl. Beat 1 min., until smooth. Pour into pans. Sprinkle half of crumb mixture on each layer. Bake 30 to 35 min. Cool. Put layers together crumb-side-up with Custard Sauce as filling.

**Quick Spice Squares:** Make Quick Spice Cake (above) —except bake in greased and floured oblong pan, 13x9½x2″ about 40 min. Omit Custard Sauce and serve cake warm or cool in squares topped with a lemon sauce.

## RANCH PUDDING

| | |
|---|---|
| 2 cups brown sugar (packed) | 1¼ cups Bisquick |
| | 1 cup raisins or chopped dates |
| 2½ cups water | |
| 2 tbsp. butter | ½ to 1 cup chopped nuts |
| ½ cup milk | 1 tsp. vanilla |

Heat oven to 350° (mod.). Mix 1 cup brown sugar, water, and butter in saucepan. Boil 5 min. Pour into 8″ sq. pan. Mix rest of ingredients in bowl. Spoon batter on top of sugar mixture. It will sink into the liquid and spread out as it bakes. Bake 45 min. Serve warm with either plain or whipped cream. *9 servings.*

# Index